Destination Florida...

The Guide to a Successful Relocation

by Lee Rosenberg, CFP
with Saralee H. Rosenberg

Rex Publishing Company
P.O. Box 390
Clearwater, Florida 34617-0390

Rex Publishing Company
P.O. Box 390
Clearwater, Florida 34617-0390

Library of Congress Catalog Card Number: 89-63292

ISBN 1-878214-02-0

To Zachary and Alexandra

"When you wish upon a star
makes no difference who you are
Anything your heart desires
will come to you."

Like a bolt out of the blue
fate steps in and sees you through
When you wish upon a star
your dreams come true."

Contents

I. Putting Your "Financial" House In Order Before You Relocate

IV. The Big Move

V. So This Is Florida: You're Going To Love It!

VI. What Every New Resident Should Know

VII. And In Conclusion...

Acknowledgements

Behind every "byline" is a chorus of voices...those who contribute their thoughts, insights and knowledge. For *Destination Florida*, hundreds of local experts across the state chimed in. I am grateful for their honest assessment of Florida's growing pains, and their relentless enthusiasm for all its attributes.

I'd like to thank all of the cooperative staff members at the state government agencies who instantly provided facts and figures. The local Chamber of Commerce offices were also terrific about sending the latest information on their communities.

A special thanks goes to John Fink, a Development Representative with the Florida Dept. of Commerce Business Assistance Program, for his continual updates on the state's economic conditions. He also served as a gateway to many other valuable sources. I only wish I'd had his rolodex!

I'm also grateful to have had the counsel of two talented attorneys. Jim Gallagher in Baldwin, Long Island (a member of the Florida Bar) and Nick Jovanovich, the head of the tax practice for English, McCaughan & O'Bryan in Ft. Lauderdale, provided interpretations of the state's most complex laws on estate planning and taxes. Harold Hymen, the founding partner of Presidential Insurance Associates, Inc. (Bradenton) lent his invaluable expertise on the perplexing subject of health care coverage in Florida.

I am also eternally grateful to my clients. They have been the true catalysts for this book. When so many expressed a desire to retire to Florida, our firm was faced not only with an enormous professional challenge but a personal one as well. These people are our extended family. Without their trust and confidence, we wouldn't have had the opportunity to develop the financial plans that became the basis for helping so many others with the same dream.

I want to also acknowledge my devoted business partner and friend, Anthony Spatafore. Through his diligent efforts day in and day out, we have accomplished so many positive results for our clients. His unending patience and support of this project has not gone unnoticed.

We are extremely grateful to the people at Rex Publishing, who believed in *Destination Florida* from the very start. George, Maaret, Mia, Liz, Rose, Victor and an ever increasing staff have supported this project as if it were their own personal "baby." Ditto for the incredibly devoted people at Fine Lines. Jo Ozdemir was the kind of editor one could only hope for. Under her direction, Saban, Cheryl, Eileen, Vijay and the rest spent untold months transforming 1000 plus pages of manuscript into two very special books. We really lucked out when they stepped in.

As with any chorus, there is always a star soloist. My wife, Saralee, worked singlehandedly and tirelessly for over a year compiling research, checking facts, conducting interviews and keeping the "Florida" project on track. Her constant interest and support, as always, was music to my ears.

Foreword

Growing up in Brooklyn during the 50s, I can recall the excitement whenever friends or family spoke of moving to a faraway place called California. I didn't know much about the place other than it offered constant sunshine, open spaces and unlimited opportunities (whatever that was). Everyone, it seems, was picking up stakes and joining the "gold rush." Even our beloved Brooklyn Dodgers couldn't resist the call from the west.

Today that "gold rush" has moved south to Florida. It is our generation's "Garden of Eden," offering the same warm climate, bright new houses, communities that spring up like weeds, and new businesses that open overnight.

But unlike California, Florida is not the "Great Beyond." Due to reasonable air fares, many of us have visited so often that Florida is practically a suburb, albeit 1300 miles from New York or Chicago. We can recite the names of favorite restaurants and shopping malls, and even consult doctors there. It's simply a home away from home.

Yet no matter how familiar, the decision to move to Florida will probably result in one of the most dramatic lifestyle changes you will ever make. The problem is that no one teaches a course in how to deal with turning your life upside down. This book will be your course.

As a financial advisor for the past 15 years, I've written hundreds of financial plans for people who were planning a move to Florida. This is due largely to the fact that my offices are based in Nassau County (Long Island), which feeds more migration to Florida than just about any other county in the country.

Because I've worked with countless Florida-bound families, a very unique and rewarding process, I've been able to test and develop numerous strategies that have helped clients make the most successful adjustment possible.

If you are considering moving to Florida, this book will be invaluable. Rather than your journey being a once in a lifetime experience, you will benefit from someone who has lived the transition hundreds of times.

That is why I have dedicated this book to all of you who have been dreaming of Florida as the place to change your life—and maybe your luck. Now you don't have to be included with those who are so overwhelmed with the task that they never get past wondering and wishing. Here's your chance to "take the course" and pass with flying colors. It's probably never mattered more.

Governor Bob Martinez, State of Florida

STATE OF FLORIDA

Office of the Governor

THE CAPITOL
TALLAHASSEE, FLORIDA 32399-0001

BOB MARTINEZ
GOVERNOR

Greetings:

As Florida's Governor, it is a great pleasure to welcome you to the Sunshine State. Florida offers a high quality of life and an unmatched diversity of activities, events and lifestyles. Young families moving to Florida quickly find they have choices.

If they prefer an active lifestyle, they can choose to indulge in their favorite outdoor sport or activity, whether it be attractions, golf, tennis, boating, fishing, swimming or any of the other forms of recreation for which Florida is famous.

If they prefer to take it easy and live the laid-back lifestyle, they can choose to enjoy the vast array of cultural amenities and natural wonders that the state offers or just stroll along a beach and soak up the sunshine.

Florida has one of the fastest growing economies in the nation, one that has created jobs and a thriving business community. Working families find they don't have as much worry about finding employment here as they do in other areas of the U.S.

Florida has it all. The living is easy and the costs are low. I think you'll find it to your liking--you'll never want to leave.

Best wishes on your new life in Florida. We're glad you're here.

Sincerely,

Governor

BM/rcm

Introduction

Pick a day, any day. If the statistics are right, 1000 people woke up for the first time this morning as official Florida residents.

Why did they move from comfortable homes in Long Island? Chicago? Atlanta? Detroit? What convinced them to leave family and friends? To give up jobs and businesses... the old neighborhood?

And why Florida? What is it about this popular vacation state that is motivating endless flocks of people to fly south for the winter... and stay?

The answer is simple. Florida is the only place in the eastern half of the United States that looks, smells and feels like paradise. It has the only sub-tropical climate in the country, a booming real estate market and some of the most beautiful planned communities ever built. There's an abundance of big business. Growth and opportunity. Year-round outdoor recreation. Championship golf courses and tennis clubs. Beaches. The ocean.

Florida's lifestyle offers the promise of a dream vacation that never ends.

So, who needs a book about making a successful transition? If Florida is paradise, how can problems exist?

All too often the excitement of poring over developers' brochures, of dreaming about sand and surf, and of saying good riddance to endless winters up north leave little time to be concerned with some harsher realities.

If you've been yearning to make Florida your home, the first question to ask is "Can I afford to move?" I'll help you answer that, and also figure out how much you'll need to live on in your new home. It's important to remember that livng and working in Florida will have both an immediate and long term impact on your financial status.

Are you aware that many people come down and take a cut in pay? Sometimes a deep one. Tax obligations change. So do mortgage commitments. New banking relationships have to be cultivated and new creditors dealt with. There are costly moving expenses to pay for. And often there are the ramifications of selling a business up north and purchasing a new one in Florida. These are just some of the financial considerations to plan for.

You'll learn that relocating involves more than packing up the household goods and saying good-bye to friends. It also means packing up the financial goods— the investments, the savings and the assets. This is the backbone of your family's existence, and the key to a successful transition.

I want to show you how you can plan ahead, really prepare for this move so that your personal financial structure arrives safe and sound. And more importantly, that it is ready to go to work for you during those crucial first months.

Your move to Florida will be a once in a lifetime experience. As a financial advisor in the New York area for the past 15 years, I've made the journey hundreds of times. I've worked hard at developing ideas and strategies to help scores of clients make a successful move to Florida—emotionally, psychologically and financially speaking.

In these pages, we'll address every major aspect of a successful relocation—from sizing up your net worth to establishing credit to shopping for new health insurance. We'll look extensively at Florida real estate—how and where to buy—whether it's a new condo, an old house or something in between. We'll talk about avoiding mortgage traps, and we'll also look at different strategies concerning your home up north. We'll look closely at job and business opportunities across the state—even tips on buying a franchise. We'll show you how to keep moving costs way down and how to keep your sanity during the process. We'll look into Florida laws and introduce you to Florida's "hottest" regions. Finally, we'll share advice from the real experts...those people who have made the move to Florida. It's their wit and wisdom you will truly benefit from.

   Destination Florida is dedicated to each and every one of you who has ever dreamt of calling the Sunsine State home. You can succeed in Florida. It can be a paradise. It can fulfill every desire you've ever had about the ultimate place to live and work.

   We're going to make it happen together.

Lee Rosenberg, CFP
July 13, 1989

Putting Your "Financial" House In Order Before You Relocate

CHAPTER 1

Can You Afford To Move To Florida?

STRATEGIES FOR MAKING IT HAPPEN

Unless you are a recent lottery winner or have the benefit of using Rockefeller as a surname, a successful move to the Sunshine State will depend an awful lot on your *financial* state. Forget about whether your belongings will get to Florida in one piece; you should be wondering if your money is in good enough shape to make the move!

Over the years I've heard many intelligent people make light of this discussion. They anticipate that huge profits on the sale of their home will take care of all their financial needs. Now it's not that I enjoy playing the role of killjoy, particularly when people are enthusiastic about moving to Florida, intent on living the good life. The problem is, too many Florida-bound residents become victims of their own enthusiasm. They fail to understand the tax implications of a house sale, and the general upheaval of their financial affairs caused by a move. Ultimately, they find themselves in hot water—which has nothing to do with their new heated pool.

Regardless of the size of your personal wealth, all new Florida residents must become accustomed to an entirely different set of living expenses. Rent and mortgage payments change. The costs of utilities, food, travel and recreation, medical care, among other essentials, are different. While Florida's tax structure can be highly advantageous (there's a $25,000 homestead exemption on property taxes and no personal state income tax), there are tangible and intangible taxes which you've probably never paid before. New banking, financing, and investment arrangements need to be structured. Finally, anticipate a high level of purchasing, particularly that first year.

I know what you're thinking. "Living in Florida means everything will

3

be cheaper. That's why we're going down there." While it's true that Florida is a relocation "hot-spot" precisely because it offers a lower cost of living than many areas up north, I don't recall anyone changing the state's name to Nirvana.

Every day, a thousand people start calling Florida "home." Many of them become disappointed, if not outright devastated, when their finances don't go the distance expected. And they have no idea why. Let me share some examples with you.

A client's wife died after a long illness. It was an unfortunate situation, as you can well imagine. However, even I didn't expect that less than a month later he would pack up the Flatbush apartment they had shared for 27 years, and move down to Florida. He called me from his new garden apartment in Hollywood and asked what he could do about all his non-liquid assets. He was trying to live the good life. However, according to the terms of his CDs and Municipal Bonds, unless he accepted the penalties for early withdrawal, that wouldn't begin until 1990. "I should live so long," he yelled in my ear!

Then there was the young family who was convinced that there was "gold in them thar hills" of Orlando. They bought a new quick-print franchise, faster than you could say "Xerox." The prospect of not having to contend with unreasonable bosses and endless commuting was so exciting, they somehow forgot they'd need a sizeable amount of cash to live on until the business generated income. Since they'd spent their last dime buying the franchise, they ran into a serious cash flow problem.

Just about everyone I know who moves to Florida goes on wild shopping sprees. I have clients who make Jack Benny look like Robin Hood, and even they go crazy. You'd think that Monty Hall was standing at the state border handing out fresh $100 bills! They pick out new furniture, a new car, new clothes and shoes, tennis racquets, golf clubs—the works. Unfortunately, many of these people move down with their old debts chasing right behind them. Naturally, when all the bills come due, they get a case of the cold sweats. I wish I could tell them it's because the air conditioning was up too high, but that's not the problem.

The general reaction is, these people feel cheated. They feel deprived of the good life everyone is supposedly entitled to under Florida law. It's a shame that these disappointing situations occur as often as they do, especially when the pain and aggravation could be avoided using the proper amount of planning and budgeting. That's why I can't urge you enough to put your "financial house" in order before you put your "residential house" in order.

For some of you, all this might amount to is maneuvering a few accounts in order to have enough cash for a smooth transition. For others, it might mean transferring more of your portfolio into income-producing investments to ensure a comfortable retirement. For most of you, it means trying to figure out exactly where you stand regarding assets and liabilities. The only way you and your new lenders are going to agree on what kind of housing and lifestyle is affordable is if they can review your net worth.

That's why this chapter will cover some of the basics of financial planning: establishing your current net worth, analyzing your cash flow, setting goals and priorities, and finally, creating a realistic budget before you move so that your finances arrive in great shape! Maybe even better than your belongings.

Step 1: What Is Your Net Worth?

The first step in assessing your financial health is looking at what you've accumulated over the years, your assets and liabilities, not ski equipment and gourmet cookware. Adding up your liquid and non-liquid assets then subtracting your debts from that number, will give you a personal balance sheet, or a net worth statement.

Preparing a net worth statement is an interesting task because the result of your compiling efforts is a like-it-or-not snapshot of your personal wealth. One client likened the exercise to receiving the most important report card of his life.

In many respects, net worth statements are exactly like report cards. They summarize how well or how poorly you've performed over a period of time. First they evaluate the assets department: savings, investments, personal property, etc. Then they look at the liabilities department: unpaid bills, loans, taxes, mortgages, etc. When you subtract what you owe from what you own, there's your final grade.

Once you've established your net worth, you'll not only have a good sense of how well you've managed your money but which aspects of your finances need improving. Is there a need for greater diversification? Is your insurance sufficient? Is your retirement fund growing at a steady pace? The answers to these questions will be evident, as well as the type of lifestyle you can afford in Florida.

Your hard work in determining your net worth will also pay off when you apply for a new mortgage, credit cards, etc. because all the necessary information will be in proper order.

Let's take a look at what gets factored into a net worth statement.

First on the list are liquid assets—cash resources such as checking, savings and money market accounts. Then there are the near-cash resources such as stocks and mutual funds. These are liquid by definition because they can be "liquidated" quickly without penalties or receiving less than they are worth.

In my opinion, between 15% and 20% of your total assets should always fall into this category. And at any given time, there should be enough ready cash in your bank accounts to cover your living expenses for a minimum of three months, preferably six.

Incidently, to calculate the value of income-producing liquid assets such as stocks and mutual funds, refer to recent price quotes from the newspaper. As for whole life insurance policies, CDs and annuities, review the tables in your policy or contract to determine current cash values.

Keep in mind that if you do decide to tap into income-producing assets prematurely, you will incur taxes and penalties for early withdrawal.

The next group of assets are non-liquid investments, the most important of which is your home. To assess its current value, consult with local realtors and/or refer to the real estate classified section of your local newspaper.

Appreciating assets, such as your home and investments, should make up more than 50% of your total assets.

Personal property—clothing, furs and jewels, cars, furniture, etc., can be assessed by estimating how much money they would generate if you sold them tomorrow. Be very conservative in your "guestimates." If you actually did have to sell them, it would probably be to meet an immediate need. That would make it difficult to hold out for premium prices.

To determine the value of your 401K or other company benefit programs, ask the benefits department to calculate those figures for you.

Some non-liquid assets, such as real estate limited partnerships, are difficult to place a value on since you'd have no way of knowing what your shares were worth until they were actually redeemed. It's best to place the value at the price you paid for your unit. The same would be true of vacation time-shares.

After assets come liabilities. Simply, this represents the outstanding balances on your mortgage, cars, installment loans, credit cards, etc. And also what you project you will owe the state and federal governments by April 15.

Ideally, your liabilities should represent less than half of your total assets. If that's not the case, you don't need me to point out that you are overburdened with debt.

Now it's time to go to work. Let's figure out your current net worth by filling in the blanks on the facing page. Please don't hesitate to consult with your financial planner and/or accountant for assistance.

Step 2: What Is Your Current Cash Flow?

Now that you've got a realistic sense of how fiscally fit you are, it's time to analyze where your money comes from . . . and more importantly, where it goes. It's called a cash flow analysis and believe me, you're not the only one who dreads examining such nitty-gritty details as what you make and what you spend. This process generates about as much enthusiasm as stepping on the scale in January. Still, combined with your net worth statement, the cash flow analysis will be the tool you use to create a realistic family budget.

To collect the data for your analysis, you need go no further than your home office, or wherever it is you stash your check book register, monthly bank statements, tax returns, and credit card receipts.

Then, to record your income and expenditures, use the Cash Flow Analysis chart on pages 8 & 9.

Now, dig a little deeper and track some of the more invisible expenditures—cash purchases. These are often the true culprits of cash flow problems because the proof of the purchase disappears into thin air . . . as though it never existed.

To examine where this money goes, add up your cash withdrawals for a three month period, multiply by four and then write down the type of things you usually pay for with cash—fast food, hair and nail care, movies and videos, other entertainment, health and beauty aids, etc.

When you add up your yearly living expenses and subtract those from after-tax income, what's left can be used for savings and investments. Hopefully, that number represents at least 7% to 10% of your net income. If not, take a look at your credit card payments and make a commitment to cut back. When you stop paying 18% interest on your purchases, that should free up a considerable amount of money.

Assets

Liquid
Checking Accounts/Cash	$_____
Savings Accounts and Money Markets	$_____
Stocks, Bonds and Mutual Funds	$_____

Non-Liquid
Retirement Savings (IRAs, Keoghs)	$_____
Time Deposits (T-bills, CDs)	$_____
Life Insurance (Cash Value)	$_____
Annuities (Surrender Value)	$_____
Pensions (Vested Interest)	$_____
Profit Sharing Plans (Equity)	$_____
Collectibles	$_____
House (Market Value)	$_____
Other Real Estate/Limited Partnerships	$_____
Business Interests	$_____
Personal Property (Auto, Jewels, etc.)	$_____
Loans Owed You	$_____
Other Assets	$_____
TOTAL ASSETS	$_____

Liabilities

Mortgage or Rent (Balance Due)	$_____
Auto Loan (Balance Due)	$_____
Credit Cards/Other Installment Loans	$_____
Annual Tax Bill	$_____
Business Debts	$_____
Student Loans	$_____
Brokerage Margin Loans	$_____
Home Equity Loans/2nd or 3rd Mortgages	$_____
TOTAL LIABILITIES	$_____
TOTAL NET WORTH	$_____

Cash Flow Analysis

Income

Husband's salary/bonus/commissions	$_____
Wife's salary/bonus/commissions	$_____
Dividends and interest	$_____
Child Support/Alimony	$_____
Annuities/Pensions/Social Security	$_____
Rent, royalties, fees	$_____
Moonlighting/Freelance work	$_____
Loans being paid back to you	$_____
TOTAL INCOME	$_____

Taxes

Combined Income Taxes	$_____
Social Security Contributions	$_____
Property Taxes	$_____
TOTAL TAXES	$_____

Living Expenses

Rent or Mortgage Payments	$_____
Food	$_____
Clothing and Uniforms	$_____
Utilities	$_____
Dining Out	$_____
Furniture/Electronics	$_____
Vacations/Recreation	$_____
Entertainment	$_____

Cash Flow Analysis (continued)

Living Expenses (continued)

Gasoline	$_____
Car Payments	$_____
Auto Repair and Maintenance	$_____
Financial and Legal Services	$_____
Medical Care/Medications	$_____
School Tuition/Day Care	$_____
Life and Disability Insurance	$_____
Car Insurance	$_____
Health Insurance	$_____
Property and Casualty Insurance	$_____
Pet Care	$_____
Birthday and Holiday Gifts	$_____
Babysitting/Housekeeping	$_____
Commutation (tolls, trains, etc.)	$_____
Cable TV	$_____
Household Maintenance	$_____
Telephone Bills	$_____
Religious Institutions	$_____
Books, Magazines and Papers	$_____
Clubs, Sports, Hobbies	$_____
Dues—Union and Others	$_____
Alimony/Child Support	$_____
Parental Support/Nursing Home	$_____
Personal Allowances (kids, lottery, etc.)	$_____
Other	$_____
TOTAL ANNUAL LIVING EXPENSES	$_____

Step 3: Establishing Priorities

Cash flow analyses can be so revealing.

I will never forget the client who kept complaining that he and his wife went through petty cash like water. Adding fuel to the fire, they both started calling attention to the fact that the other was getting a little thick around the middle. Not wanting to get involved in a fight about fat, but always anxious to help people take better care of their money, I suggested that they track their cash purchases for a few weeks by keeping a daily diary.

In doing so, they solved both mysteries. The culprit was Dunkin' Donuts. Apparently they had fallen into a routine of meeting friends for coffee and "Munch-kins" several times a week. Unfortunately, they had failed to consider either the health or financial consequences of this habit.

When they figured out the number of visits a week times the average cost per visit, they were astonished. They had spent over five hundred dollars that year on those teeny-tiny balls of dough. Since they loved the place so much, I encouraged them to buy stock in Dunkin' Donuts and eat the profits, not the products.

I love this story because it is a reminder of how innocent and unimportant small purchases seem—until you add them up. It also suggests how subtly we make choices about spending. We don't sit down and make deliberate decisions; we buy now and ask questions later. The result is that most people are disappointed that their money never seems to buy important things—college educations, vacations, investments. They attribute it to not earning enough, paying high taxes, etc. While this may in part be true, the real reason money fails to perform is that priorities haven't been firmly established and goals haven't been discussed. There's no clear direction as far as spending is concerned, so most of it goes toward impulse purchases and non-necessities.

It's time to determine what your financial goals are. We already know you are interested in moving to Florida. Wonderful. We'll make it priority #1 and put it at the top of the list. What else is important to you and your family? Fill in the blanks on the facing page and start talking about the future.

Once you've established your priorities, your next step is to determine which goals are to be short, medium, or long-range.

Voila! You're created a roadmap for your money. Now it has a destiny with you in control behind the wheel!

Step 4: The Dreaded "B" Word

Look how much you've learned about your finances. You know how much you're worth and what it buys you. Not enough! But you're going to change now that you know what are your financial goals. As a way to achieve those goals, it's time to take the most important step of all—establishing a budget and learning to live on it.

One client's definition of a balanced budget is that it occurs when the month and the money run out at the same time. That's not exactly what I mean. A budget is a contract you make with yourself to spend up to a certain amount per month in order to live within your means.

Establishing Your Goals

Goals	Not Important	Important	Very Important	Absolutely Necessary
MOVE TO FLORIDA	☐	☐	☐	☐
Chop Debts	☐	☐	☐	☐
Build Savings	☐	☐	☐	☐
Get More Insurance Protection	☐	☐	☐	☐
Buy a first House	☐	☐	☐	☐
Buy a bigger House	☐	☐	☐	☐
Buy a New Car	☐	☐	☐	☐
Start a Family	☐	☐	☐	☐
Save for Children's Education	☐	☐	☐	☐
Have a Better Lifestyle	☐	☐	☐	☐
Take a Great Vacation	☐	☐	☐	☐
Open Your Own Business	☐	☐	☐	☐
Retire Early	☐	☐	☐	☐
Retire Comfortably	☐	☐	☐	☐
Other:	☐	☐	☐	☐

As a financial planner, you would expect me to extol the virtues of budgeting under any circumstances, but honestly, with a major relocation in your plans, this is a critical time to take control of the money reins.

I know that in some households the mere mention of the "B" word brings out foot-stomping, head-shaking, finger-pointing gyrations—and that's just from the kids! Unfortunately, with today's high-priced lifestyles and unending material desires, your toughest, but most important job, will be rallying the troops to cooperate.

But wait just a minute. Before you start your campaign, consider this. Budgeting has gotten a very bad rap over the years. When you strip the word bare of all its associations, the truth is a budget is a plan for spending money. It doesn't mean you can't spend money, it simply means you'll decide *in advance of spending it,* where it's going to go.

A budget helps you take control, resulting immediately in increased savings, reduced debts, and most important . . . less fighting. Just think of what you'll save on broken dishes alone!

You've already started the budgeting process by taking a good hard look at what you've got coming in *vs.* what's going out. The next step is to forecast your income and return-on-investments for the year in order to lay the groundwork for your budget.

In addition, don't make the mistake of waiting to see what's left over in savings at the end of the year. The secret of saving money is to pay yourself every month, as though you were a creditor. Pretend you're paying another utility bill. However you decide to trick yourself, earmark a certain amount each month in your budget for savings. At the end of the year, you'll be quite proud of your nest egg.

At this point you may be wondering, what's the point in setting up a budget if the numbers are going to be entirely different in a few months? Practice. It will be a great warm-up exercise for the permanent budget you'll set up when you arrive in Florida.

BUDGET SYSTEMS

The first step in creating a working budget is deciding what it should look like.

I have a client who set up an elaborate budget tracking system on his IBM personal computer. He had spreadsheets and forecasting tools and year-to-date figures and variance analyses . . . and you guessed it—he never entered a single piece of data. "Takes too much time," he told me.

That's an important lesson. Here are some less complicated ideas for keeping a budget that might work for you. If not, try to devise your own methods.

- *Monthly Reviews* . . . Every month add up what you spent in each category *vs.* what you were budgeted to spend. Compare the numbers to see where you've overdoing it, or not spending what you anticipated. After 3 months, look for trends and readjust the budget accordingly. While this system may not keep you from splurging, you'll be able to count on having a good sense of where the money is going—12 times a year. If things start getting out of control, just apply the brakes.

- *Accountant's Spreadsheets . . .* This is an extended version of the monthly review, but in this case, all the information is confined to ledger sheets, which can be found at any office supply store. The advantage of using this format is that you can put an entire year on one sheet, or "spread it out" on a quarterly basis. The other major difference is that there is room on the spreadsheet to record your banking transactions, paychecks and investment income—giving you a complete birdseye view of your finances at a moment's glance. If you are computer literate, you can set up the system on your PC and let the software calculate your year-to-date totals and projections. By the way, projections are made by adding "actual" expenditures in a category to the amount that is budgeted for the remainder of the year. An overspending situation will be immediately indicated.

- *"The Envelope, Please" . . .* Borrowed from immigrants running cash businesses, this system is simple yet effective. It involves cashing your paychecks or other income, dividing the cash into envelopes which are labeled by expense categories, and paying the bills from that cash. When the envelope is empty, you stop spending in that category. Of course you can always rob Peter to pay Paul, but you get the idea. This method is probably best for those on a fixed income, whose financial needs are uncomplicated and predictable.

- *The Bank Account Method . . .* This is a more sophisticated but similar version of the envelope method. It involves setting up 3 different bank accounts: a savings account for long-term goals (investments), an interest-bearing checking account, or money market fund, for short-term goals (tuition payments), and a checking account for bills and cash withdrawals. Budget how much is to go into each account on a monthly basis, and withdraw a certain allotment for bills. If your withdrawals exceed the budget for the month, stop taking the money out.

Truthfully, the final execution is the least relevant matter. What's important is that the tracking system you set up is simple enough to use on *a continuing basis.*

BUDGET TIPS

Once you and your budget are comfortable with each other, there are some suggestions for ways to keep the ball rolling:

- *As in Monopoly — Pick the Banker First . . .* If the wrong person is in charge of the funds, all your intentions and efforts could be wasted. Decide which family member is the most organized, has the better memory for dates and obligations, likes working with numbers, has the most free time to handle the record keeping, bill paying, etc. and is preferably the saver not the spender. If both adults are equally capable, or incapable, of these functions, split the chores to keep each other in check.

- *Build in a Reward System . . .* There has to be both small and large payoffs for good behavior. Make sure that rewards are given as often as possible. Perhaps a family membership in a health club is a way to say thanks, or a nice vacation, dinner out . . . you get the idea. Keep 'em happy. Everyone deserves a break now and then.

- *Charge Yourself a "Check" Fee . . .* Some people find that they can save small amounts of money by deducting $10 or $20 every time they write a check. They call it a check fee, and after a month of bill paying, they've accumulated a few hundred dollars, which can be placed into an interest bearing account.

- *Leave Home Without It . . .* That's right. You can leave your American Express card home, along with your other credit cards, and you *will* survive. You'll also cut back on credit card spending in a big way. Use your cards for planned purchases only. Also think of it this way—if you're not always carrying your cards, you'll be less likely to ever report them lost or stolen.

As with anything experimental, you can expect the first few months of money watching to have its ups and downs. You'll discover luxuries you absolutely can't live without, expenses you overlooked, and overall bad ideas, like serving macaroni and cheese every third night. But at least your heart and your pocketbook will be in the right place. And when you work out the glitches, you'll be thrilled at the surplus remaining at the end of the year. That's exactly what you need to make a successful move to Florida.

CHAPTER 2

Organizing Your Financial Records:

WHAT TO KEEP AND WHAT TO TOSS

In some respects, we humans are a pretty predictable species. Every time we move or relocate we inevitably make two important promises to ourselves. The first vow is to clean up, throw out, donate and otherwise discard our years of accumulation. That vow is immediately followed by a second promise which sounds something like this: "I am never going to let things get so out of control again. My new home is going to be organized!"

It's a wonderful fantasy for most of us to envision a tidy garage, a basement you can walk through, and closets you can open without fear of a concussion from falling debris. And too, we like to dream about keeping our personal files in order. No more rifling through shoe boxes for a birth certificate. Or pulling apart an underwear drawer for last year's check registers. Yes sir. With this move we do solemnly swear to keep a well-organized record keeping system.

The nice thing about being a financial planner is that this particular goal is one I can help everyone achieve. Yes, getting your financial files in order takes time, but not only is there an immediate payoff with respect to having information at your fingertips, but being organized will save you money as well. For example, people with organized records pay less to have their tax returns prepared. They are less likely to forget insurance bills and other quarterly or annual payments, and they don't keep paying interest on small credit charges because they're paying those bills in full.

It happens that there is no better time to get organized than when you're moving to a new home. I have one client who is quasi-fanatical about this theory. He thinks January 1 should be National Moving Day so the whole country can start the new year in a clutter-free environment (it's one of his better ideas). He knows that under the intense pressure of a moving date, you have no choice but to go through all your personal belongings and decide what to keep, what to toss and what to unload on your unsuspecting Aunt Elsie. Although I can't offer guidance on your junior high school yearbook or your bowling shoes, I can tell you what informational records you should maintain and organize, and what others are no longer necessary to have.

Listed below are the major categories of records the average person should be keeping at home and when to eliminate them.

Banking

ITEMS TO KEEP:

- Canceled checks;
- Deposit, withdrawal and transfer receipts;
- Cash Machine (ATM) transaction records;
- Monthly statements.

WHEN TO TOSS THEM:

Hang on to the canceled checks which are pertinent to your tax records for a minimum of three years. After three years, the government cannot challenge your tax return unless they have reason to believe you understated your income by 25%. In that case, they have up to six years to come after you. If they have reason to believe that there is genuine fraud involved, they have the right to go back to the first year you ever filed. Only you can decide whether you need your checks for any more than 3 years.

Other checks to retain for a period of time are those which serve as your only receipts for a purchase or for charitable contributions. They need not be kept after a year. If you intend to sell your house before you move to Florida, you should hang on to the checks you've written for permanent improvements, such as central air conditioning. That way you have proof of how you've added to the property value. Also, the cost basis and improvements are valuable for capital gains calculations.

Everything else can be tossed. It may be hard at first, but once you look through your voluminous archives of old checks, you'll see that they've served no purpose all these years.

All receipts for deposit, withdrawal, transfers and cash machine transactions can be thrown out each month after you've reconciled your monthly bank statement. Hang on to the monthly statements for one year.

Employment And Business Records

ITEMS TO KEEP:

- Paycheck Stubs;
- W-2 Forms;

16

- Pension Documents;
- Profit Sharing Statements;
- Travel, Entertainment and Business Gift Expenses
  (with complete documentation and receipts if the expenses are more than $25 each);
- Business Diary or Appointment Book.

WHEN TO TOSS THEM:

After you've checked your W-2 wage form for the year, and it reconciles with your year's accumulation of pay stubs, throw them out. The only pay stub to keep is the last one of the year because it serves as a complete summary of social security, union dues and other taxes.

Monthly and/or quarterly pension and profit-sharing statements can be discarded at the end of the year, provided they jibe with the final statement of the year. Keep the annual statements in a permanent file.

Receipts and documentation for tax deductible business and travel-related expenses should be kept with your tax records for a period of 3 to 6 years.

FOR FURTHER INFORMATION ON BUSINESS EXPENSES:

Call your local IRS office for a copy of Publication #463, "Travel, Entertainment and Gift Expenses." For information on car expenses, get a copy of their Publication #917, "Business Use of a Car."

Taxes

ITEMS TO KEEP:

- Tax Returns;
- Receipts and Canceled Checks for All Deductible Expenses;
- Records of All Assets and Liabilities.

WHEN TO TOSS THEM:

Remember that the IRS can audit a return within 5 to 6 years after filing. If you are still hanging on to records older than that, get rid of them. If for any reason you want a copy of an old return (they keep them for six years), the IRS can supply you a copy for a nominal fee.

Individual Retirement Accounts And Keoghs

ITEMS TO KEEP:

- Statements showing deductible and non-deductible contributions;
- Statements showing withdrawals.

WHEN TO TOSS THEM:

Never! These documents should be kept in permanent files for tax purposes as well as to keep a current accounting of how much you've accumulated, and what your tax liabilities are for early and/or allowable withdrawals.

Insurance Records

ITEMS TO KEEP:

- ALL POLICIES: Life, Health, Auto, Homeowners and Annuities; create yearly reminders to yourself to review policies for possible coverage updates (to take care of new purchases and to keep up with inflation).

WHEN TO TOSS THEM:

Obviously if you drop an insurance company for a new one, toss the old policies. Same goes for insurance booklets from previous employer's health plans. You only need current information.

Investments

ITEMS TO KEEP:

- All sales receipts or cancelled checks for tangible investments (antiques and other collectibles, real estate, etc.);
- Monthly or quarterly capital gains statements;
- Transaction slips and canceled checks that show the cost of investments;
- Investment account statements.

WHEN TO TOSS THEM:

Once you review your annual 1099 forms which summarize the year's investment activities, you can get rid of your monthly and quarterly statements.

Keep the transaction slips which show the actual purchase costs of your investments with your permanent tax-keeping records. That way you can prove the amount of profit or loss so you don't have to pay more taxes than necessary. Also, hang on to the statements which show the amounts of reinvested dividends.

Investment Account Statements should be kept until you receive the end-of-the-year statement. Each year's summary statement should be kept until the account is liquidated and that year's tax return filed.

Investment Property

ITEMS TO KEEP:

- All K-1 Forms and records documenting passive-loss allocations;
- Rental Journal (showing number of days the second home was rented during the year);
- All tax-related records (property taxes, mortgage payments, utility bills, etc.).

WHEN TO TOSS THEM:

If you have passive-activity losses from limited partnerships or rental real estate that cannot be deducted until some future year, then you should keep all K-1 forms since 1987.

Keep your rental journal and other tax records for 3 to 6 years.

Medical And Dental Bills

ITEMS TO KEEP:

- Medical records (medical histories, lab reports, prescriptions, hospital stays);
- Pharmacy bills;
- Records of travel expenses incurred when handling medical problems;
- Insurance forms summarizing medical reimbursements.

WHEN TO TOSS THEM:

Medical records should be kept permanently. They will be of particular importance when you move and start seeing new doctors and dentists. Certainly you can request that your records be transferred, but it always helps to have a duplicate copy of the information so that you can present it in emergencies or in case the records should be lost or misplaced by the doctor's office.

You do not need to keep years and years of physician's statements showing various medical services for which you have paid. Your canceled checks and insurance reimbursement forms are all that's necessary.

Records of travel expenses should be kept with your tax files, as should the bills from your pharmacy. These receipts are important in case the IRS ever asks for proof that you haven't deducted non-deductible items such as toiletries and cosmetics.

Your Residence

ITEMS TO KEEP:

- FOR RENTERS: Copy of your lease and rent receipts or canceled checks.
- FOR HOMEOWNERS: All records pertaining to the purchase, including the deed, closing documents, appraisal, mortgage and property survey, canceled checks for mortgage payments;
- Annual statements showing interest and principal;
- Home improvement records;
- Casualty losses;
- Sales of easements and condemnation actions.

FOR PEOPLE WHO USE THEIR HOME
FOR BUSINESS PURPOSES:

Contact the IRS for their booklet #587, "Business Use of Your Home." This spells out all the acceptable deductions, such as the cost of computers, provided you've kept meticulous records.

WHEN TO TOSS THEM:

Again, the items mentioned above are pertinent to your tax return so you must keep them for the 3 to 6 year period. This is of particular importance if you sell your home or investment property within that period because you need a basis from which to compute your gains or losses.

ONE LAST NOTE: If you postponed the tax on a gain from a previous home sale, then you must keep all the records pertaining to that residence or property because the basis of your current home is affected. A copy of IRS Form #2119, "Sale or Exchange of Principal Residence," will show any postponed gain and should be kept indefinitely.

Your Career

ITEMS TO KEEP:

- Transcripts of grades, courses, and credits (in case you ever decide to go back to school, you'll want proof of your educational background or proof of completion of a job training program);
- Letters of recommendation, Diploma;
- Employment records; Resumes.

WHEN TO TOSS THEM:

Not until you are independently wealthy or retired, whichever comes first.

Miscellaneous

Here are some other items that are probably lying around the house that are doing nothing but taking up precious space. Immediately drop these in the circular file:

- Warranties and guarantees that have expired or are for products that have expired;
- Old Blue Cross/Blue Shield cards from previous employers;
- Old checkbook registers.

Once you've cleaned house, I highly recommend that, when you get to Florida, you rent a safe deposit box at the bank where you establish your checking and/or savings accounts. This is the best possible place to store vehicle titles, birth certificates, marriage and adoption records, stock and bond certificates, property deeds, a list of insurance policies and their related account numbers, military records, trusts, power of attorney, living wills and other important legal papers. The only thing you might want to keep elsewhere are your own Wills since the deposit box could be temporarily sealed by the bank or tax authorities after your death (although that might not happen if the box is jointly held). Check with the bank before you include your Wills.

Good luck in your mission to get organized. This is one resolution that will be well worth your efforts.

CHAPTER 3

Big Brother Knows What's In Your Credit Report...

AND SO SHOULD YOU

Today, for many of us, running to a cash machine (Automated Teller Machine) has become as much a part of our routine as stopping to pick up milk. My wife does all her banking by machine and in fact has become such a familiar ID number to the bank's computers that she swears it recently asked her, "What did you do with the $50 I gave you yesterday?" (Couldn't have said it better myself.)

From the ever-increasing lines at the ATMs, she is obviously not alone in relying on this convenient method of banking. Yet just because our cash is more readily available today doesn't mean we are giving up our love affair with credit cards and borrowing. Living in a cashless society is still the American way (isn't our national battle cry "CHARGE"?). During the course of the year more than three-fifths of the adult population have outstanding installment debts.

Given that most of us could never acquire our homes, cars, major appliances and other purchases without credit cards, bank loans and other forms of borrowing, it is always helpful to be aware of your and your spouses's creditworthiness. When you have plans to relocate, however, the need to know where you stand with creditors is essential, because moving will almost always mean establishing new sources of credit.

For example, unless you plan to move in with relatives or into an already-owned home, right off the bat you'll either be applying for a mortgage or signing a rental agreement. Credit check No. 1. This will be followed by more credit checks if you buy a new car, appliances and other major household items on time. As a next step, you may find that you'll want a new MasterCard or Visa, particularly if you find the interest rates favorable or you are just looking to fatten your credit limit over and above your existing cards; another credit check. Finally, there's a good chance you'll be interested in establishing credit at one or more of the department stores in town. Hello TRW. Good-bye privacy.

Have you ever had serious credit problems due to a bankruptcy or a long period of unemployment? Or a history of making late payments? If you've never established credit in your own name before, or if you are applying for joint credit for the first time as a result of a remarriage, checking your credit rating becomes doubly important.

Also, if you believe you have very little or no credit in your name, you should check your credit rating anyway. You'll be amazed at how much is known about you.

GETTING TO KNOW YOU

Who is keeping tabs on you? To begin with, there are thousands of credit bureaus across the country which keep files on local borrowers. There may be several agencies in your area who all maintain the same basic information on you.

What's inside your file? Surprisingly, more than you can imagine, yet not everything you'd think would be in there. For starters, there is ample personal data: name and address, date of birth, age and sex, race, ethnic background, marital status, employment history, education, etc. In addition, these reports contain matters of public record such as tax liens, judgments, arrests and convictions, and any serious delinquencies and defaults. Most importantly, from a prospective lender's viewpoint, the records show your financial payment history.

To obtain this information, the majority of credit bureaus subscribe to one of five national reporting services. The largest are TRW, Inc. of Orange, CA. and Trans Union in Chicago. Combined, they maintain files on over 135 million consumers. Bear in mind that credit bureaus and reporting agencies do not make the decisions on whether to grant you credit. They simply provide information so that the creditor can make the decision based on independent and hopefully accurate records.

Credit bureaus are authorized by law to turn over your files to any person or organization with a legitimate business need for the information. This is contingent on the fact that they will be using it in connection with a financial transaction involving you. What this means, of course, is that if you apply for a loan of any sort, or for a new job, or for insurance, etc., you are giving permission for those people or companies to open your files.

At a time when so much is at stake—a new mortgage, new credit cards, etc., you cannot afford to be surprised by your report. As a consumer, you must protect yourself by confirming that your files contain factual and accurate information. In today's data-oriented world, you just can't depend on flawless files. Since computerization, there are more mistakes than ever. But now there's no one to blame!

The first step in assessing where you stand with the credit bureaus is understanding what you are entitled to know about yourself.

YOUR RIGHTS AS A CONSUMER

First and foremost, *you have the right to examine your own files!* The Fair Credit Reporting Act of 1970 stipulates that you have access to the information at any time and for a reasonable fee. The average cost for receiving a copy of your credit report, or at least a summary of it, is between $10 and $20.

Before you move, I can't encourage you enough to ask your banker for the name or names of the credit agencies used by the bank when conducting credit checks. Then sit down and write to them, requesting a copy of your file. In the unlikely event that you are not in their files, check the yellow pages for other large credit bureaus in your area and write to them. NOTE: Don't ask your banker to obtain the report for you. Under federal law, bankers are prohibited from releasing this information to anyone, including you.

Should it happen that a prospective lender has already declined your application as a result of unfavorable information in a report from a credit agency, the law requires that the lender give you the name and address of the agency that provided the report. If you request a copy of your credit report from that agency within 30 days of being turned down, you are entitled to receive your report from that bureau at no cost to you. The law also requires that the credit bureau reveal the source of its information so that you can dispute any inaccuracies directly with the source(s). Finally, you are entitled to know everyone who has received a copy of the same report in the past six months (two years for employment reports).

UNDERSTANDING THE TRWs OF THE WORLD

According to some lenders, credit reports are the best non-fiction reading around. These comprehensive reports can reveal quite a story about you—your staying power on a job, where you like to shop, how often you shop and what you spend, your reported income, and much more.

The problem occurs when this non-fiction is wrong. Really wrong. If you are unaware of what is being released about you, you could be rejected by a lender for up to 7 years based on a single negative mark that shouldn't be there. It happens more often than you think.

Last year, *U.S. News and World Report* (6/29/87) recounted the story of an Ithaca, NY couple who applied for a mortgage and were declined. They were positively stunned. Despite their scrupulous efforts to pay their bills promptly and stay within their budget, their credit report showed them to be seriously delinquent in paying a Sears bill. The postscript to the story was that this serious delinquency was a one dollar service fee that was erroneously added on when Sears billed them for merchandise that was never delivered. Can you imagine the outrage upon discovering that that's all that was standing between you and a new mortgage?

Still, it is a good example of the kind of information that showed up in a TRW report. Here is an overview of what else you might expect to find:

- All Your Credit Cards: Dead or Alive;
- Credit Card Balances;

- Late Payments and the Extent of Your Delinquencies;
- Current Employment Status and Earnings.

A sample credit profile provided by TRW is on the facing page. The problem is not necessarily what's on file, but where it comes from. While we are led to believe that these big credit agencies are like the omnipotent "Big Brother," in truth, they are dependent solely on the very clients who subscribe to them for their information, i.e., TRW counts on the department stores, credit card companies, insurance companies and employers to submit information on you on an ongoing basis in order to maintain their files. The catch is that lenders do so at their convenience and on their timetable, so a lot of what shows up in your file may very well be obsolete and inaccurate.

For example, a client recently showed me his TRW report. I looked at it and said, "What do you do? Collect department store credit cards as a hobby?" He did not. The reason his report listed so many different creditors was that his job had taken him to several different cities in the past five years. With each move, he and his wife had applied for charges at the local department stores. When they moved, they had no use for the old charges, but according to TRW the accounts were all active. And when a prospective lender saw how much credit was potentially available to my client should he have decided to cross the country on a helluva great shopping spree, he was considered a risk and not worthy of further credit.

I have subsequently learned that most department stores continue to report on and hold open inactive accounts for marketing purposes. If you want to close your account, then, you must personally inform them of your decision. In light of my client's experience, this sounds like a good idea before you move.

With respect to credit card balances, again the credit bureaus are dependent on receiving up-to-date information from the lenders. Since they all report in at different times, if at all, your report is not likely to be completely current. For example, if you paid off a loan three months ago, it will probably show a balance owed well after that. The only saving grace is that the report will also indicate "last date reported" so that at least the lender is aware if your file is dated.

When it comes to your payment habits, here is an area where the creditors don't seem to miss a trick. It's entirely possible that if you are even one day late on a MasterCard or Visa payment, that "delinquency" could show up in your report for the next 7 years. Ironically, if you've defaulted on a student loan, that might not show up at all.

As for your current employment, if you have not applied for a loan or credit cards since you've been on your current job, the records will not reflect this position or your increased salary, if that's the case.

Interestingly, there are important financial transactions you would expect to find that don't show up at all. Student loans, a prime source of indebtedness for some people, are not likely to appear (although the Department of Education is starting to go after delinquent loans with a vengeance). Neither is your mortgage payment history. The reason is, the credit agencies are convinced that if you're going to pay any bill late, it won't be the bank or the mortgage company (and they're probably right). Debit cards also don't appear, because they are believed to be an exten-

26

Updated Credit Profile
Disclosure

TRW CREDIT DATA/TRW INC.
5 CENTURY DRIVE
PARSIPPANY NJ 07054

INQUIRY INFORMATION

TCR2

DFD2 1999999ABC CONSUMER JANE Q..,1825 H 08638,P-2234 W 08638,S-135999999,
Z-MN,M-1825 HILL STREET?TRENTON NJ 08638

IDENTIFICATION NO.

LINE NO	PAGE	DATE	TIME	PORT	H/V	CONSUMER	TNJ1	IDENTIFICATION NO.
	1	08-01-86	15:19:14	AL11	A14	CONSUMER	TNJ1	11-999999/99

LINE NO		
1	1-86 JANE Q CONSUMER	1-85 A & B SALES · SS#135999999
2	1825 HILL STREET	1350 4TH STREET
3	TRENTON NJ 08638	1240000 TRENTON NJ 08638 · YOB-1952

LINE NO	ACCOUNT PROFILE POS NON NEG	SUBSCRIBER NAME/COURT CODE / STATUS COMMENT	STATUS DATE	DATE OPENED	SUBSCRIBER #/COURT CODE / TYPE	ASSN. CODE / TERMS	AMOUNT	BALANCE	ACCOUNT/DOCKET NUMBER / BALANCE DATE	AMOUNT PAST DUE	PAYMENT PROFILE NUMBER OF MONTHS PRIOR TO BALANCE DATE 1 2 3 4 5 6 7 8 9 10 11 12
7	A	MIDLANTIC NATL			1121515	2			20245566789		
8		CUR WAS 120	3-86	6-84	SEC	36	$8600	$3800	4-10-86		C 4 3 2 1 C C C C C C C
10	A	CITIBANK			124000	2			892939495969		
11		NO STATUS	6-86	5-80	C/C	REV	$1000				
12		**ACCOUNT IN DISPUTE– REPORTED BY SUBSCRIBER									
14	A	SOUTH WESTERN S&L			1270905	4			4021345600		
15		PAID SATIS	1-84	8-81	CRC	REV	$800				
17	A	JC PENNEY			1300000	2			5969794939221		
18		CURR ACCT	6-86	2-79	CHG	REV	$100	$32	6-5-86		C C C C C C C C C C C C
20	A	SEARS			1319117	2			8384858687777		
21		CURR ACCT	3-83	3-75	CHG	REV	$500	0	6-15-86		
23	A	BAMBURGERS			1370450	1			7700041223333		
24		CURR ACCT	6-86	1-83	CHG	REV	$200	$54	6-28-86		C C C C C C C C C C C C
26	A	CHASE MANHATTAN			1102076						
27		INQUIRY	4-08-86								
29	A	B OF A M/C			3270450						
30		INQUIRY	2-10-86								
32	)))))	CHECKPOINT))))) SS# IS 139599999/OTHER FILE IDENT: MID INIT IS Q/STREET INIT IS W, ZIP IS 08638									
34	A	B OF A M/C			3202121	2			5254002260565104		
35		CR CD LOST	12-85	10-78	CRC	REV	$3000				
37	M	NJ CO REG			1031217				11135699		
38		FED TX REL	11-17-81				$2100		IRS		

*CONSUMER STATEMENT*04 & 02-10-86
THE FOLLOWING STATEMENT HAS BEEN ADDED AT THE CONSUMER'S
REQUEST:
"REGARDING MIDLANTIC NATL. THIS ACCOUNT WAS AWARDED
TO MY EX-SPOUSE IN THE SETTLEMENT. AS SOON AS I LEARNED
IT WAS DELINQUENT, I ASSUMED THE RESPONSIBILITY OF PAYING
THE PAST DUE AMOUNT AND WILL CONTINUE TO MAKE PAYMENTS."

- - - - - END

TRW does not provide general credit ratings or make credit granting decisions. We will check any item of information
you dispute by contacting the source. This will take approximately 3 to 4 weeks and we will send you the results.

Consumer Copy (Keep for your records)   **Confidential**

sion of your checking and savings accounts, and not a source of debt. The exception is if you have a line of credit attached to your bank account.

Until January, 1988, American Express stayed away from reporting to credit bureaus. Now, however, they cooperate fully, providing both positive and negative information to the major credit reporting agencies. They report members with past due accounts who canceled the card as well as cardholders with excellent payment records. According to a spokesperson at American Express, the reason they began to report credit history was that they felt they were doing a great disservice to members with excellent track records by not having that information appear in their credit files.

Even the government is joining in the personal data parade. Last April, Fannie Mae (Federal National Mortgage Association) told the 40,000 lenders servicing its mortgage loans to report 90-day payment delinquencies and foreclosures to the big credit bureaus. And state agencies that enforce child support payments are now beginning to report delinquencies as well.

All in all, there is room for a huge margin of error. A credit bureau's files, with all that they contain, are still viewed as skimpy and unreliable by most legitimate lenders. This is why you still need to fill out a lengthy application each and every time you apply for credit or a loan. Now you know why it's in your best interest to do so. At least that gives you a fighting chance of relaying accurate information.

HOW TO TAKE ACTION IF YOUR CREDIT REPORT IS WRONG

When you receive a copy of your report, you will also find a reference to the 1971 federal law that describes the necessary steps to correct any out of date or otherwise inaccurate information. If a credit agency does not have reasonable procedures for correcting a consumer's file, you could sue them for both real and punitive damages.

Upon reviewing your report, should you find information that is incomplete, obsolete or simply inaccurate, write a letter outlining the inaccuracies and/or fill out the dispute form provided to you. The onus is then on the credit agency and the lender to prove that their information is correct. You should expect to hear the results of their findings within 30 days. Within that time, they must verify the report or delete the information from the files. If you don't get a response within 30 days, the disputed information must automatically be removed from your file. But follow up as often as necessary to verify that this has been done.

If the credit bureau's reinvestigation of an item you dispute does not resolve the matter, you can file your version of the story in a brief statement (100 words or less); the credit bureau must include this statement in all future reports containing the disputed item. Ideally, if you do have a dispute with a particular creditor, you should try to reconcile with them directly. That way, if you're successful, the negative mark can be permanently removed from your file without having to write a letter explaining the dispute.

ONE LAST NOTE: Most adverse information that is more than 7 years old, including suits, court judgments and tax liens, cannot be included in consumer credit reports unless the reports are furnished in connection with a credit or life insurance transaction involving a principal amount of $50,000 or more. The exception to this rule is for bankruptcies, which may be reported for up to 10 years.

CREDIT REPAIR CLINICS

Recently there has been a proliferation of clinics that promise to have derogatory information removed from a person's credit file for a fee. I've seen fees that run as high as $1200. But let the buyer beware. A congressional subcommittee was recently informed that many of these operations are shams. Consumers can do anything that a credit clinic purports to do, at no cost. If a credit clinic tells you they can remove a bad credit history or records of a bankruptcy and this sounds too good to be true, most likely it is.

THE FUTURE OF CREDIT

With the explosion of bank credit cards, vanity cards, home equity loans, private label cards such as Sear's Discover Card, plus expanded uses for oil company cards, credit bureaus are going to be inundated more than ever in the years to come. Couple that with the highly-sophisticated computer capabilities that allow for cross checking consumer files, and you'll see why your credit file is something to be reckoned with... *before you apply not after*. You can do yourself a very big favor by making sure that your non-fiction reading does not become science fiction.

CHAPTER 4

Establishing Credit:

HOW LENDERS SIZE YOU UP

I f you are a widow, a divorcee, or even newly remarried, and are considering moving to Florida so you can start your life over, good for you! With proper planning, it can be the best move of your life!

As with any move, it will probably be necessary to establish new credit with the banks, credit card companies and department stores (unless, of course, you've recently won the state lottery, in which case you could probably buy your own bank or department store).

If credit is already in your name and you are in good standing with the lenders, then applying for new credit should not be a problem.

However, if your marital status has recently changed, or you are in a situation where you will be establishing your own credit for the first time, you might feel you have cause to be concerned. While I can't sit here and tell you that obtaining a loan or credit card will be a piece of cake, I can tell you that in today's competitive marketplace, lenders are hungry for business.

Five years ago, less than half of those who applied for credit cards were approved. Today, more than 60% get an okay, and some banks that are very aggressive marketers approve 80% of all applications.

What's with the sudden compassion for borrowers? It's pure bottom-line thinking. If the banks can pay 6% for money and lend it out at 18%, there is a little more margin for error in deciding who is creditworthy and who is not. It also doesn't hurt that the Equal Credit Opportunity Act (ECOA) guarantees that your credit application cannot be discriminated against.

31

WHY YOU NEED CREDIT

Over the years, I have worked with many clients who have expressed total disdain for credit. In their view, the only people who borrow are those who either can't manage their money properly or are "spendaholics," or both. Maybe you know the type: they paid cash for their home 30 years ago. In fact, they pay cash for everything— cars, food, travel and entertainment, etc. Their thing is not to owe anyone anything. They came into this world without debts, and they plan to go out without debts. Unfortunately, times have changed. And in this complicated and costly world of ours, having credit in your own name is a necessity.

Here's an example. A client, a divorcee in her 40's, decided to move down to Florida to start a new life with her two children, far from the anger and strife in their old home. When she flew down one weekend to try to rent an apartment, her application was turned down. Why? All her credit had been in her ex-husband's name. The credit bureaus had no record of her personal payment history.

Then there is the possibility of facing an emergency when you're not carrying enough cash to handle the crisis. It could be anything from car trouble to a medical emergency to needing to fly home immediately for some reason. If there's no time to run to the bank, you're stuck. A bank credit card at that time could be a lifesaver.

Finally, relocation is another good reason to want credit. When you move to Florida, you should anticipate making greater-than-average purchases: furniture; appliances; possibly a new car. You might need your cash reserves for basic living expenses until you get settled and your income becomes replenished. With credit cards, you would have the option of borrowing for a short time and then paying off the balances.

WHAT EXACTLY DO CREDITORS WANT?

Before you fill out your first loan or credit card application, it helps to have an understanding of what the banks and other lenders are looking for when determining creditworthiness. Here is an overview of the criteria used to make a judgement call:

- *ABILITY TO REPAY*...What is your current job or other source of income? How long have you worked or how long is your income guaranteed? How much do you earn or receive? How does that amount stand against your current overhead (mortgage or rent payment, other fixed expenses, other loan or credit repayments, etc.)?

- *CREDIT HISTORY*...How much do you currently owe? How often have you borrowed? Do you pay your bills on time? Have you ever defaulted on a loan or credit card? And finally, does it appear that you live within your means?

- *ASSETS*...Do you have a home and car that can be used as collateral against your loan? What other sources of income do you have, such as savings and investments, to help you repay your debts?

- *SIGNS OF STABILITY* . . . How long have you lived at your current and/or former address? How long have you been employed? Do you own or rent?

CREDIT SCORING

The thing to remember is that lenders examine combinations of these factors to reach a decision on extending credit. This process is called "Scoring." Each element of your credit application represents a certain number of points. If the points add up to an acceptable number and no serious credit problems show up, credit is usually granted. Traditionally, the banks scored based on the 5 "Cs": collateral, cash flow, capitalization, conditions and character. But now the scoring system is becoming more complex.

Citibank makes lending decisions based upon huge statistical models that supposedly identify potential credit risks. TRW, the giant credit checking bureau, recently introduced a new computerized scoring model that ranks an applicant's potential for delinquency on a scale of 0 to 1300. The higher the score, the greater the chance of being a good credit risk. Sears has almost 700 different scoring models, one for each store.

Where does that leave you, a person with very little or no credit history? Probably in a very good position, since you've never abused the privilege of borrowing. But to increase your chance for approval, it helps to begin building a good credit history by opening a checking and savings account. After that, you should be eligible for local department store charges. For several months, you might want to run up a small balance and pay it off . . . on time.

The best strategy is to arrange for a bank loan from a bank with which you or your spouse have had a relationship. You shouldn't have any trouble getting approval if you apply for a collateralized loan, where you pledge an asset equal to the value of the loan. Apply for the loan in your name only and then pay it back exactly as scheduled.

The Equal Credit Opportunity Act (ECOA)

To overcome years of discrimination, the law forces the hand of those banks and institutions who would just as soon not give credit to women and other minorities even if they meet the lender's standards of creditworthiness. The Equal Credit Opportunity Act forbids discrimination against a credit applicant based on age, sex, race, religion, national origin, marital status or receipt of public assistance. Further, no one can be:

- Discouraged or prevented from applying for a loan;
- Refused a loan if they otherwise qualify;

- Lent money on different terms than others with similar "risks";
- Given less money than applied for, if other people with similar "risks" apply for and receive the whole amount.

WOMEN AND DISCRIMINATION

In times long past, women with credit in their own names were either rich old spinsters, or married women with husbands who co-signed for them. But, as the advertising slogan says, "You've Come a Long Way Baby!" Thanks to years of consciousness-raising while becoming a tremendous force in the workplace, today there are millions of women, young and old, who apply for and receive bank loans, mortgages, credit cards, car loans, etc. Many of the ECOA's provisions were stipulated specifically to address the charges of past discrimination that made credit so inaccessible to women.

The main thrust behind the law is that a person cannot be denied credit because of their sex or marital status (married, single, divorced, separated, or widowed).

Here are other provisions related to sex discrimination:

- Credit applications cannot require you to list your sex, nor do you have to refer to yourself as Miss, Ms. or Mrs.

- Loan applications to buy or build a home are the exception to this, because the government monitors *housing discrimination* and keeps track of female versus male home purchasing.

- You have the option to disclose your child support or alimony payments, depending on whether you *want* the lender to count this as income.

- An application cannot inquire about your plans for a family or your method of birth control.

In effect, men and women are viewed as equal in the eyes of the law.

Marriage

Whether you are married or not, you have the right to maintain separate credit card accounts and other loans, provided you can prove your own ability to repay. Actually, whatever your current marital status, you should be aware of the following:

- You cannot be refused credit because of your marital status (married, single, widowed, divorced).

- Unless you live in a community property state where spouses are equally responsible for each other's debts, you cannot be required to have your spouse co-sign for a loan.

- A credit application can not inquire about your spouse or ex-spouse when you apply based on your own income. The exception is if your income comes from alimony, child support or other separate maintenance payments from that spouse.

WHEN YOUR MARITAL STATUS CHANGES

Lenders are well aware that marital statuses change for most people at some point in their lives. But the law protects you from credit discrimination when it occurs. The most important condition of the law is that should you become widowed, separated or divorced, a creditor without just cause, cannot:

- Require you to reapply for already established credit;

- Close your account or change the terms of your account.

The factor that determines whether your credit status will change is if your income becomes substantially reduced as a result of the change in marital status. If this is the case, the lender has the right to ask how you will repay the debt(s) and to decide if you are a credit risk or creditworthy. The lender must allow you to use your account while the matter is pending.

Age Discrimination

Many of my clients who plan to retire to Florida and are 60 years or older, express real concern about being turned down for credit because of their age. I tell them that they must realize that age alone cannot be a factor for denying credit. There are exceptions, of course. I once had to explain to a client why I agreed the bank was justified in turning him down for a 30-year fixed mortgage. He was 92 at the time.

When it comes to age discrimination, the ECOA specifies that a lender may ask your age, but may not:

- Refuse to approve credit or decrease your amount simply because of age;

- Refuse to calculate your retirement income in rating your credit application;

- Discontinue your credit account or require you to reapply for credit just because you have reached a certain age and/or have retired.

The law does allow for age as a consideration with respect to how long your current income will continue or how many years it will be before you reach retirement age. In other words, if you are applying for a long-term loan two years before a scheduled retirement, and there is no guarantee of adequate security to pay back the loan, you will undoubtedly be considered a credit risk. As long as you can prove you do have the means to repay, your age cannot work against you in the pursuit of credit.

When Credit Is Denied

The ECOA is also very specific about helping individuals who have been turned down for credit and who feel it is due to discrimination.

First you should be aware that a prospective lender has only 30 days to make a decision about granting or declining your credit application. Should you be turned down, the notification must be in writing and it must explain the reasons for being refused.

If you are turned down as a result of what appears in a credit report, you must be given the name and address of the credit agency who supplied the report so that you can write and request copy of the damaging report. This is also true if an existing account is closed or a credit line reduced.

If you feel that you are being discriminated against, you should inform the lender that this is your belief and try to resolve the problem through negotiation. If you are still denied credit or credit has been taken away and the lender has not given you just cause for this action, then you have the right to obtain help from a federal enforcement agency. Refer to the list below to determine which agency is the proper one to contact based on the type of institution you want to file a claim against.

FOR PROBLEMS WITH CREDIT BUREAUS, DEBT COLLECTION PRACTICES, ANY RETAIL STORE, SMALL LOAN AND FINANCE COMPANIES, PUBLIC UTILITIES, STATE CREDIT UNIONS OR CREDIT CARD COMPANIES, WRITE TO:

Federal Trade Commission
Debt Collection Practices
Washington, DC 20580

Or, you can write to one of the regional FTC offices:

ATLANTA
1718 Peachtree St., N.W.
Atlanta, GA 30367
(404) 347-4836

CHICAGO
55 E. Monroe St.
Chicago, IL 60603
(312) 353-4423

BOSTON
10 Causeway Street
Boston, MA 02222
(617) 565-7240

CLEVELAND
118 St. Clair Ave.
Cleveland, OH 44114
(216) 522-4210

DALLAS	**NEW YORK**
8303 Elmbrook Dr.	26 Federal Plaza
Dallas, TX 75247	New York, NY 10278
(214) 767-7050	(212) 264-1207
DENVER	**SAN FRANCISCO**
1405 Curtis St.	901 Market St.
Denver, CO 80202	San Francisco, CA 94103
(303) 844-2271	(415) 995-5220
LOS ANGELES	**SEATTLE**
11000 Wilshire Blvd.	915 Second Ave.
Los Angeles, CA 90024	Seattle, WA 98174
(213) 209-7890	(206) 442-4655

If you feel that a financial institution has violated a banking law or regulation, there are numerous regulatory agencies that can help you. Who you contact is dependent on whether you're dealing with a national or state chartered bank, a federally insured bank, etc. Refer to the list below to determine which agency is the appropriate one for your particular problem.

NATIONAL BANKS (look for "National" or "N.A." in the bank's name)

Comptroller of the Currency
Consumer Affairs Division
490 L'Enfant Plaza, SW
Washington, DC 20219

STATE CHARTERED BANKS/MEMBER OF THE FEDERAL RESERVE (look for sign that says "Member, Federal Reserve System" and "FDIC")

Federal Reserve System
Division of Consumer and Community Affairs
20th and Constitution Ave, NW
Washington, DC 20551

STATE CHARTERED BANKS/NON-MEMBER OF THE FEDERAL RESERVE (sign will still say "FDIC" but not Member, Federal Reserve System)

Federal Deposit Insurance Corp.
Office of Bank Customer Affairs
Washington, DC 20429

CHAPTER 5

Cleaning Up Your Debts Before Cleaning Out The Garage

I f the 1970s conjure up memories of the "jet set," then the 80s will sure bring to mind the "debt set." This year the national debt topped two trillion dollars. Consumer debt represented over $666 billion of that (not including mortgages). Hopefully the amount you owe your creditors pales by comparison.

But regardless of how much you do owe, if you see that your bills are choking you every month and you don't have the vaguest idea of how to get back in control, you have more in common with Congress than you thought. Small consolation, no doubt.

What's the answer to getting a handle on your indebtedness? The answer is simple whether you owe $5000 or $5 million. Stop spending on all but the basics. I know. I know. If the government with all their resources and braintrusts can't seem to reduce the country's debt, how can you, one single adult, master the task?

It's easy. Just make the commitment to work at it and realize that whoever invented the credit card was probably the same guy who invented the boomerang. Seriously, if you are prepared to be honest with yourself about your spending habits and you genuinely want to resolve the problem before you move to Florida, then there are numerous steps you can take to correct the problem. Even more important, I can show you ways to stay out of debt once and for all.

The first step in reducing your debt is to determine on how bad your credit situation really is. I'm not just talking about the extent of your indebtedness (although that is critical information). I'm talking about coming to terms with your month-to-month pay-back habits, the fancy footwork you do to get by. In other words, are you constantly robbing Peter to pay Paul? Are you playing "eenie meenie miney mo" when it comes to deciding which bills to pay?

To truthfully examine your financial picture, please answer YES or NO to each of the statements on the following pages.

Scoring

Now add up the number of statements to which you answered YES. To obtain your score, multiply the number of YES's times 5. For example, if you answered "YES" to 15 statements, your score is 75. Look at the analysis below for your score.

75 or Higher: You're drowning. You need a life jacket only a financial planner or a reputable credit counselor can provide. If you don't seek professional advice, your only other option will be working with an attorney and filing for bankruptcy. Admittedly, the stigma of bankruptcy is not what it used to be, but it's still a very serious matter. It can impair your credit record for the next 10 years. In some instances, you could lose your house and property. Do not pass go, do not collect your $200 until you get help.

50 to 75: You are in over your head, but the problems can be controlled. The first step is to halt all but essential expenses. Cut the credit cards up. Work out a repayment plan with your creditors and don't make any major purchases until you can break the cycle of living on credit.

25 to 50: You are over-extended but you've been able to dodge the bullets. You're in a good position to consolidate your debts. By using restraint from now on, you can avoid more serious problems. Setting up a budget, and following it, could make a world of difference.

Below 25: Congratulations, you're on safe ground (but you already know that). However, please keep in mind that with the new tax laws, much of your credit may not be deductible. So why pay 12%-18% interest while you've probably got savings accounts earning 6%-8%? Cut back on credit card purchases and put your savings into money market accounts.

Although your score will be quite revealing with respect to your financial status, it will probably not tell you anything you didn't already know in your heart. And that is, in order to reduce your debt and *stay out of debt*, you are going to have to make changes. Drastic though they will seem, the best present you can give yourself is having your finances under control before you leave for Florida. Even if you are in less trouble than you thought, do yourself a favor and remember one thing— borrowing isn't what it used to be.

Credit Cards

_____ I pay the minimum amount or less each month.

_____ I've reached my credit limits on my Visa and/or MasterCard.

_____ I'm charging purchases I used to pay cash for.

_____ I'm taking cash advances from one credit card to make payments on another.

_____ My credit card balances keep going up, not down.

_____ It's been months since I paid my credit card bills on or before their due dates.

_____ I've applied for more credit cards to increase my borrowing capacity.

_____ My spouse and I each have our own separate accounts for the same department stores so we have access to more credit.

_____ Dunning letters and late notices are a real fixture in my mailbox.

_____ I've been threatened with legal action or repossession.

_____ I honestly don't know how much installment debt I have and I'm afraid to find out.

_____ One or more of my creditors has turned me over to a collection agency for non-payment or for a substantial balance I can't seem to reduce.

_____ I've considered going to a lending agency for debt consolidation.

_____ My brother-in-law knows this loan shark…

_____ I've considered filing for bankruptcy.

Checking And Savings

_____ I've stopped contributing to my savings account.

_____ I frequently take money out of the savings account to pay bills.

_____ The balance in my savings account would not cover expenses for three months, let alone the optimal six months.

_____ I no longer have a savings account.

_____ I consistently tap into my overdraft checking in order to pay bills.

_____ I play Russian Roulette with the bank (writing checks before payday and then rushing to deposit a paycheck in order to cover them).

_____ I postdate checks so my payments won't bounce.

_____ I "forget" to sign my checks in order to buy time, knowing that the creditors will forgive an occasional "honest" mistake.

Loans

_____ I've borrowed money to pay for household expenses, including the rent or mortgage.

_____ I've taken out a loan from a new source to pay off an old loan or debt.

_____ I've been paying bills with money earmarked for other financial obligations.

_____ I've been turned down for a loan in the past year.

Income

_____ More than 20% of my take home pay goes to pay off my debts.

_____ The amount of take home pay I use to pay off my debts is increasing.

_____ My liquid assets total less than my short-term debt.

THE PRICE OF BORROWING

With the implementation of the new tax laws, deducting interest payments on your installment debt from your income taxes is becoming a thing of the past. In 1988 only 40% of the interest paid was deductible. In 1989, the deductible will drop to 20%; a year later, 10%. After 1990, you'll be totally on your own.

Furthermore, interest on installment debt is still hovering between 18% and 20% on unpaid balances, while our savings accounts are earning a not-very-exciting 8%. When you further add the cost of annual membership fees, and the exhorbitant penalties for late payments and over-the-limit charges, in another era it would have been called highway robbery.

The bottom line is that borrowing is a very expensive proposition today. If you're buying something on sale and throwing it on your Visa card, it would probably be cheaper if you'd paid full price in cash. That's one of the reasons it is so important to control your borrowing habits. The other reason, of course, is that if you are planning to move, you'll be doing yourself an incredible favor if your debts don't move with you. Having a lighter load, fiscally speaking, will make your transition so much more rewarding and enjoyable.

HOW MUCH ARE YOU SPENDING ON CREDIT?

Let's take some positive steps to remedy your credit problems.

The first thing to do is figure out what percentage of your after-tax income you're spending to pay off installment debts. The conservative school of thought is that you should be spending no more than 15% to 20% of your take-home pay, not including your mortgage payment. If you are currently spending 20% to 30%, or higher, it's time to apply the emergency brakes.

The best way to analyze how much of your income and savings are being eaten away every month by credit debt is to write down every creditor on a piece of paper. Next to that put the interest rate being paid, the average monthly payment and the total amount due. If there is a maturity date (when the loan will be retired), list that as well. Add it all up, and that's exactly where you're at.

Another way to determine the extent of your indebtedness is to prepare a personal balance sheet, or net-worth statement. This is a list all of your assets—liquid and fixed—in one column, and all of your debts and liabilities in another. Subtract the total liabilities from the total assets, and you'll arrive at your net worth. (See Chapter 1 to prepare a net worth statement).

Whatever the bottom line, don't give up. If you're willing to fight this battle, there are any number of ways you can win.

Strategies For A Successful Turnaround

I have a client who swears that the only way to acquire a second home, a second car, and a second vacation is to get a third income. I told him that's the hard way. Here are some practical suggestions to get you started on the road to fiscal fitness and to remain in good standing with the creditors you don't ultimately cancel out on:

- *Cut, Cut, Cut...*Find the biggest, sharpest scissors in the house and start cutting up credit cards—all but the ones you need for emergencies such as gas cards, one bank card (MasterCard or Visa), and one dining card (American Express, Diners Club, etc.) Anything else will get you into deeper trouble. Remember one thing: Credit cards don't extend your paycheck. They actually give you less money to work with because they eat away at your income month-in and month-out. Remove the temptation of overspending by destroying your cards (and your spouse's), and you will rediscover the true meaning of a good night's sleep.

- *Look for Better Rates...*If you don't have the money to pay back the balance on your high-interest bank card, shop for a lower-rate card and use that to pay off the more expensive one. There's one caveat. Be sure that the interest rate on a cash advance isn't higher than borrowing on term. For example, Citibank charges 19.8% for cash advances and 16.8% on credit charges. Shop the best deal and you won't get burned.

- *Shop for Better Deals...*Even better, shop for lower-rate, no-annual-fee bank cards. There is a non-profit organization in Washington that publishes a list of about 45 creditors who market cards with no membership fees. They have another list of banks around the country that charge the lowest interest rates. To get copies of these lists, write to Bankcard Holders of America, 333 Pennsylvania Ave., S.E., Washington, D.C. 20003. Send $1.50 for each list requested.

- *Look into Home Equity Loans...*Explore the possibility of applying for a home-equity loan. Interest rates are not nearly as high as they are for credit cards and at least the interest is fully deductible (provided your loan doesn't exceed $100,000). A very strong word of caution before you do this. These loans put your home up as security. You cannot afford to further jeopardize your life by lavishing more things on your family. The only reason you should be borrowing against the roof over your head is to reduce and consolidate your debts. If all you can envision is packing for a Caribbean Cruise, you better pass on this option.

- *Get Rid of the Nuisance Bills...*Try to pay off as many of your small debts as possible. They may not amount to much money in total, but at least you'll feel like you're making progress by scratching creditors' names off your list, and you'll also feel relief knowing there are going to be less threatening letters waiting for you in the future.

- *Pay with the Green Stuff...*Introduce yourself to the concept of "pay-as-you-go." It's one of the last credit bargains around because it offers the privilege of borrowing without the added expense of high-priced finance charges.

- *Keep Track*...Get out of the habit of throwing away your credit receipts. Aside from the fact that they will come in handy if you return purchases, they will help you keep track of monthly spending. If you take each of your receipts, put them in an envelope for the month and then write down the amount of each of those receipts on the back of the envelope, you'll know exactly how much you owe before the bill shows up. Not only does that call immediate attention to billing errors or discrepancies, you'll know in advance if you're overdoing it for the month.

- *It's Time for the "B" Word*...last but not least, you must create a realistic family budget. The first stab at doing so should represent the amount of income you currently generate and a complete breakdown of where it all goes each month. The second version, the one you might call "Future Shock," should indicate what spending will take place (if any) based on how much there is to go around after the anticipated monthly bills have been paid. See Chapter 1 for budget tips.

If you feel that the only way to get out of your mess is to talk with your creditors, by all means do so. The key is to be up-front and honest with them, rather than waiting for them to turn you over to a collection agency. When you talk with them, tell them what you can realistically send them each month to reduce your debt. If they argue with you and threaten that your bill has to be paid in full, get to a supervisor or someone in management. In most cases they will be happy to work out some kind of a payment plan with you rather than risk getting nothing back at all. Or better yet, let your financial planner make the calls. I can tell you from experience that when creditors get assurances from a professional money manager who is supervising a customer's debts, it helps a lot. Further, working with a certified financial planner can make a big difference when it comes to getting back on track. A CFP can help you assess which are the best assets to sell off, and which methods work best to create savings from tax deductions. CFP's can assist you in setting up a realistic budget, developing a total program for restructuring debt, structuring savings plans and reducing overhead and expenses.

It could also be helpful to work with one of the 356 non-profit consumer credit counseling services across the country. Their advice is either nominal or free (they are supported by the government, creditors and even the United Way). Further, they can help you negotiate loan payments, show you how to consolidate your debts, and basically help dig you out of the hole. To find out about a nonprofit counseling center in your area, call or write the National Foundation for Consumer Credit, 8701 Georgia Ave., Suite 507, Silver Spring, MD. 20910. (301) 589-5600.

Be careful of the "for profit" credit repair centers. Many are known to charge outrageous fees (how about $50 an hour?), make impossible promises about fixing your problem (yes, but at what price?), and end up creating even bigger problems for you than the ones you originally presented.

Filing For Bankruptcy

If working with a professional advisor does not provide sufficient relief from the clutches of your creditors, you have the right to file for bankruptcy. It is a drastic measure, and it should only be viewed as a last resort. The first thing to realize is that it *will not* necessarily wipe away all of your obligations. Student loans, overdue taxes, alimony, child support and loans obtained fraudulently by lying about your income are not erased from the slate.

There are two kinds of personal bankruptcy: Chapter 7 and Chapter 13. Deciding which way to file will depend on the kind of debts and assets you have, and your earning power.

If you own a home and you've built up equity in it, you should probably lean towards Chapter 13, which allows you to keep the house while you repay your debts. However, you can only qualify for this provided you earn enough to pay back those debts. Chapter 13 works this way. You submit a budget and a detailed plan for repaying your obligations to the courts. Upon their approval, creditors are obligated to take whatever amount they've been scheduled to receive and must then relieve you of the remainder. Creditors will receive money from a court-appointed trustee, to whom you direct all future payments.

Chapter 7 is more drastic, and is for those who offer an acceptable repayment plan either because they are so deep in debt or because they are currently unemployed. Here, the court cancels all of your debts but takes over your estate in the process; liquidating your assets and dividing them among your creditors. You are entitled to keep some assets and a portion of the equity in your home.

My only hope is that you never get to the point of going through bankruptcy proceedings. While you'll undoubtedly learn your lesson, the heartache and hardship is a very high price to pay.

If you know you're in trouble, whether it be a little or a lot, don't let the problem continue to fester. Take action immediately. Use the prospect of starting over in Florida as your incentive. What a reward it will be for cleaning up your debts before cleaning out the garage!

CHAPTER 6

What's This Business About Choosing A Financial Planner?

If you don't have a financial planner, don't know a financial planner or don't think you can afford a financial planner, you're probably sick and tired of hearing all about financial planners. It seems you can't pick up a newspaper or magazine anymore without reading how they're going to save the world. What's the big fuss? Doesn't your accountant and your attorney take care of everything?

Unfortunately, it's very difficult for CPAs and lawyers to be totally immersed in your finances unless certain events precipitate the need. Your lawyer gets involved when you draw up a Will or start a new business venture. Your accountant comes into your life once a year at tax return time; of course by then it is usually too late to do anything about reducing your tax burden. And when was the last time your accountant called and suggested sitting down to put together a secure retirement plan? Or your lawyer called to make long-term investment recommendations? I guarantee you this has not happened, and I also guarantee that if you are relying solely on an attorney and an accountant, your finances are not being "handled"— they're being "shuffled." It's not their fault. It's not because they don't care. And it's not because they're not competent. It's because legal and accounting professionals have little or no investment training, nor have they been trained to advise people on the fundamentals of financial planning. They also don't maintain the software and hardware to track investments. If you still feel, in spite of this, that you're getting adequate financial counsel, you might have a case of "psychoschlerosis"—a hardening of the attitudes. In today's volatile and complicated economic environment, that line of thinking could really hurt you financially.

Just look at what's happened in the last decade. In the late 70s and early 80s, inflation started to soar, driving up millions of incomes artificially while doing a hatchet job on purchasing power. Interest rates didn't sit still for one minute; then real estate values began to climb and we saw more and more Americans being pushed up into higher tax brackets, forcing them to deal with increasingly complex tax laws and hidden "penalties" for "doing better." Now, through the new tax simplification program, there are people who are in lower brackets but because they have fewer deductions, they're actually paying higher taxes. And what about the proliferation of financial products? You don't need me to tell you it's a whole new ballgame out there!

Financial Planning Is Not A Product...It's A Process

That's precisely why the financial planning profession was born—because it's a whole new ballgame out there. What's so great about financial planning? First of all, it is not another product; it's a process—a long and rewarding ride towards your financial future with an experienced driver behind the wheel...the Financial Planner.

As an overview, financial planning is a complete and objective analysis of your current financial and personal circumstances: your assets and tax liabilities, your income and investments, your savings story, your family needs and cash flow, your retirement goals and your hopes for the future. Do you want to travel? Buy a second home? Put money away for college? Financial planning involves setting goals, selecting coordinated strategies for achieving those goals, implementing the strategies and monitoring the results. This ongoing effort will result in the building and preservation of your estate and will guarantee a financially independent retirement. When you sit down with a financial planner to discuss your needs and your goals, the outcome will be a highly organized, realistic program for accomplishing your objectives. The recommendations will be outlined in a written document: the financial plan. This plan is your roadmap, a guide to your financial security.

Financial Planning: Who Is It For?

In my private financial planning practice, I meet hundreds of nice people every year who tell me that financial planning isn't necessary for them. These same people then complain that their mortgage-interest deductions are tapering off with nothing on the horizon to lighten the tax load.

I've talked to people who haven't the vaguest notion of how they're going to pay for their children's college educations. A single mother told me she encourages her 6-year-old son to blow part of his allowance on lottery tickets. "Maybe we'll hit the jackpot and the state will pay his tuition," she says! Or how about the father of twins who told me that he begged them not to study so hard when they announced their intentions to apply to Ivy League schools? "Can't you goof off a little more?" he pleaded. He said it half in jest. But he, too, was sure a financial planner couldn't help him.

Then there are the investors, both small and large, who have portfolios full of "dinosaurs"—money sitting in outdated and virtually useless investments because they don't have the time or the expertise to select anything else. And they tell me that financial planning is for people who don't know what they're doing!

I've talked to people who summer where they winter even though they once had high hopes of buying a vacation home. Somehow that second home never materialized because over the years money disappeared like water. They've missed out on years of pleasure, not to mention significant tax savings…and they tell me that financial planning is only for the rich.

Then there are the six-figure professionals who bring home $10,000 a month but manage to spend $15,000. On top of this, they often have trouble covering a $100 check for the week's groceries. And they tell me that financial planning sounds great as soon as they can put enough money together to pay for it.

The people I am most concerned about are those who are financially unprepared for retirement. Unfortunately that represents every nine out of ten Americans. It is a tragedy that only one tenth of the population is financially independent at retirement today. Everyone else relies solely on charity, friends and family and their minimum social security benefits. Otherwise they must keep working at a part-time, or even full-time job. And these people tell me they can't afford financial planning. To them and to the rest I say, "In today's money-maddening times, you can't afford not to have a financial planner. Financial planning is no longer a tool for the wealthy. It's for anyone and everyone who wants to be fiscally fit!"

And Now That You're Moving To Florida...

If you're reading this book, I assume it's for one of three reasons: you're considering a move to Florida; you've already decided to move; or you're going to help someone else make the move—perhaps your parents. Wonderful! It's going to mean the start of a very exciting, rewarding lifestyle change. And it's the perfect time to get your financial house in order. You see, making a long distance move means not only packing up your personal belongings, it also means packing up and moving your financial belongings. If you're like most people, you will probably move your money into new checking and savings accounts. You'll eventually get new credit cards, transfer your stock certificates to a local brokerage house…get the picture?

The point is, if you expect to take a hard look at your furniture and household goods, you should also take a hard look at your finances. Decide what you want to sell off. Give away. Take with you. How about some updating? If you can reupholster your living room furniture so it has that "Florida" look, why not spruce up some of your investments? The enhanced value will give you years of service and pleasure!

How can you do all of this by yourself? The answer is you can't. You'll need the guidance and expertise of a professional. A certified financial planner. Consider it a housewarming present to yourself.

A Financial Planner's Credentials

Today there are an estimated 150,000 people practicing financial planning. Not all who hang out their shingles, however, have the credentials or educational requirements to be certified by the College of Financial Planning or the Institute of Certified Financial Planners (ICFP). This is possible because there are few current state and no federal laws requiring any specific education, training, or qualifications to be a financial planner. Of those who call themselves planners, only a few thousand have qualified for membership in the Institute of Certified Financial Planners (ICFP), which requires extensive course work of their members as well as the passing of rigorous examinations.

The problem for consumers in the past was what I called the "alphabet soup" dilemma. Everyone in the industry seemed to have initials after their name—CFP, CPA, ChFC, RFP, RIA, CLU, etc. Then there were the people with advanced degrees in real estate, law and business. Add that to the MBAs, the GRIs (Graduate of the Real Estate Institute), and the MSFSs (Master of Science in Financial Services). To sort out the confusion, the ICFP and the IAFP (International Association of Financial Planners) have been working to restructure their organizations so that they speak to consumers with a unified voice. Their aim is to help establish who is a qualified financial planning professional with acceptable credentials.

Certified Financial Planners (CFPs) receive their professional designation after studying and demonstrating competency in the most crucial areas: tax planning and management, investments and securities, estate and retirement planning, financial planning, insurance, and risk management. The designation "Certified Financial Planner" is more than a title; it's a precise definition of the person's knowledge, experience, competence and overall understanding of the complexities of financial planning.

Anyone who is a Certified Financial Planner has enrolled in very difficult training programs offered by either the College for Financial Planning in Denver or similar accredited colleges. To receive the designation, the candidate must have passed six different three-hour tests and, be approved by the IBCFP—the International Board of Standards and Practices for Certified Financial Planners. Once a planner has received this professional certification, he or she agrees to abide by one highly-principled Code of Ethics established by the IBCFP and other affiliated organizations. These are not laws but standards by which the CFP will determine the propriety of conduct in relationships with clients, colleagues and the public.

Briefly, the Code promotes these doctrines:

1. *CFPs must place the public interest above their own.*

2. *They must continually maintain and improve their professional knowledge, skills and competence.*

3. *They must obey all laws and regulations, avoiding any conduct or activity which causes unjust harm to others.*

4. *CFPs must be diligent in the performance of their occupational duties.*

5. *They must establish and maintain honorable relationships with other professionals, those with whom the members serve in a professional capacity and with all those who rely upon their professional judgement and skills.*

6. *CFPs must assist in improving the public's understanding of financial planning.*

Finally, CFPs are the only planners whose credentials are continually monitored by the IBCFP. They confirm that every CFP is meeting certain professional standards and has passed 60 credits in continuing education courses every two years.

As a Certified Financial Planner in private practice for 10 years, I can attest to how much dedication and knowledge it takes to be called a CFP. And I can say with complete confidence that anyone who has reached this pinnacle is worthy of your consideration and trust. Therefore, I will refer to the CFP when speaking of professional financial planning help. For the sake of readability, the CFP may be referred to as "he."

What Does A CFP Do Exactly?

The role of the Certified Financial Planner is to manage your financial team, not eliminate it. You still want the expertise of your lawyer and accountant, but with a CFP, you'll have a professional coordinating their efforts. Now you can be sure that everyone is working together in your best interests. Your planner will study your investment needs and can either implement a new program, or work with your agent to guarantee the best possible coverage.

Finally, with one professional, you can cover all the bases. You can work with a leader who will look at every aspect of your financial life and take the responsibility to coordinate them so that the various money managers on your team are working toward the same goal!

Just remember that the CFP holds a pencil in his hand, not a wand. There's no magic in what he does; he just relies on good old-fashioned planning strategies combined with today's sophisticated knowledge.

Financial Planning Works For All Generations

A family's financial goals will often be dictated by the age of the income earners, their assets and most importantly their aspirations. Like a baseball game, your life is divided into innings.

THE FIRST 3 INNINGS: YOUR 20s AND 30s

Anything can happen at the beginning of your adult life. Your choices are wide open to you: careers, marriage, children. That's why anyone who starts the financial planning process early in the game will have a tremendous jumpstart on his future. The payoff will be in the ability to acquire more and larger assets, meet interim financial goals such as buying a first home, and ultimately establish a healthy nest egg for retirement. *Your parents and grandparents would have done anything for that opportunity!*

INNINGS 4, 5, & 6: YOUR 40s

It's the middle of the game now. You still have time to make choices, but you're probably working against a score that's already on the board. At this point in your life you have a pretty good sense of where you're going. Your career or business has been established; often the children are heading to college or are already independent (though unfortunately they may not yet be *financially* independent); your assets have accumulated and grown; etc. In essence you have a realistic understanding of your potential earnings, liabilities and investment returns. Use that knowledge to plan for the next 40 years. If you have not yet set up a retirement program for yourself and your spouse, you and your CFP need to make that priority No. 1!

THE FINAL 3 INNINGS: YOUR 50s AND 60s

As Yogi Bera says, "The game's not over till it's over." There's still time to come from behind if you haven't evened the score yet. It's never too late to take advantage of the financial planning process. In fact, it can be a tremendous boon to pre-retirees who make last minute adjustments that reward them with longer-lasting income. A case in point is the retiring client who was offered the choice of either a $1450-a-month life annuity or a $190,000 lump-sum payment from his company pension plan. He didn't know which "pitch" to take; they both looked like fast-balls to him. When he got the help of a CFP, the answer was simple.

What he hadn't realized was that when you elect to annuitize your pension benefits, you forego the possibility of passing on the remainder of the assets at your death. Payments stop at your or your spouse's death, depriving your heirs of the entire sum owed you. When we did the math, he saw that the monthly payments offered little more than the interest on the lump sum. Further, he wasn't aware of the fact that he had several other options, including taking the money in a lump sum and rolling over the pension proceeds into an IRA, which would defer taxes until he started withdrawing. Another option we explored was taking advantage of 5- and 10-year forward averaging, which reduced his tax bite and gave him enough capital to invest in tax-exempt bonds.

In his case, it was more advantageous to take an IRA rollover. It deferred taxes, kept all of his principal intact and ultimately generated a higher payout than any other option. *That's how a financial planner thinks and works in your best interest!*

What Are Your Immediate Needs?

Before you sit down with a Certified Financial Planner, you should take some time to consider your personal family circumstances as well as your immediate needs. What have you been putting off that can't wait any longer? To start, ask yourself these 10 important questions:

1. Are you paying too much in taxes?
2. Do you still spend more than you earn?
3. Do you ever have enough left over to invest?
4. When you invest, do you have specific objectives in mind?
5. Are you happy with your return on investment?
6. Are the things you own properly protected?
7. Do you have an up-to-date Will?
8. Do you have enough assets to retire?
9. Do you have too little or too much life insurance? Is it the appropriate kind?
10. Do you have adequate disability coverage to protect your income should you ever find yourself unable to work due to an accident or illness?

These "financial planning basics" will cover a lot of important ground and give you a good indication of the planner's capabilities.

Translating Goals Into Accomplishments

Once you have a sense of the basics that you need to accomplish, your next step will be to work towards your long term financial goals. Regardless of your station in life, here are some very specific objectives you and your Certified Financial Planner can work together to achieve:

- *Cash Flow*…What do you need to do now to generate enough cash flow to make investing possible? You'll be shown how tax planning and careful budgeting can help you get there. You'll learn how to get a better grip on your expenses and spending habits and how to better manage your income.

- *Retirement Income*…You may be dreaming about retirement, but you're probably not dreaming about paying for it. How much income will you need to maintain your current lifestyle after you retire? You'll discuss all the ways you can extend your pension plan and social security income.

- *College Educations*…By 1990, public colleges will cost $6500 a year. Private colleges will be twice that. How much will it cost you to send your children to college? You and your planner will figure out how much you have to put aside and by what time, taking inflation and other rising costs into consideration.

- *Home Equity*...Figuring out how to finance a home and build equity in it is an enormous challenge for most young families today. Or wanting to move into a larger home as the family grows. Or trying to buy a vacation home. Or all of the above. If these are your goals, your planner will show you how to get there.

- *Estate Planning*...Securing your assets is one of the most important components of a financial plan. You want a way to pass down an inheritance or a family business in a way that will provide for your beneficiaries without burdening them. Your CFP will work with your attorney to make certain that your estate is consistent with changing laws. He will also work with your accountant to minimize taxes while ensuring the best possible distribution of assets.

- *Investment Strategies*...What are your growth objectives? How fast must your money grow in order to provide the things you want? What is your risk tolerance in the market? To borrow from an old commercial, "only your financial planner knows for sure."

Show And Tell: What To Provide Your CFP

Everyone knows the ropes when they visit a new doctor for the first time. They expect a complete physical examination and a thorough discussion of their medical history. A meeting with a CFP will call for the same attention to detail (except that the only thing you'll ever be asked to remove is your jacket).

To give you an idea of the types of hard information financial planners need in order to give you a "complete examination," here is a checklist:

- *Family Data*...including number of children, ages, and information about living parents of spouses;

- *Federal and State Income Tax Returns*...from the past 3 years; also corporate returns, if applicable;

- *Federal Gift Returns*...any that have been filed within the last few years;

- *Financial Statements*...personal net worth statements for you and your spouse;

- *Partnership Agreements, Articles of Incorporation, and Financial Statements*...any business data and financial documents pertaining to your own corporation(s);

- *Wills, Trusts, Divorce Settlements, Buy and Sell Agreements, Stock Redemption Agreements*...and any other agreements related to Testamentary Disposition;

- *Real Estate*…anything owned by either yourself or your corporation. Include locations, purchase dates, costs, current fair market values and reasons for owning;

- *Income*…breakdown of any and all income sources brought in by you and your spouse;

- *Assets*…including savings accounts, stocks and bonds, mortgages, Notes Receivable, educational trusts, etc. Indicate purchase dates, purchase prices, reasons for owning;

- *Employee Benefits*…copies of pension plans, profit sharing plans, deferred compensation plans, group insurance plans;

- *Insurance Policies*…copies of life and disability insurance owned by both you and your corporation;

- *Personal Property*…anything of significant value such as an art collection, jewels, furs, rare coins, etc.;

- *Inheritances*…information and documents pertaining to present or anticipated inheritances.

Understanding The Financial Plan Itself

After you have established your personal financial goals and reviewed your personal data, the next time you meet with your planner will be to review a very important, personal document: the written portion of the financial plan. This confidential plan will offer specific recommendations on how to achieve your stated goals. Don't expect a "boilerplate" agenda. As with fingerprints, no two financial plans are alike. Contained in the plan will be ways to implement the recommendations; it will also provide for ways to coordinate with other specialists. For example, if you need to significantly increase your tax deductions, the plan will point out tax allowances which you and your accountant may have overlooked. Or it might suggest specific investments that will increase your cash flow by building capital more efficiently.

Once you have had the opportunity to review and ponder your financial plan, you'll undoubtedly be impressed. However, no matter how well thought-out the program, it will be rendered useless if the plan is not put into action. The whole idea behind having a CFP work for you is to allow him to use his true talents by implementing the plan he has devised. You won't be helped one iota if the plan gets stashed in a drawer for a rainy day.

Finally, it is important to understand that your financial plan is a living, breathing document. It is not set in stone. It will be updated, reviewed, revised, and otherwise changed to accommodate changing tax laws, changing lifestyles, current economic conditions etc. This is contingent upon your desire to work with your financial planning team. Once you get started, however, it's hard to imagine that there will be any turning back. Why would you ever want to go back to the days when your accountant phoned you with the bad news and said, "Maybe we'll be luckier next year?"

Evaluating Your Financial Plan

Here is a list of important criteria for judging the caliber of your financial plan:

1. Each section should be neat, organized and include some narration in plain English. If it's just a collection of statistics, you'll have a difficult time understanding it.

2. There should be a series of present-value computations. In other words, in order to amass a certain amount of money in a certain time period, you want to know how much to start investing, how frequently, and at what rate of return.

3. Does the plan include an analysis of how much life and disability insurance you need? Unless you are protected with enough coverage, the rest of the plan will never be complete.

4. Is there a balance between investment risks and rewards? If only "best case" scenarios are shown, you're not getting the whole picture. It's better to have probable middle-of-the-road projections that take best and worst cases into consideration.

5. Do the projections make sense to you? Even a non-expert can see a problem if inflation is pegged at 5% but a real estate investment is expected to prosper because of 15% annual rent increases.

6. Finally, does the plan seem realistic to you? Is it based on earnings, savings and investments you can live with? Does the plan address your needs and goals? Does it motivate you to want to stick with it?

It's Time To Find Your Certified Financial Planner

OK, you're in Florida now and you want to look for a CFP. How do you find the right person or firm? Here are some suggestions for starting your search:

1. Ask your new neighbors, business associates or family members in the area if they are working with a CFP.

2. Write or call one of the following national associations for lists of CFPs in your area.

   The Institute of Certified Financial Planners
   10065 East Harvard Ave., Suite 320
   Denver, CO 80231
   (303) 751-7600

   The International Association for Financial Planning
   P.O. Box 467879
   Atlanta, GA 30346
   (404) 395-1605

3. Finally, you can refer to the Yellow Pages. A word of caution, however: under the heading of Financial Planners you'll find accountants, bankers, lawyers, insurance agents, real estate and securities brokers, and eventually, the genuine article: the Certified Financial Planner.

You'll also see exciting buzz words like "wealth management," "dynamics," "resources," etc. which sound nice, but don't tell you anything about the firm's approach to financial planning. For a clue, look at the designations of the members of the firm. Are they mostly accountants? That could suggest that they will be expert in tax matters but conservative in their investments. If the planners are listed as CLUs, their insurance background has trained them to limit risks. Stockbrokers who are now planners may be partial to stocks in their investment choices. CFPs are less likely to have biases because they've been trained to evaluate a wide variety of investment strategies.

Interviewing Financial Planners

The only way to decide on a financial planner is to set up a meeting for a free consultation. In that meeting, the planner will go over his or her credentials as well as the capabilities and resources of their firm. Equally important will be the opportunity to discuss your problems, goals and overall outlook on your situation. That one session should be revealing enough to give you a sense of your "comfort level."

FULL DISCLOSURE DOCUMENT

If for any reason you're the type of person who has difficulty "drilling" someone on their credentials and philosophy, or you just want to consider a firm in the privacy of your home, request a copy of the firm's Full Disclosure Document. This is a brochure which will describe in detail the company's basic working philosophy, types of clientele the firm serves, payment requirements, potential conflicts of interest and complete background on the firm's staff: background, education, credentials, licenses, and expertise.

If the firm has no such literature, let the buyer beware. Or, if in examining the document there is no indication that the planners are Registered Investment Advisors (RIA) with the Securities and Exchange Commission (SEC) or with an appropriate state agency, the value of their investment advice is not very high. Finally, you want to see if the firm is affiliated with professional trade organizations such as the IAFP and the ICFP. This tells you that they are fulfilling annual continuing education requirements and are being kept current on the latest information involving financial planning.

QUESTIONS YOU WANT ANSWERED

I recommend that you meet with at least two different planners before you decide who you'll ultimately work with. All this should cost you is your time. Over and above your own gut instincts about the person, here are 10 categories of questions you can go over with a financial planner so you can determine in your own mind if this person is acceptable to you.

1. *Background...* What is the planner's education, experience, reputation and track record? It's in the Full Disclosure Document, but you want to hear it from the horse's mouth to be sure it's the same story.

2. *Remuneration...* Inquire how the planner is compensated. Does the firm work strictly on a fee basis, with fees and commissions, or strictly on commissions? If this is an all-commission firm, for obvious reasons their advice will be awfully biased and thin on planning.

3. *Communication...* Do you understand what the planner is saying or are you being "jargonized" to death? If you've ever had a doctor or lawyer who spoke in a "foreign" language, you'll recognize the problem immediately. Also, take a look at samples of the firm's financial plans. Are they clear, concise and well communicated? Are they neat and organized? This is all a reflection of the company's philosophy and strengths.

4. *Specialization...* Does anyone in the firm have a specialized expertise in the area of employee fringe benefits (pensions, stock options, etc.)? Is the firm known for its work in a particular category, such as pre-retirees, professionals, etc? Does their specialization match your needs?

5. *Size of the Organization...* While the number of people in the firm is not an indicator by itself, the growth of the company is. If the company has increased in size in respect to employees and clients,

that says a lot about their track record and their respectability. That's more important than glossy brochures and plush offices. Also, if you're meeting with a solo practitioner, be aware that anyone who has to do everything himself—answering phones, doing all the computer work, etc.—will have less time for the most important work.

6. *Accessibility*…How easy will it be to get to your planner? Is the person you have your initial consultation with the same person who will be working on your plan? If not, will that person be supervising the work on your plan? If not, who will be?

7. *Competency*…Is the planner trained in all types of investments, tax-advantaged vehicles, insurance and tax strategies? Is he or she comfortable working with complicated legal documents? Is the planner fluent in retirement plans, estate planning, wills, trusts, and business partnership agreements?

8. *Independent Recommendations*…How are strategic decisions arrived at? Is it through a detailed study of your needs involving research, or does it derive from a computer-generated program that is applicable to anyone? Is the planner influenced by a preference for a particular type of investment? Is he or she an independent thinker?

9. *References*…Are they readily available? Are you offered several names or just one? References can be tricky because you can expect that the names will be carefully selected. Still, they may be helpful if you are undecided about a planner.

10. *Likeability*…You will eventually share the most personal information with your financial planner. You will confide in him, express your fears, etc. That's why in addition to everything else, there has to be chemistry. A rapport. A mutual trust and confidence. The bottom line is do you like and respect the planner both as a person and as a professional? Sometimes all the other criteria will be fine, but it's that last hump—liking the person—that stops you. Or it can be the other way around: you really the like the person but question his qualifications. Take your time deciding. You want this person to be a part of your life for many years to come.

Finally…You Probably Want To Know What This Is Going To Cost!

If anyone can appreciate the subject of what things cost, it's going to be a financial planner. That's why the subject of fees should be an easy one to discuss, once the planner has a solid understanding of your case. It would be unfair of you to expect any reputable firm to quote prices without first having a sense of you and your needs. The way they determine that is by having you fill out a questionnaire they use to start a plan. If you are seriously interested in the planner, take the time to fill it out. It's really the only way to provide enough details to size up your case.

As far as specific fees are concerned, sometimes it will be based on your income and net worth. If that is the case, find out exactly how that is calculated so you aren't surprised by a whopping bill. In most instances, however, fees will depend on how many hours it will take to generate your plan. The more complex a plan you need, the more it will cost, and rightfully so. Time is money. What you can review in detail is how the firm earns its money. As we discussed briefly, there are three methods of compensation.

FEE PLUS COMMISSIONS

The largest sector of financial planning firms charge an upfront fee to develop a financial plan for new clients. This fee can range from $500 to $1500 for the average plan and go up to several thousand dollars if the plan delves into extremely complex issues and requires extraordinary research and strategic planning.

After your plan is completed, you are free to go to anyone for implementation. If you are satisfied with the planner's work, however, you may find it advantageous to have him do the follow-through by personally handling the investments. This way you can be assured that one person is continually monitoring and updating the investment strategies. Many consumers like the idea of "one stop shopping" because of its convenience (make one call to get several answers), and the opportunity it gives the planner to become totally involved in your case. That can really work to your benefit. The planner is compensated for handling the implementation through commissions earned from the sales of the investments. That's why they are called "Fee Plus" planners. They are licensed to sell mutual funds, insurance policies, real estate partnerships, and other financial products. In doing so, they earn a percentage of those sales. This extra source of income helps to keep the cost of the financial plan down. Some Fee Plus firms also charge by the hour or an annual retainer fee for continual updating and monitoring of the investments.

FEE-BASED PLANNERS

Some planners work *only* on a fee basis. They charge a set amount for developing a financial plan and do not earn commissions on the sale of investment products. As a result, their fee structure tends to be the highest in the business. You can expect to pay anywhere from $1000 to $6000 up front, plus an hourly fee ($100 an hour) for future consultations. If you agree to the hourly charges, find out if the clock starts ticking as soon as you pick up the phone or if you're only charged for formal consultations.

With Fee-Only planners, their claim of total impartiality is valid, but they may have less incentive to select winning investments. The reason is they will not have to answer directly to you if their recommendations don't work out. They will refer you back to the firm that actually made the investments.

COMMISSION ONLY

There are still some financial planning firms that charge nothing for a financial plan if you allow them to handle your investments. In other words, they earn no fees. Their income is based solely on how much revenue they generate from the sales of investment products. I would caution you about this setup. It sounds great because your up-front financial commitment is zero. On the other hand, the recommendations they make can unfortunately be more in their interest instead of yours. In the end, that could cost you plenty. As with anything else, you get what you pay for. Advice that costs you nothing is often worth nothing.

Summing Up

Today we are living and working in the richest, most productive country in the history of the world, yet we are faced with more complex financial problems than those that faced any previous generations.

Today we work shorter hours and earn more money, but the dollars buy less and less.

Today our children can look forward to better jobs and wonderful opportunities for advancement, but those opportunities depend on higher education, which is becoming prohibitive for even middle class families.

Today, through modern medicine, people are living longer. Retirement can last 20, 30 or perhaps 40 years, but most people are not prepared to pay for their retirement and must be supported by family or Social Security. It's hardly a great existence.

Today taxes take an ever-increasing bite out of our income and passing on an estate to one's heirs is even more difficult and expensive.

You know all this. So does a Certified Financial Planner. Why not let one show you how he can deal with these very important concerns? Investing in a CFP will be the single most important investment you have ever made in a lifetime!

CHAPTER 7

Financial Planning Mistakes You Didn't Even Know You Were Making

In his hit Broadway show, "The World According to Me," Jackie Mason brilliantly summed up the human condition when he referred to the single biggest financial mistake people feel they've made. "Everyone I know could have bought a building thirty years ago for nine dollars, but didn't." Then they cry, "Do you know what that building is worth today? One hundred and eighty-seven million. They talked me out of it, those —!" It's funny but true.

Haven't we all lived to regret an investment we could have, should have, would have made, but didn't?

Unfortunately, nothing is more disheartening than discovering we've made mistakes along the path to financial freedom. When those well-meaning decisions come back to haunt us, wouldn't it be nice if we could sell our mistakes for the same price they cost us? I say whatever and whenever the missed opportunities, poor judgments, and uneducated decisions took place, it's never too late to learn from your mistakes and correct the problems. It also never hurts to learn from the mistakes made by others. Lord knows none of us will live long enough to make them all ourselves.

Why not review this list of the most common financial planning errors the average person makes? The recommended solutions are all common sense ideas, but not always common practice.

See if you recognize any errors that you may have made, were about to make, or if you know someone else has made. When you're done, if you move to correct even a few, you'll be ahead of the game.

Investment Planning

KEEPING TOO MUCH MONEY IN CHECKING AND SAVINGS ACCOUNTS

There's nothing easier than keeping large sums of money in non-interest bearing checking and 5¼% savings accounts. They're safe havens. But there's no reason to keep more than the minimum balance required to take advantage of free checking or interest-bearing benefits. You may recall when savings rates didn't keep up with inflation; with a small yield coupled with taxes on the interest, many people experienced negative or no growth on their money. That's why it's more profitable to open accounts that are tied to money-market rates so you can increase the after-tax yield on cash balances. Or, ask your financial planner or brokerage firm about money market accounts that pay interest that is exempt from federal taxes.

INSUFFICIENT LIQUIDITY

On the other hand, some people are apt to keep only the amount they need to cover a month's expenses in their accounts, and not a dime more. Obviously it makes more sense to have enough of a reserve on hand in case of an emergency. Exactly how much to have available depends on how secure your income is and how much insurance protection you have. But for argument's sake, the optimal amount to keep liquid is enough to cover expenses for three to six months. This way you are less likely to ever have to sell off an investment before it comes due. Otherwise you could realize a substantial loss and/or penalty for early withdrawal.

NOT DIVERSIFYING YOUR INVESTMENT PORTFOLIO

Everyone likes a sure thing, which is why some investors continue to put money into an investment which consistently performs well. The problem occurs when that investment suddenly stops providing the anticipated returns. Then it's the old "putting too many eggs into one basket" dilemma. That's why the backbone of any sound financial plan is diversification. And by diversification I do not mean an assortment of savings accounts. I mean having a balance of savings, stocks, bonds, real estate and tax free investments. This strategy helps ensure that your assets are insulated from inflation and the weak performance of a single investment. Continued diversification within those categories will further shelter you from downward trends in a particular investment.

THE GREED FACTOR

For some investors, seeking out the highest possible yields is their only strategy. It's called the "greed" factor, and although sometimes it works in their favor, more often than not it doesn't. For example, one client bought municipal bonds because of the impressive 9% yield, but he had to pay a premium over par value. What he failed to recognize was that the bonds could be redeemed or called at any time at par, resulting in a loss of the premium paid. Within the year, that's exactly what happened. The investment had no net gain! Other times people get very involved with utility stocks that pay 13%, but no sooner do they buy than the stock stops paying 13% dividends. Those high yield CDs from Texas banks also seemed irresistible until many of the banks folded their tents.

This is why the most fundamental lesson of finance is that the higher the return, the higher the risk. And that risk has to be weighed with every investment, particularly with the falling interest rates we've seen over the past few years. This resulted in millions of people moving out of money markets and into these higher-yield investments, unaware that there could be severe pain with their gain. Their net worth was drastically affected as soon as interest rates took a turn upwards because lower yielding fixed incomes are worth less. To protect yourself, consider other features of the high-yield investment such as call protection, risk of default, and whether there is private insurance on the return of principal and a spread of both long- and short-term maturities.

EXCESSIVE DEBT

The more you borrow, the more your financial picture is affected because the debt-to-equity ratio is thrown off balance. The key is to be fully aware of your assets-to-liabilities; in other words, your net worth statement. You should always be aware of the percentage of disposable income used to reduce your installment debts, and put on the brakes if you see that more than 15% to 20% is going out the door each month (not including your mortgage) to pay creditors. One telltale sign is if you are creating additional debt in order to pay off other debts.

RUNAWAY DAILY EXPENSES

It's human nature to spend today in the hopes that tomorrow will bring a higher income, an inheritance, a winning lottery ticket, etc. This is called financial planning by default or living on "F.I.": Future Income. Deficit spending is costly in terms of paying out high interest rates on installment debts, but where you really get hurt is by spending in lieu of saving...for your children's education, for home improvements, or, more importantly, for your retirement. The prudent approach is to have a balance of spending and saving, and to be committed to that for the long haul. If you really don't know where your money is going, it's time for family members to keep a notebook recording daily expenses. Even a week's worth of notes will shed enough light to help you figure out where you can cut corners. Another strategy is to work towards a balanced budget each month, with savings added in as an "expense."

INVESTING FOR TAX-FREE INCOME
AT THE WRONG TAX BRACKET

It is a natural assumption that tax-free income is the ultimate asset, and it does sound good in theory. However, for some taxpayers, it's important to examine the after-tax alternatives before jumping to any conclusions. In other words, depending on your tax bracket, it may be more advantageous to get a higher taxable return than a lower tax-free return. For example, if an investor who is in a 28% tax bracket had a choice between buying a 7% tax-free bond or a 10% taxable bond, the *after-tax* return on the taxable bond would be .2% higher than the tax-free. Have your certified financial planner or CPA help you determine whether tax-free income is the right investment strategy based on your tax bracket.

OVERLEVERAGED REAL ESTATE

If you've had real estate investments for ten or more years, then you know all too well that Congress has drastically changed the rules of the game. In the good old days, you could put down 10% in an investor mortgage, buy a house and rent it out. Your income was then sheltered with big write-offs, depreciation and interest. Maybe you had some negative cash flow, but you balanced that with very respectable capital appreciation. Within seven years the sale price covered your tax gain, paid off the mortgage and closing costs, and still left you with a 25% or higher annual return. Today tax rates are lower, but there's no tax break on capital gains and families with adjusted gross income of $100,000 or higher have lost their right to offset all or a percentage of real estate losses against earned income. Furthermore, property values are slower to rise than they were years ago, and in some cases they are completely flat. That's why the route to take today is investing with less debt.

Here are some suggestions. If you already own rental property and can't use the write-offs, you should either sell to cut your losses, or restructure your deal to create a low-leverage investment. If you have substantial equity in your home, another tactic is to borrow against it to pay down your rental-property mortgage. Remember that interest on your home mortgage is still deductible, up to a certain level. But interest on rental property is only deductible against income generated.

NOT TAKING ADVANTAGE OF COMPANY BENEFIT PROGRAMS

Many companies offer optional benefit programs to employees such as forced savings programs, stock plans, supplemental group life insurance and long-term disability coverage. Typically these programs are extremely beneficial, yet go untapped by many employees because they don't want to have less net income. In truth, however, money that doesn't come home will not get spent (and will probably not be missed). So why not sign up for these programs via painless payroll deductions? Here is why these programs are so great. First, with respect to insurance, group rates will always be significantly lower than anything you could purchase as an individual policy holder. Further they could make it easier to provide guaranteed coverage at a time when you are uninsurable due to an age or health-related problem. As for stock and savings plans, many employers will actually match your contributions, thereby doubling your efforts. Finally, if the company performs well in the stock market, you'll profit from the favorable returns. Obviously you have to evaluate the benefit program to determine if it's advantageous to you; in all probability, you'll find that it is. After all, they're not called employee "benefits" for nothing.

NOT SEEKING THE ADVICE OF PROFESSIONALS

Even in today's complex financial world, there are people who feel that no one other than themselves can help them achieve their financial goals. Or they feel that no one could possibly have their interests at heart as much as they do. Or they feel that the out-of-pocket expense of professional advice will be too great. All of this is short-sighted thinking and actually costs people by way of expensive mistakes. Everyone should have at least one professional advisor today, and preferably more. The most versatile professionals are the Certified Financial Planners because they have a broad understanding of all financial matters. But it can also be advantageous to use a Certified Public Accountant, an attorney, and an investment advisor. These professionals pay for themselves over and over again by charting a sound, profitable course of action for your financial future. If you still think their fees are costly, wait until you figure out what *not* having access to them costs you.

Tax Planning

NOT ITEMIZING TAX DEDUCTIONS

Often taxpayers who rent, as opposed to own, perceive that they don't have enough deductions to itemize on their tax returns; but in many instances, this assumption is wrong. It's possible that there are enough deductions through business and medical expenses, state income taxes and other items. Or, even if you're a homeowner but you always take the standard deduction, it pays to double-check with an accountant or competent tax preparer to make sure that you are not losing out on thousands of dollars of savings every year. Once the tax year ends, those savings are non-recoverable. Just remember to keep good records throughout the year so that you will be able to take advantage of every deduction owed you.

NOT CONSIDERING THE ALTERNATIVES
WHEN YOU RECEIVE LUMP SUM DISTRIBUTIONS

When a retirement plan pays benefits, it's often in the form of a lump sum. This is particularly true of employment plans when an employee leaves or retires. If you are 50 or older, find out whether you are eligible for a special tax treatment called capital gains/ten-year forward averaging, or five-year forward averaging. Alternately, you can "roll over" the taxable portion of the distribution into an IRA (Individual Retirement Account), thereby completely deferring income taxes until the money is used. The benefit of an IRA rollover is that it allows you to defer taxes on the lump sum distribution until you actually start receiving the funds. This is typically at retirement when most people are in lower tax brackets. If you use this special tax treatment, it can result in an immediate lower rate of taxation. The only downside is that you forgo the benefits of the tax deferral on the principal and the earnings. Your financial planner can help you determine which options are available to you and work to your advantage; the proper execution can save you thousands of dollars; the wrong one can cost you more than that in lost income. Since this option is allowed only once, and the decision is irrevocable, you cannot afford to make a mistake.

USING THE WRONG ASSETS TO MAKE ANNUAL GIFTS

In order to take advantage of the annual $10,000 gift tax exclusion, some taxpayers give assets to friends or family members. The problem is when people use previously taxed cash to make such a gift. The better route to take is to give appreciated securities and have the donee pay the capital gains tax. This is very advantageous if the recipient, perhaps a grandchild, is in a much lower tax bracket than you, the donor.

NOT CLAIMING ENOUGH WITHHOLDING ALLOWANCES ON A TAX RETURN

If you have a substantial number of itemized deductions and/or business losses, you should be sure that you are withholding enough allowances from your income. If you are only withholding for yourselves and your dependents, it will probably result in an overpayment of taxes by the end of the year. To see if this is what is happening to your paycheck, review the worksheet on Form W-4. You obviously want to withhold what is legitimately owed the IRS. On the other hand, you are not in the loan business; surely you could put the additional take-home pay to better use.

OVERPAYING ON ESTIMATED TAXES

If you are a taxpayer who has to make quarterly tax payments, then you already know that there are several methods you can use to calculate your taxes to avoid penalties for underpayment. Each method, however, can result in coming up with a different number, depending on income fluctuations that occur from year to year. That's why each year, you and your accountant or financial planner should decide which method will require the payment of the lowest permissible amount for that year. Again, this gives you and not the IRS use of your money.

Retirement Planning

INEFFECTIVE PLANNING, OR NO PLANNING AT ALL

Nothing is more heartbreaking than knowing that millions of Americans have retired or will soon retire with inadequate income to have an acceptable standard of living. Years ago people didn't understand the need to plan that far in advance, but today there is no excuse. There are numerous options for setting up a retirement savings plan and there are many types of professionals who can guide you in the right direction.

The most important thing to do in advance of your retirement is to set realistic income goals for the retirement years. This means calculating the capital base needed to achieve a certain income level at age 65 and then determining the methods you will use to save that amount. This is a crucial aspect of financial planning and one that cannot be neglected. The earlier you start preparing, the easier it will be on you and your loved ones.

The other important consideration today is preventing the rapid reduction of principal, resulting in outliving your money. With the long life expectancies of today's generations, you want to prevent draining all your capital while it is still desperately needed.

Estate Planning

NOT HAVING A WILL

A Will is one of the simplest legal documents to have drawn up, and yet there are so many Americans who never take care of the matter. Then, at their deaths, their estate comes under the jurisdiction of their state's succession laws. If the decedent had any wishes with respect to possessions, assets, etc., they will not be recognized. The state of Florida has very clearcut laws governing intestate succession (dying without a valid Will), and this could leave family members open to expensive legal and court costs as they attempt to settle the estate. This could be avoided if a formal Will were written. If you haven't taken care of this matter, do it as soon as you arrive in Florida. Your beneficiaries will thank you and the state will thank you.

HAVING AN OUTDATED WILL

Just as bad as not having a Will is having an outdated Will. The laws changed since 1976, and changed again in 1981 regarding the minimizing of estate taxes. No doubt your family situation has altered as well. Perhaps there are more children, or grandchildren. Perhaps new beneficiaries need to be named due to death or divorce. Whatever the changed circumstances, this matter needs to be attended to ensure maximum protection for your loved ones.

Please refer to Section VI, "What Every New Resident Should Know." In it, you'll find a very comprehensive overview entitled, "Florida Laws: Wills, Trusts and Everything In Between" (Chapter 29).

INACCESSIBLE DOCUMENTS

Some people are very private and have always tended to keep their personal business to themselves. This is fine until there is an untimely death, making it difficult for a spouse or grown child to pick up the pieces. Without access to important documents, the executors of your state cannot do the job they were asked to do. They may not be aware of all assets, which would then be lost forever. That's why even if you have a secret "nest egg," there should be a record of the account in a place where your executor can find it and then work to preserve it. It's your decision if you wish to die with secrets, but not if your financial papers remain hidden as well.

Risk Management
(Life, Property, Medical And Disability Insurance)

It helps to remember the basic principles behind life insurance. The first is to provide estate liquidity. The second is to provide sufficient assets for a surviving family after a wage earner has passed away. Unless substantial assets have been acquired along the way, only life insurance can provide adequate income for survivors. In addition, if an estate is not liquid enough, other assets may have to be sold at a loss in order to pay estate costs when a death occurs.

PERSONAL RESIDENCE IS UNDERINSURED

Once most homeowners buy their initial homeowner's coverage, they never look at it again. And that means they are failing to acknowledge an annual inflation rate of 8%. For example, the replacement cost of your property doubles every nine years, not to mention that the addition of home improvements and furnishings have added to the value. If your home was originally insured for only 80% of its replacement cost, you'll be covered only for that lesser percentage, *regardless* of the dollar limits of the policy. And since homeowner's policies usually cover a stated dollar value, this results in gross underinsurance.

NOT HAVING PERSONAL PROPERTY "FLOATERS"

It's not news to anyone that homeowner's and renter's insurance policies have personal property limitations. This means that there are dollar maximums paid out for such luxury items as furs, jewelry, artwork, cameras, electronic equipment, etc., so even if your losses in one category, such as jewelry, were less than your total personal property coverage, you would still only be covered for whatever is the maximum allowable in that category. That's why the "floaters" can be so important, and they are usually available at a reasonable cost. Another type of "floater" is umbrella liability coverage which protects you from lawsuits, especially against personal injury.

MEDICAL INSURANCE WITH INADEQUATE COVERAGE FOR LONG-TERM HOSPITALIZATION AND CATASTROPHIC ILLNESS

It doesn't take a very long hospital stay these days in order to run up an outrageously expensive bill. You should know whether your medical insurance policy covers up to $150,000 or more. The minimum acceptable coverage you want today is between $250,000 and $500,000, and even then you should make a point of reviewing your policy every two years to guarantee that your coverage is keeping pace with rising medical costs. Additional coverage has been made available from both private carriers and if you are of retirement age, through the new government catastrophic coverage.

DISABILITY INSURANCE WITH TOO MANY RESTRICTIONS

Everyone buys life insurance to protect their families from huge financial risks in the event of death. Ironically, the odds are far greater that you will be disabled, not die, before retirement. Yet the decision not to buy disability insurance is a very common financial mistake. Disability insurance provides replacement income when an income earner cannot work due to an accident or illness. The problem with some policies is that they stipulate that if the person can perform any kind of a job after the second year of coverage, regardless of whether it is the person's stated profession, the insurer can discontinue coverage. Your disability policy should provide income until you can go back to your current occupation and it should provide enough income to cover your monthly overhead. One last note. You can't assume that if your employer provides disability coverage for you that is sufficient. Typical group policies offer the bare minimum, and should you leave that job, you'll be left with no coverage. Further, your health status will determine your ability to purchase coverage. The best time to buy is when you are in good health and gainfully employed.

HOLDING ON TO A DISABILITY POLICY AFTER RETIREMENT

Many disability policies cease when the policyholder reaches retirement age and/or retires. If you are 65 or older, make sure you are not paying for coverage that is not available to you. Insurance companies claim they can't automatically notify you because they have no way of knowing whether you've elected to continue working or not.

Funding For Education

PAYING FOR CHILDREN'S EDUCATION WITH "EXPENSIVE DOLLARS"

For convenience's sake, many parents put money away for their children's college education that has already been heavily taxed, such as earned income. It would be much more advantageous to spin off income to the child so that it is taxed at much lower rates and use that money to pay for tuition and living expenses. The way to do this is through the $10,000 gift exclusion, gifting income-bearing assets to the child. Current rules allow a child to earn $1000 of interest income at a lower rate each year. Anything above $1000 in interest income is taxed at the parent's tax bracket.

Business Planning

SELF-EMPLOYED PERSONS WITHOUT A RETIREMENT PLAN

The law currently allows self-employed individuals to make substantial annual tax-deductible contributions towards a retirement plan. These are commonly known as Keoghs or IRA/SEPs, for Simplified Employee Pensions. Not only is this a legitimately good away to shelter income during the year, it's an important step towards a financially secure retirement. Anyone who is self-employed and not taking advantage of this opportunity is missing the boat. Keep in mind that current tax laws treat qualified retirement plans for incorporated and unincorporated businesses very similarly.

NO BUSINESS INSURANCE

It's not unusual to find big, successful businesses that have a large portion of the company's net worth tied to the daily operation. This could prove to be a disastrous strategy if some of the operating capital hasn't been allocated for casualty insurance, or enough of it. All it would take is a fire, vandalism or a serious personal injury to shut the business down, either for a short time or permanently. Either way this is avoidable by protecting the business with liability coverage, key-man life insurance, key-man disability and business property insurance. This type of coverage has to be viewed as part of the overhead—on par with merchandise, advertising, payroll, etc.

If you are aware that you are making mistakes which will ultimately lead to your financial demise, there's no time like the present to do something about it. Perhaps this is the time to seek the help of a qualified financial planner so that he can help you right the wrongs and at the same time structure a personalized plan for you and your family that assures you of a secure financial future.

CHAPTER 8

A Few Words About Disability Insurance:

DON'T LEAVE HOME WITHOUT IT!

Before NBC pulled the plug, one of my favorite television shows was the hit drama series, "St. Elsewhere." It's not that I love hospitals. The truth is, anything to do with medical procedures makes me ill. Still, I tuned in every week to keep up with the assortment of interesting characters and their real life crises.

If you were a viewer, you'll recall the last few episodes which followed the emotional and financial demise of Dr. Mark Craig, a crotchety but highly successful surgeon. At the height of his brilliant career, a self-inflicted injury to the right hand permanently prevented him from ever doing the only thing he was trained to do: surgery.

It is unfortunate, but this type of life crisis is not a fabrication of Hollywood. Each year, thousands of families are forced into drastic lifestyle changes because a serious illness or injury prevents an income earner from working.

Looking at it from a pure numbers perspective, the odds of being disabled at some point during your life are fairly high. If you are 30 or younger, there's a 50/50 chance you'll be disabled for more than three months at least once before you reach the age of 65. And if you are 42, you stand a 3 times greater chance of becoming disabled than of dying. If you are 50 and older, you already know the incidence of serious illness and injury increases with each year.

If you think this message is directed to skydivers and other risk takers, you're wrong. No one, absolutely no one, is immune from a disaster that could wipe out their earning power. No one has a written guarantee that they won't be involved in a serious accident or afflicted with a disease at some point in their life.

The intent here is not to dwell on a morbid subject or to appeal to people's worst fears. Instead, I want to point out the seriousness of the problem and to convince you to take action if you are one of the three-out-of-every-four employed Americans who has no disability coverage!

Ironically, I'm sure these are the same people who firmly believe in other insurance coverage. They probably have auto, property and casualty, life, hospitalization…the works. The only thing they haven't protected is simply their *MOST VALUABLE ASSET: THEIR INCOME!*

Each year, thousands of income producers, from factory workers and farmers to entrepreneurs, professionals, and white- and pink-collar personnel, discover too late that either they have no means of replacing their income when they become disabled, or their coverage is woefully inadequate. As a result, the unexpected and sudden loss of income jeopardizes not only their financial future, but their financial present.

If you were without a guaranteed income for six months, or even three months, would you still be able to keep up with mortgage payments, installment loans, and other fixed monthly expenses? Would you be able to maintain any kind of status quo? And could you do all this without depleting a huge chunk of your savings and investments? We both know the answer. You'd hurt as much financially as you would from the disability. Maybe more.

As a Certified Financial Planner in private practice for many years, I can attest to the fact that in spite of its tremendous importance, the concept of disability insurance is unclear to most people. Because of some common misconceptions, the typical family is wide open and vulnerable to financial collapse if one or both of the income earners were unable to work—even for a few months. When a new client visits our offices, we immediately address the need for disability insurance if we see that none has been secured. We are not amused by their responses:

> *"The state already deducts money from my paycheck for disability. I must be covered."*

> *"If I become disabled, I can just apply for social security benefits."*

> *"Doesn't Blue Cross take care of everything?"*

> *"I have long-term disability coverage through my employee benefits package. I'm sure that's sufficient."*

> *"I bought a disability policy a few years ago. No, I don't recall what I'm covered for, but I'm sure the coverage is adequate."*

> *"If I had to, I'd just take out a loan to cover my expenses until I went back to work. I'm sure that would be cheaper than paying for another insurance policy every year."*

Upon further investigation, we find that in the vast majority of cases, none of the above is true! Here's why.

STATE DISABILITY INSURANCE (SHORT-TERM DISABILITY)

States that provide benefits at all will pay an average of $150 per week (or less) for up to 26 weeks. If your disability exceeds 26 weeks, you're not even eligible for that amount. Thus, the state's short-term disability is fine as a supplement to other coverage, but it doesn't even come close as the only source of income. You should also know that the state of Florida offers no short-term disability insurance whatsoever.

SOCIAL SECURITY BENEFITS

If a breadwinner with two or more dependents became disabled and was therefore prevented from working at any type of job, the Social Security Administration could pay up to $1615 a month. "That's pretty nice," you say. Unfortunately, 70% of the applicants who apply for this disability protection are refused because they don't meet the stringent requirements. In order to collect even a dime, the disability has to be totally crippling or terminal. If you are capable of *any* type of employment, you are disqualified. And if such a disability actually occurs, the $1600 a month they provide won't even begin to cover expenses.

BLUE CROSS AND OTHER MEDICAL COVERAGE

Medical coverage pays for hospitalization, physicians' fees, laboratory tests, and other related costs. There is no denying its importance, but it should not be confused with *income replacement*. Only disability insurance offers this type of protection.

BANK LOANS

Many people feel they can always turn to their bank in times of need. But even if your banker has a heart, you could still find yourself in a Catch-22 situation. You see, it may be difficult to obtain approval for a loan when you have no guaranteed income to repay it. Or you may get the loan but it could mean putting your house up for collateral or taking some other risk that would extend your indebtedness for years after.

You must remember that borrowing money is a very expensive remedy, possibly costing thousands of dollars a year plus interest. A disability insurance premium will cost a good deal less and involves no risks.

Long Term Disability Coverage

Long Term Disability, in my mind, should be mandatory, just as auto insurance is in many states. There are two types of LTD (Long Term Disability) Coverage: 1) a group policy, usually sponsored by an employer or union; 2) an individual policy, available for purchase from a financial planner or insurance agency. Both policies typically commence anywhere from thirty to ninety days after the onset of a disability. Coverage varies from two years to age 65, or can even provide lifetime protection. No two plans are the same because the variables are all determined by you or your employer-sponsor. The only thing you cannot "buy" is a total payout exceeding your gross income. In other words, if you earn $50,000 a year, you cannot insure yourself against the loss of $100,000 a year. Otherwise you'd hear about scores of people suddenly contracting rare tropical diseases with no known cures.

GROUP POLICIES

With respect to group policies, it is important to know that each time you start a new job, you may be required to "qualify" for the company's plan by submitting to a physical exam. If you've developed a condition since a previous check-up, it's possible you won't qualify for the company's LTD plan, or your premium will cost considerably more. Although some large group policies cannot restrict entry, they can waive pre-existing conditions. Further, with some group plans, it's possible that there could be a six-month waiting period before coverage becomes available to you. This means that for a six month period you will be extremely vulnerable. Would you be willing to wait this long without health insurance? Probably not. The same is true with disability coverage. That's why it's so important to have your own individualized coverage.

Finally, most group programs will only cover up to 60% of your salary.

INDIVIDUAL POLICIES

Although group protection is still better than no protection, the ideal set-up is to purchase an individual policy while in good health and gainfully employed. This will give you the greatest flexibility with respect to benefits plus the greatest peace of mind. Your own policy can be tailored to specific income needs, starting as early as thirty days from the onset of a disability, and can offer continuity of coverage, regardless of job changes or job termination.

Evaluating Your Disability Coverage

When you begin to explore the different types of policies available, or if you want to determine whether your current coverage is adequate, following is a checklist of questions to ask:

1. Is your coverage commensurate with your current earnings?

2. Do you have both short- and long-term coverage? If you only have LTD, do you have sufficient savings or investments to cover your overhead until you are eligible for benefits? And if so, can you really afford to tap into your personal savings for this purpose?

3. What is the waiting period for receiving benefits from your disability policies? Can you wait that long?

4. What is the maximum benefit period you are entitled to? Is it one year? Five years? Until age 65? Or is it a lifetime policy?

5. What are the terms and conditions of your policies? How does the insurer define "disability?" Some policies stipulate that if your actions are to blame for your disabilities, such as a car accident where you are charged with driving "under the influence," the insurance company might not be obligated to pay. Or, if you are able to return to work part-time while still recovering, you may lose your benefits because the insurance company will only pay out when you are prevented from working full-time. Other policies will pay partial or residual benefits which provide for payments until your full earning capacity is restored.

6. Is the policy non-cancellable and renewable? The ideal policy is one that can never be cancelled and the premiums never raised. Some policies are renewable only. This means they are non-cancellable but the rates will increase with age and health conditions.

The Nine Most Important Aspects Of Disability Coverage

At this point, it's probably much clearer why disability protection is so important. I believe it is the cornerstone of any sound financial plan. Hopefully you are now in agreement and will make a concerted effort to comparison-shop for the best policy. To ensure that your final choice offers the greatest possible protection, here is a review of the ten most important components of any disability policy:

1. *Benefit Period...* You want a policy that protects you with monthly income until at least age 65. Policies which limit benefits from one to five years are cheaper, but they leave you very vulnerable as you get older, as well as in cases of permanent disabilities.

2. *Lifetime Benefits...* You can opt for a plan that pays you full benefits indefinitely. This would be of great importance to accident victims confined to a wheelchair, for example. This option is allowable if your claim starts before age 55. This benefit is of great importance because it serves the same function as a pension plan. It can be your "substitute" pension if you never had the opportunity to work for one. If your disability occurs after age 55, you'll receive full benefits until age 65. At that point, your payments will be reduced by 10% each year because social security and your pension plan will presumably pick up the slack.

3. *Waiting Period*...Similar to a deductible, you have to pay your own way until the policy goes into effect. The average waiting period is 90 days. Most people choose this because they can count on savings as well as paid sick leave from their employer up to that point. Should you want your policy to start sooner, say at 30 days, count on paying a 20% higher premium. You can also opt for a one year waiting period, but I highly recommend you pay no attention to it. It will only bring your cost down 20% and by then your financial state could be in ruins. Further, it would exclude the most common claims, therefore being of little benefit.

4. *Benefits Even If You Take a Different Job*...Your policy should state that you are entitled to full benefits if you cannot perform the main duties of your regular occupation but are able to draw a salary from some other line of work. For example, a surgeon whose arthritis prevents him from operating could still possibly earn a living doing consultations. If his policy called for replacing partial loss of income, he would be free to do that without jeopardizing his benefits.

5. *Residual Benefits*...Residuals refer to payment of partial benefits. If you are able to work at your current occupation one day out of five, you'll presumably earn 20% of your current income from the employer. In this case you would still want a policy that paid 80% of the full benefit. In other words, you don't want your policy to penalize you for attempting to go back to work. Some companies pay at least 50% from six to nine months.

6. *Premium and Renewal Guarantees*...As stated earlier, you should only consider policies that are non-cancellable with guaranteed renewals. You don't need an insurance company that can drop you or suddenly bump up your premiums if they decide to label you "high risk." Also, be sure that you are excused from paying your premiums while you are in the middle of a claim. This is called "waiver of premium."

7. *Cost-of-Living Adjustments*...If your policy doesn't keep pace with inflation, it won't do you much good during a long-term claim. In other words, you want to count on the policy paying you at the rate of inflation if you're being paid out for several years in a row. Make sure your basic benefits rise automatically by a certain percentage each year.

8. *Standard of Living Adjustments*...Similar to cost of living adjustments, you will want a policy that allows you to increase the value of your payments to reflect raises and bonuses. This option

permits you to increase them by a standard amount at your discretion, no medical questions asked. This is similar to what many people do with their homeowner's coverage.

9. *Social Security Supplements*...Most companies offer a $500-a-month supplement after you've been disabled for six months to a year. This tides you over until your social security benefits commence, obviously provided you are eligible.

Disability Premiums

I don't say this often, but when it comes to buying a disability policy, money is no object. You are talking about protecting an asset that will be worth hundreds of thousands of dollars over the course of your lifetime, perhaps much more. When you view the issue from that perspective, the policy won't seem so expensive. And relatively speaking, it's not. For example, a 40-year old man earning $55,000 will pay approximately $1500 a year for a decent disability policy.

Let's establish the value of his earnings over a lifetime or a career.

$$\begin{array}{ll} \$55,000 & \text{Annual Income} \\ \underline{\times 25} \text{ Years} & \\ \$1,375,000 & \text{Earned Income During Career} \end{array}$$

This doesn't even take into account any raises or cost-of-living increases that will invariably be paid him. But if an accident or long-term illness occurred, how could he replace even a portion of those earnings? He couldn't, unless he had a good disability policy. With a policy that paid out $2500 per month, for example, the insured would be guaranteed 60% of his income, or $30,000 a year. Over a 25 year period, that would equal $750,000 of tax-free dollars (provided the individual paid for his own premiums). With standard-of-living and cost-of-living adjustments, the policy would pay out even more.

Given this life saving coverage, it's amazing that people will spend a couple of thousand dollars a year to insure a car that's worth $15,000, but can't justify spending even less than that to protect their earning power worth ten to twenty times more.

PREMIUM COSTS

To get a sense of what a top-quality, non-cancellable policy would cost, here is a chart which compares rates between two of the largest disability insurers, Paul Revere Life and Connecticut Mutual Life. The subject is a 40-year-old non-smoking man or woman in a professional or managerial occupation. The benefits here will pay $2500 a month, up to age 65, starting 90 days after the disability occurs. The costs indicated are for the annual premiums.

Features	Paul Revere Life	Connecticut Mutual Life
Monthly benefits to age 65	$1,032.25	$810.00
Lifetime benefits	257.28	175.50
Adequate residual benefits	0	121.50
"Disability" (you can't perform the main duties of your regular job)	61.50	151.20
$500/mo. extra until Social Securit benefits pay off	100.80	210.60
Automatic cost-of-living increases while you are totally or partially disabled	266.34	249.30
TOTAL PREMIUM	$1,718.17	$1,718.10*

* Dividends, at the current rate, would reduce this premium by 10% in the third year.
  SOURCE: *Money* magazine, August, 1988

You'll note that even though there is a big disparity in costs between the basic benefits, the bottom line is that the two policies cost the same when you add the other important options.

Oh Yes...Did I Mention That Most Benefit Payments Are Tax-Free?

If I haven't sold you on the benefits of disability insurance by now, give me one more chance. I've been holding the trump card in my hand the whole time. Disability income plans are subject to a variety of tax laws. Premiums and benefits are taxed differently depending on who pays them and who receives the benefits. However, it is safe to say that benefits paid out in individual disability policies, employer-sponsored plans where the employee contributes to the premium payments, and disability policies for key persons and partners of businesses and corporations are 100% tax free! They are not tax deductible, but they are tax exempt.

How does that grab you?

Please Follow Up...

I can't urge you enough to review your current disability coverage today to make certain that you are insulated from financial disaster if another type of disaster, an accident or illness, ever prevents you or your spouse from earning the living to which you've grown accustomed. Remember Dr. Craig on "St. Elsewhere?" There's no need to worry about his disability. He was lucky enough to have scriptwriters bail him out of his dilemma. Most of us aren't that lucky.

CHAPTER 9

Who's Got You Covered:
SHOPPING FOR HEALTH INSURANCE
IN FLORIDA

Can you guess the most popular topic in Florida? It is not the weather. It's not even where to find the best early bird specials (although this probably comes a close second). It's health. If such a designation existed, health would probably be deemed the official state conversation, sharing status with the state bird (the mockingbird) and the state tree (sabal palm).

One of the things you might notice when you first move down is that lots of folks, both young and old, talk about their health. How it is, how it should be, how it might be next week...

It's not that people get sicker in Florida than anywhere else. But typically, seniors talk about what ails them. And since Florida is a retirement haven, there is a tendency for people to become well versed in a subject that affects a large portion of the population. Thus it is that Floridians seem to be more aware of their health insurance needs and why you'll find a seemingly large number of private health insurance companies doing business in the state. The market offers such enormous sales potential that it attracts a large number of insurance carriers. Depending on how you look at it, these choices can make shopping for new coverage easier or more difficult.

If you are moving to Florida on a permanent basis, are under the age of 65, and will not be employed by a company that provides group health benefits, this chapter is for you.

The first step to take is to purchase private health insurance coverage, or make arrangements to convert your current group coverage to an individual policy.

For the sake of an easy transition and continuity of coverage, I recommend that you initially convert your group coverage and then shop for private health coverage in Florida once the dust settles.

CONTACT YOUR GROUP BENEFITS MANAGER

To convert your current health insurance group policy from your employer, union or other organization, contact the Group Benefits Manager and inform him that you are relocating to Florida and will therefore be leaving the company, union, etc. Advise him that you wish to convert your group policy to individual coverage.

Even though you are severing ties with your employer, by federal law you must be given the option to maintain whatever coverage has been a part of your policy, provided you agree to make the payments on the premiums. Under this COBRA law, for Consolidated Omnibus Budget Reconciliation Act, you are entitled to continue coverage at a cost of 2% over the current premium for up to 18 months. To be eligible, you cannot be covered by any other group health insurance and you cannot be leaving a company due to gross misconduct.

Continuing a group policy under your own auspices can be a costly proposition, particularly if you are unaccustomed to footing the bill. But imagine how expensive it is to *not* be covered for even one day. Do not, I repeat, do not make the mistake of leaving yourself and your family unprotected for any length of time. In a worst-case scenario, the consequences for this oversight could bankrupt you. Holding on to this group policy is only a temporary measure until you have the opportunity to shop for your own health insurance in Florida.

HOLD ON TO YOUR MEDICAL RECORDS

Whether you purchase a private insurance plan in Florida or convert your group policy to an individual plan, be sure to hold on to all your medical records and correspondence with the current insurance carrier, especially regarding any outstanding claims. You never know when questions or problems will arise that can be resolved through your copies of paperwork.

Your Total Health Insurance Package

At the point that you are ready to shop for individual coverage in Florida, there are several things to look into. Again, this is only in instances where you are not joining an employer or union that provides health benefits. The minimum health package you should purchase for yourself and your family would include Major Medical and Hospitalization. Here is a brief description of what these and other types of coverage provide in the majority of Florida health plans.

MAJOR MEDICAL POLICIES

Major Medical insurance can cover hospital, medical and surgical expenses, and may include coverage for outpatient doctors' visits, nursing care, medicine and other medical expenses. The biggest difference between major medical and hospital/medical/surgical insurance is that major medical has a combination of a deductible and co-insurance (you pay 20%, they pay 80%), and usually pays up to a certain dollar amount over the life of the policy.

In Florida, the standard major medical policy covers semi-private hospital rooms, miscellaneous hospital expenses, physician and nursing care and convalescent care. Plans will vary in terms of the extent of coverage allowed.

The standard plan pays 80% of the first $5000 of covered charges after a $500 per illness deductible has been met. They will pay 100% of other covered expenses in the two year period following the first expense credited to the deductible, with a lifetime maximum of $1,000,000. There is a $20,000 lifetime maximum for alcoholism or mental illness. These policies generally *do not* cover dental treatments (except for injury); eyeglasses, contact lenses or hearing aids; cosmetic surgery (except to correct normal bodily functions); and pregnancy, except for complications, which are covered like any other illness.

HOSPITAL/MEDICAL/SURGICAL POLICIES

Basic hospital/medical/surgical policies pay a certain portion of hospital room and board costs each day, or an amount equal to the supplies, such as lab tests, medicine, X-rays and other items in an amount equal to at least 10 times the amount the policy pays for daily room and board.

The medical expense portion of the policy pays a set *per diem* amount for doctors' visits during the hospital stay, and provides this type of coverage for a minimum of 21 days.

The surgical expense portion pays at least 75% of reasonable charges for a surgeon's fees, or up to a set amount for certain operations listed in your policy. When you review this fee schedule, you'll find coverage information for anesthetic services and operating room charges as well.

This type of hospitalization coverage has a deductible in an amount determined by you, the purchaser. These policies provide coverage for a certain length of time or in a certain dollar amount, and you must then be responsible for anything over and above that.

HOSPITAL INDEMNITY PLANS

In addition to standard hospitalization plans, you can purchase indemnity insurance which pays an extra daily amount specified in your policy for hospital room and board over the payment you receive from other health insurance policies. Between the two plans, 100% of your hospitalization expenses should be covered.

LIMITED BENEFIT POLICIES

There are insurance plans called Limited Benefit Insurance which pay only for costs resulting from specific accidents or diseases, such as car accidents or cancer.

A common type of Limited Benefit Insurance is a cancer policy which would presumably pay for cancer treatments or procedures in addition to hospital benefits. However, if your cancer has already been diagnosed or treated, you are ineligible for coverage. There is also a waiting period before benefits can begin.

STATE COMPREHENSIVE HEALTH ASSOCIATION

The Florida Legislature has created a State Comprehensive Health Association plan (SCHA) for permanent residents who are unable to get adequate health insurance coverage in the private market due to their mental or physical conditions.

SCHA offers three different plans, all of which provide the same basic benefits, but differ according to annual deductibles and the amount of out-of-pocket expense limitations. The SCHA pays a maximum of $500,000 in benefits for all injuries and sicknesses combined over the policyholder's lifetime. There is a 6-month exclusion of pre-existing conditions. For more information, call this toll-free number (in Florida only): 1-800-422-8559.

ACCIDENT POLICIES

Finally, you can purchase Accident-Only Insurance, which limits payments to a stated amount for specific losses such as the loss of a limb, eye or accidental death. It may also pay some medical costs resulting from the accident. All policies have certain exclusions, such as suicide attempts or deaths related to military duty. Some will only pay up to a certain age.

Health Insurance Options And Premiums

People who have difficulty faring with all the options on a new car aren't going to have any better a time shopping for health insurance. "Options" is the industry's middle name. Still, many of them are not only worthwhile but extremely important. It just goes without saying that the more options you go for, the more expensive your coverage. You should also be aware that health insurance costs will vary depending on your age, sex, health, *and* where in Florida you choose to live.

This is something you may not be aware of, but it's true. Insurance carriers determine rates in part by the zip code of your home address. In other words, if your plans call for moving into Dade County (Miami area), you can expect to pay higher premiums than those who move into Northern Florida (Gainesville, Tallahassee, etc.).

Again, this is due to the overbalance of elderly that live in the Miami area. Typically, they submit claims with greater frequency, and their medical costs are far greater. To protect themselves against heavy losses, insurance companies have set up their rates so that all policyholders in these areas bear the burden. We'll discuss the issue of zip code pricing in greater length further into the chapter.

REVIEWING YOUR OPTIONS

Similar to any health insurance policy you've ever purchased or participated in, there are options which affect the price. These include the amount of the deductible, your percentage of the coinsurance, pre-existing conditions, waiting periods, exclusions, renewals and rate increases.

With respect to renewals, the optimum policy is one that is *non-cancelable and has a guaranteed renewal.* In other words, once you've been approved for coverage and continue to pay your premiums, the insurance carrier cannot change, cancel or refuse to renew your policy no matter what! They can still raise the rates as you get older, but they have to pay your claims.

How To Buy Health Insurance

There are some very important steps to take to not only find the best possible coverage, but to protect yourself from buying the wrong kind of policy. There are plenty of charlatans out there who see newcomers as easy prey. It's not that Florida has a corner on the market of unscrupulous salespeople, but there are more than 450 companies selling health insurance in the state; it makes sense that if there are more salespeople out there, there are bound to be more bad apples. Thus, the Florida Department of Insurance offers these suggestions for shopping for health coverage, or for that matter, any type of insurance policy.

- *Shop, Shop, Shop*...Take the time to compare policies. Yes, this can be time-consuming and boring. But the time spent will invariably lead to price savings and better coverage.

- *How's the Service*...Rates aren't everything. Compare how companies are set up to service claims and how long it takes for them to process the paperwork and reimbursements.

- *Get the Facts Straight*...Talk with several agents and make sure you're getting the same story with respect to the laws and other general information. If this is all foreign to you, ask a trusted friend or family member to help you sort out the facts from the fantasy.

- *Your License, Please*...Ask every agent to provide proof that his agency is licensed with the state of Florida.

- *Coverage Summary*...The best way to comparison shop is to get a summary of the policy benefits from each agent you talk to. Before you compare price, you want to be sure that any policy you are considering has all of the benefits you're looking for.

- *Tell the Whole Truth*...Don't jeopardize your coverage by making false statements and claims on your application. If the truth is ever uncovered, you'll have big troubles. Any agent who tells you it's OK to alter the truth a little has probably altered the truth a little about what he or she is selling!

- *Pay by Check*...Never pay for insurance premiums by cash. Pay only by check or money order and make them payable only to the insurance company—never the agent or agency.

- *When the Policy Arrives*...Don't throw anything out, including the envelope. The postmark will verify the approximate time you received it. If you haven't received the policy after one month of making your first payment, it's time to start asking questions.

- *Put on Your Best Reading Glasses*...Do not stash the policy when you get it. Read it immediately to make sure that you've bought what you've been promised. That means reading all the fine print and comparing the policy to the summary of coverage the agent originally gave you.

- *Keep Your Policy Safe*...Store one copy of your policy in an easy-to-find place in your home and store extra copies in a safe-deposit box or with an attorney.

- *Free Looks Are OK*...Ask each agent about a free-look period. This entitles you to review the policy before committing to it. All life and health policies must have a minimum 10-day free-look period.

- *No Obligations Necessary*...If you decide against a policy after your free-look period, just return the policy to the company by certified or registered mail with return receipt requested within the allowed time frame. This entitles you to a complete refund.

- *Beware of Ads that Promise the World*...If something sounds too good to be true, it probably is. Look out for newspaper ads that make big claims but have little asterisks next to them. When you read the fine print, that's where you'll find the real story.

- *Put Your Foot Down*...If you find yourself up against high pressure tactics, "Just Say No." If you are undecided, sign nothing and commit to nothing. If you are uncomfortable with the agent's tough sell approach, insist that he leave. Report any harassment or other unprofessional behavior to the Florida Department of Insurance.

- *Call Toll Free*...To report any problems with insurance policies, insurance agents or agencies, or to just get more information, you can call the Florida Consumer Service Hotline. It's toll-free. 1-800-342-2762. If you want to file a formal complaint, ask for the Insurance Consumer Complaint Request form. This form will outline the information you need to provide in order to submit the complaint.

CHECKLIST OF QUESTIONS YOU WANT ANSWERED

You'll probably have a list of your own questions, but for starters, here are the basics to cover when interviewing an insurance agent. If you ask everyone the same questions, you'll have an accurate means of comparing.

1. Are there waiting periods before certain illnesses are covered?

2. What is the deductible, and is it for each treatment or on an annual basis?

3. What is the co-insurance? In other words, what percent of the claim must you pay after the deductible has been met?

4. What are the renewal conditions?

5. Under what circumstances can the company raise your rates?

6. What is the maximum amount the policy will pay for each illness and for the entire time you hold the policy?

7. What types of services are covered under the policy, and which are not?

8. Will the policy cover routine doctors' office visits? What about house calls?

9. How do the benefits compare with actual costs for doctors' visits, hospital care or surgery in the area?

10. What are the limits on the amount paid for daily hospital room and board, medicine, tests, surgery, doctors' visits, etc.?

11. What are the limits on the maximum number of hospital days paid for and the number of doctors' visits during a hospital stay?

Blue Cross And Blue Shield Of Florida

If your health insurance is currently covered by a Blue Cross and Blue Shield plan and you want to continue the coverage, there are several things you need to know.

The first is that Blue Cross and Blue Shield programs in every state operate autonomously. As a courtesy, however, Blue Cross and Blue Shield of Florida will allow you to transfer your current policy. This means that there will be no disruption of service or coverage, there will be no need for a new physical examination, nor will there be a need to start the deductible over again. Understand, however, that you will not be transferring identical coverage. In all likelihood, because of the high rate of claims in Florida due to the overbalance of elderly, you should expect to pay higher premiums for inferior coverage.

Should you stick your Blue Cross policy anyway? One determining factor in deciding to hold on to your current Blue Cross policy or purchase an entirely different plan in Florida is the state of your and your family's health. If you or a family member are in poor health or have a pre-existing condition, the best strategy is to continue your affiliation with Blue Cross. What's the point in trying to find lower costing premiums through a different carrier when it means subjecting yourself to applications, waiting periods, new deductibles, physicals and even the possibility of being turned down?

If you want to continue with a Blue Cross policy in Florida, they offer three insurance products. The first is called, appropriately enough, "New Florida Resident Coverage." This plan is for those of you who are currently covered by BC/BS in another state. As such, if you transfer your policy you are guaranteed coverage. But again, don't expect the same type of coverage.

For example, your New Florida Resident plan provides for a $1500 maximum per surgical procedure, a maximum hospital room allowance of $150 paid at 80% and hospital charges paid at 80% of the billed charges. There is a $700 deductible for this product and a $1000 out-of-pocket expense. Premium costs are based on a family/single rating structure and are age-rated as well. You'll notice immediately that these benefits are quite different from your current coverage. You're getting less coverage but paying higher out-of-pocket costs. Thus, if you are eligible for the New Florida Resident Plan but are looking for something less costly, BC/BS has two other types of policies you can apply for.

DIMENSION IV

Blue Cross's "Dimension IV" is a full access product, i.e., policyholders are not limited to a specific network of physicians and hospitals. It carries a $1 million lifetime maximum and pays for a semi-private room based on a discounted allowance that they have negotiated with hospitals. Physician's charges are reimbursed at usual and customary rates. Unmarried children are covered until they reach their 20th birthday—23 if they are a student. Maternity coverage is optional but complications in pregnancy are treated as any other medical condition.

PREFERRED PATIENT CARE

This is Blue Cross's version of an HMO. Preferred Patient Care provides policyholders with a network of physicians and hospitals who have agreed to provide medical care at pre-negotiated fees and who will file claims for you. If a subscriber receives services from a source outside the PPV Network, you'll be reimbursed but it will be at a lower rate than when you stick to their network. Preferred Patient Care offers a variety of deductibles and out-of-pocket expense options. There is a 24-month pre-existing condition clause. Applicants are rated according to age, geographic region in Florida (there are 26 areas), by sex and number of dependents.

Florida's HMOs

If you are joining a company that offers HMO benefits, and you have never participated before, this section will familiarize you with their services. Health Maintenance Organizations, or HMOs, are a health care alternative which offers consumers pre-paid health plans. The primary benefit is that for a fixed monthly fee, most of your medical needs will be taken care of. This makes health care affordable for many people. In fact, according to the Florida Department of Insurance, over one million residents have chosen to participate in HMOs.

To participate, you have to work for a company that has 10 or more employees. In fact, according to Florida law, any company with 25 or more employees *must* offer you the choice between joining an HMO or subscribing to private health care insurance. As a rule, individuals are not permitted to join.

THE DIFFERENCE BETWEEN HMOs
AND PRIVATE HEALTH INSURANCE

The biggest difference is that if you are a member of an HMO, you must use the physicians and facilities under contract with that particular health organization. Although you can choose the doctor at the HMO that you would like to see on a regular basis, you can not select a doctor in private practice and then expect that your HMO will pay the bills. The other major differences involve benefits and fees, and these can be very advantageous. Many HMOs provide prescription drugs, eye exams and other services not generally provided by private health insurance plans.

In addition, HMOs usually result in less out-of-pocket expenses for members. Instead of paying deductibles, participants pay nominal costs for doctors' visits, usually between $2 to $5. And because HMO services are pre-paid, members don't fill out and submit claim forms.

The biggest disadvantage is being limited to HMO physicians. Sometimes you will not even be seen by a physician, but by a nurse practitioner or physician's assistant. In addition, HMOs generally pay for medical treatment outside their service areas only in emergencies. If you travel back north a great deal, your routine medical care will not be covered.

Our research shows that HMOs are not as widely accepted or as successful in Florida as they are up north. It seems that in the major metropolitan areas in the midwest and the east they fill a crying need, particularly among the working middle class. In Florida, they just haven't caught on, although they are somewhat more successful on the east coast than the west coast.

The problems with HMOs in Florida seem to stem from the fact that many are not as well-run as they could be. There have been enough cases of complete mismanagement to give the whole concept a questionable reputation, even though in theory they can provide a valuable service to the community.

The real problems occurred when the rapid growth and competitive strategies of HMOs undermined their services several years ago. Many of them ran into serious financial trouble and were forced to close their doors. This left their members high and dry—without any medical coverage. Subsequently, the Department of Insurance has stiffened their regulations regarding HMOs and requires that they must carry insolvency insurance and/or post bonds with the Department.

In 1988, proposed legislation called for the establishment of a "superfund" which would help pay claims if an HMO failed. To generate revenue for the fund, the state would charge HMOs an annual assessment of 1% of their gross revenue. As of this writing, the bill had not yet been passed. And although it would help protect members to a greater extent than before, it unfortunately wouldn't begin to address the serious jeopardy and inconveniences it would place on the participant when an HMO suddenly closed.

Mail Order Health Insurance

In Florida you'll find a particularly large number of insurance companies that sell healthcare policies through the mail. These direct mail agencies have no offices in the state and no local agents. Although they are licensed to do business in the state and must maintain a registered agent within the state, these programs can only be purchased by mail. Offerings are generally found in local newspapers or magazines, and via direct marketing campaigns.

The only advantage of mail order health insurance is that it offers inexpensive premiums. Because these companies do not have to pay agency commissions, their biggest expenses are mailing and advertising costs. This is how they can afford to offer very competitive prices.

However, you should be careful when examining mail order policies. They are very cleverly worded to give the impression of offering comparable coverage to private health insurance sold by agencies. In truth, they offer reduced benefits. In many instances, the benefits are so unrealistic in terms of deductibles, pre-existing conditions, waiting periods, etc. that they are of little or no value at all.

As with anything you buy through the mail, let the buyer beware. When it comes to protecting you and your family's health, the lowest price should not be the top priority. Further, by buying insurance through the mail you are agreeing to waive having a personal agent to explain your policy and benefits, or to assist with claims. Your only communication with the company is through the mail or by phone. Lack of personal contact, and not having an agent who knows you and your circumstances can be a serious disadvantage.

More importantly, you should also be aware that some of these mail order insurance programs are set up by Trusts or by associations which have the right to discontinue, change or modify a policy at the discretion of the insurance company. This could leave a policy holder without coverage after a 30-day notification.

Although changes and modifications are also possible with agency-distributed companies, it is less likely. And at least with an agency there is someone available to advise you about replacement insurance, if necessary.

What's All This Business About Zip Codes?

As I mentioned earlier, Florida's major medical insurance carrier calculate premiums based on a number of factors. One of the key criteria is geography: what area you live in, and more specifically, what your zip code is. The point is that if you reside in an area which is a known haven for medical claims, all residents in the area will carry the burden.

For example, here are the sample rates of a major medical carrier in Florida. This particular policy has a $150 calendar year deductible, paying 80% up to $5000. The age of the policyholder is 40-44 and the plan is for the member and the spouse. These are the costs of the annual premium based on the last three digits of the policyholder's zip code.

Major Medical Policy

County	Zip Code	Premium
Dade County	All	$218
Broward County	334, 337	$154
Broward County	320, 322, 325-329, 335, 336, 338, 339, 342	$142
Broward County	All Other	$199
All Other Counties	All Other Zip Codes	$120

Please remember that the addition of children to the policy, the election to take maternity coverage, age, sex, and health will also affect the prices above. Typically, however, you can expect that Dade and Broward County residents will pay the highest health insurance premiums in the state. Palm Beach and Monroe County residents are next in line.

The Florida Department Of Insurance Is There To Help

You'll find Florida's State Insurance Commission very helpful in securing information and advising you about your particular insurance needs. In addition, while they can not recommend a particular company, they can advise you with regard to a carrier's reliability and integrity, based on any files of customer complaints.

If you have a complaint about a company, this office will investigate your problem and is usually successful in satisfying it. These services are available without charge and there are several regional offices throughout the state to serve you. Overall, the Department of Insurance is a very effective body which enforces state insurance regulations strictly. They serve the buying public well by keeping Florida a safe state in which to buy and use insurance. Listed in alphabetical order are the Florida Department of Insurance's Consumer Service Offices:

Daytona Beach	(904) 254-3920
Ft. Lauderdale	(305) 467-4339
Ft. Myers	(813) 337-5339
Jacksonville	(904) 359-6146
Miami	(305) 377-5235
Orlando	(305) 423-6105
Pensacola	(904) 436-8440
St. Petersburg	(813) 893-2351
Tallahassee	(904) 488-0030
Tampa	(813) 272-2351
West Palm Beach	(305) 837-5045

The State Commissioner's Office is located in Tallahassee. The new Commissioner is Mr. Tom Gallagher.

Again, if you have questions or problems regarding any insurance agency, agent, or mail order firm, you can call the Insurance Consumer Hotline at 1-800-342-2762.

NOTE: Mr. Harold T. Hymen, founding partner of Presidential Insurance Associates, Inc. served as contributing editor for this chapter. His firm handles life and health insurance sales and service, and specializes in the areas of supplemental care for seniors and long-term convalescent care. For more information on this important coverage, contact him in care of:

Presidential Insurance Associates, Inc.
4835 27th St., West
Bradenton, FL 34207
(813)758-0423

SECTION

II

If You Have To Earn A Living Somewhere... It Might As Well Be Florida

CHAPTER 10

An Overview Of Job And Business Opportunities In the Sunshine State

I t may be hard for you to think of Florida as a workplace, or to imagine being there and concentrating on something other than a tan. It's understandable when people's only association with the state is sundrenched vacations. The concept of working in Florida may be a difficult one at first; yet for the tens of thousands of people moving there every year, finding a job or starting a business is what they've come to do!

LOOKING THROUGH THE CRYSTAL BALL

Isn't it great that opportunity abounds? "Help Wanted" signs are as much a part of Florida's landscape as palm trees and beaches. It's no wonder that according to a recent survey in *Changing Times* magazine, Florida is ranked second only to Nevada in job growth until the year 2000. They estimate more than 113,000 jobs will open up across the state by 1990 alone. By the end of the century (just 11 more years and counting), Florida will have 1.4 million new jobs to offer, with an overwhelming 80% of them in the service sector. To give you a sense of how this compares with the rest of the nation, Tampa has just been ranked by *Changing Times* as the third fastest-growing job market in the country! Ft. Lauderdale is ranked number six, and Miami ranks number 13. No other state has as many cities ranking in the top 15.

Growth is only part of the story, however. The high marks given these regions, as well as the rest of the state, is due to the fact that the unemployment rate has remained well below the national average. Most indications point to the fact that it will continue to be one of the lowest in the nation, hovering around 5% to 6% a year.

These are just some of the reasons that Florida's business climate is as sunny as its weather climate. Although the forecast does call for intermittent cloudiness in some industries, and in some areas, most experts agree that Florida will continue its reign as the second fastest-growing state in the nation.

Today you'll find a veritable Who's Who of Fortune 500 corporations with Florida addresses, including IBM, Martin Marietta, Westinghouse, Harris Corp., Honeywell, General Electric, AT&T, and United Technologies, to name a few. It's no wonder that Florida was also ranked second in the nation for new manufacturing jobs created between 1976 and 1986. However, the manufacturing and hi-tech industries don't by any means have a corner on all the action.

The entertainment industry is making plenty of waves. Disney-MGM Films and Universal Studios have built new motion picture studios and sound stages in Central Florida. Paramount is rumored to be purchasing land for the same reason. In 1988, 43 major TV and motion picture productions were filmed in the state, bringing in $60 million to the economy and providing thousands of jobs.

Given this level of activity, it's entirely possible that there will be more movies, commercials and television sitcoms produced in the sunshine state than in Hollywood by the end of the century. Florida's already ranked third in the country for film and TV production.

Even thoroughbred breeding has its place in the Florida sun. In fact, Ocala (Marion County) is listed as being the 4th best breeding and training center in the world! What does that mean to the Florida economy? About $1 billion a year in revenue and 29,000 jobs. That doesn't even include the farms, racetracks and other ancillary businesses that benefit from the breeding business.

THERE'S SOMETHING FOR EVERYONE...BUT AT WHAT PRICE?

All of this commerce and enterprise must be reassuring to someone who's counting on making a living when he moves to Florida, but particularly important when coming from an area of the country where there are thousands of job layoffs due to cuts in defense spending—or from an industrial area that has been economically devastated by outdated facilities, such as the Chrysler factory in Kenosha, WI. Whatever the reasons for wanting a better life, Florida seems to have something for everyone.

However, and this is a big however, as you have probably already heard, pay scales in Florida are relatively low. It's getting better, but in 1987, 40% of Florida workers earned wages below the poverty level. Yes, the cost of living is lower, but wages and salaries are not always commensurate with the standard of living you're expecting.

Interestingly, Florida's personal income ranks 19th in the U.S., but this probably has more to do with retirees moving down with large investment incomes than it does with wage earners bringing home top salaries. For example, the Gold Coast (Palm Beach and Broward Counties) ranked No. 1 in the state for personal income last year, the median annual income was $18,582.00. Not exactly "Fat City," particularly if you are comparing it to the New York metropolitan area and other major markets where salaries are considerably higher. And certainly not when you consider that Palm Beach County, for example, is ranked as the 4th costliest place to live, according to the state's Cost-of-Living Index. Monroe, Broward and Dade Counties have higher annual costs-of-living, respectively.

If you are currently earning hourly wages and are wondering where you'll do best in Florida, it appears that the Ft. Lauderdale/Hollywood area is the most generous wage payer, with Gainesville a close second. This is according to Florida's State Employment Service, which analyzed average entry-level salaries on an hourly basis.

Because of the prospect of earning less money than in the East and Midwest, many people move to Florida with the intent of "buying" a job. This means that they opt for the entrepreneurial life, regardless of whether they are experienced business people or not. In these cases, they start a business or franchise, or buy an existing one. It's not the romantic notion of being their own boss that beckons them as much as it is the economic realities. They just don't want to take a step backwards and live on the meager salaries promised by many employers across the state. So say the thousands of business owners who have incorporated in the state. In 1986, Florida ranked first in the nation for new business incorporations (more than 77,000 have been filed), representing 11% of the nationwide total!

Here's another interesting statistic. Market Force, a Longwood, FL-based business research firm, compiles business listings in the major metropolitan areas of Florida. In doing so, they determined that more than 395,000 different establishments were doing business in 1988. Perhaps the sound of ringing cash registers might someday replace Stephen Foster's "The Old Folks at Home" as the state song!

As to the nature of its businesses, Florida mirrors the rest of the country with the greatest growth occurring in the service industries. In 1984 service businesses accounted for one-third of all small businesses in the state, and that number has subsequently increased. Within the services sector, Florida's boom has occurred in healthcare and medicine. But according to *Florida Trend* magazine, you can expect to see a great demand in the state for the following industries in the immediate future: housing, consumer goods, personnel and business services, retail trade, finance, insurance, and real estate. *Florida Trend* also projects that businesses moving away from federal deregulation such as trucking, communications, and financial services will be small business superstars of the 90s.

WHERE THE GROWTH IS

Where are newcomers settling? Where do business opportunities appear most golden? According to the Goodkin Research Corp. in Ft. Lauderdale, it appears that the Miami/Ft. Lauderdale/West Palm Beach areas have captured the lion's share of growth in the state, enjoying 28% of all the new population and businesses. The Tampa Bay area (Hillsborough and Pinellas Counties) has attracted 15.1% of the growth; Orlando has reaped 13%. Finally, the Jacksonville area has captured 6.9% of the growth.

David Biddulph, President of Market Force, predicts that Pinellas County

(St. Petersburg) and all of Central Florida will be the fastest-growing areas in the state over the next decade. This includes the Orlando area, the Daytona Beach area, and surrounding Osceola, Seminole, and Volusia Counties. Other regions expected to see very respectable growth include the Sarasota/Ft. Myers/Naples area, and Bradenton to the north (Manatee County). Ocala (Marion County) and the Melbourne/Titusville (Brevard County) area—the heart of the "Space Coast"—are also taking off.

Once you know *where* you want to move, you can concentrate on what you'll do when you get there.

HOW WILL YOU EARN YOUR KEEP?

This special section is devoted to helping you find the best way to earn your livelihood. The first chapter is directed to those of you who plan to seek employment rather than go into business. We'll explore the prospect of conducting a full-scale job search in Florida. We'll look at how to flex your job skill muscles to land the position you want. We'll also take a look at the starting wages and salaries for over 100 different jobs in Florida. We've even compiled the names and addresses of the state's largest employers by category of business. Ideally you'll want to relocate to an area where your interests and skills can be matched with companies that have settled there. Finally, we'll explore the question of coming out of retirement to work in Florida—so you know what to expect.

The next chapter is for those of you who want to start your own small business. We'll examine all the basics of getting started, as well as direct you to the agencies and associations in Florida geared to helping new business owners. You'll be happy to know that the state has developed enormous resources for assisting you, both with respect to financing as well as guidance and direction. There is more new business advice available in Florida than probably anywhere else in the country. If you are so inclined, you can be inundated with information from both the private sector and public financial institutions.

Finally, we'll discuss franchising. You'll be able to find out if it's really for you by reading about how they operate. In addition, we'll review franchise activity around the state and help you understand the positives and negatives of becoming a franchise owner.

Considering what's happening in Florida today, I wonder if Horatio Alger would have changed his advice and said, "Go South, young man." It has a certain ring to it.

CHAPTER 11

Operation: Job Search

"Our ships would come in much sooner if only we would swim out to meet them"...so says a famous philosopher. I have a client, also a philosopher (just not famous yet), who feels differently. From his perspective, with most people's luck, if their ships *do* come in, they'll probably be at the airport!

Whatever your philosophy, there's no escaping the fact that when seeking the perfect job, the only way for your ship to come in is to seize the bull by the foghorns and let 'em know you're out there! Then, of course, hope that luck is on your side.

Should you decide to move to Florida and look for a job, there are some fundamental tasks you'll need to engage in before you start your hunt. I've divided those stages into: "On Your Mark," "Get Set" and "Go."

In the first phase, you'll decide the field of work you're interested in, establish precisely what your skills are, draft your resume, and compose form letters to be sent to prospective employers. Since for many of you, these are things you haven't done since Tucker was in the auto business, here are some guidelines for getting off to the best start. It wouldn't hurt even experienced job hunters to hone up on "search skills"—just to make sure they're not missing a beat.

ON YOUR MARK

    1. *Establish Your Career Goals*...Do you want to stay in your cur-

rent field, or are you anxious to make a career change? If so, consider any schooling, licenses, or certifications Florida might require so you can set a timetable for coursework and exams.

2. *Evaluate Your Skills*...Write down every job you've ever had, including volunteer work. Identify your responsibilities in each job, and ask yourself whether you liked or disliked performing them. Keep in mind that you may not only have developed skills in sales, marketing, etc., but also may have acquired experience in interpersonal applications such as time management, communication, management, etc. Next, rank your skills in order, starting with the ones in which you feel you do best. Ask your spouse and/or colleague to duplicate this activity for you and see if they assessed your skills the same way. Finally, analyze the three or four skills you do and like the best and make a decision about your next career choices. If you'd like to work all of this out in a special workbook, you can send away for one that is recommended by United Van Lines relocation experts. Send a check or money order for $1.95 plus $1.00 for 4th class postage, or $2.25 for UPS shipping, to: *Quick Job Hunting Map, Advanced Version, Ten Speed Press, P.O. Box 7123, Berkeley, CA 94707. Or Call: (415) 845-8414*

3. *Get Job Search Assistance*...Consult with a reputable job counselor to explore different fields you could move into. Find out if your spouse's company offers job-search help for transferred spouses as part of their relocation benefits. Contact employment agencies and executive search firms in the Florida communities you are interested in and explore your opportunities.

4. *Spread the Word*...Tell anyone and everyone about your plans to relocate and find work in Florida. The process of broadcasting your intent to neighbors, colleagues, family, etc. is called "networking" and 30% to 40% of all jobs are obtained through these personal or professional contacts. If you work hard at it, you'll be sure to pick up job leads, make important inroads at companies, make contacts etc.

5. *Write That Resume*...Put together a one-page document outlining your work experience in reverse chronological order (with the most recently-held position first). Each job should include dates of employment, company name, job titles held, accomplishments and responsibilities. State your career objective at the top and your educational background on the bottom. You might also want to include professional organizations you belong to and any honors you've been awarded. Other than that, give little personal information. You want to save something for the interview.

6. *To Whom This Concerns*...Draft all of your form letters—the "networking" letter to professional trade associations or people within organizations who might be able to help you, the basic cover letter, and a short thank you note for anyone who has helped you or agreed to interview you.

7. *Keep Track for Uncle Sam*...Many of your job-hunting expenses will be tax deductible. If you are expecting to remain in the same occupation in which you are currently employed, you will be able to deduct employment agency fees (provided you are not reimbursed by an employer), costs for typing and printing letters and resumes, phone calls and postage, as well as all travel expenses associated with finding a job in your new home state. Contact your local IRS office for a free copy of Publication 529, "Miscellaneous Deductions" for further details.

GET SET

Now you're ready to start the actual job hunt. Experts will tell you that there are two markets to include in your search. The first is the "advertised" market. Obviously this is where companies solicit employee applications in newspaper classified advertising, professional trade journals, college placement centers, government job banks, employment agencies and executive search firms, etc.

The second market is the "hidden" market, so called because the opportunities are available but not publicly announced. Why? Often companies are searching for replacement personnel unbeknownst to the current job holders. Or they may be expanding into a new area and don't want competitors to find out. Or they may have a need for a specific set of skills but haven't worked out enough details to advertise. Your call or letter could come at exactly the right time. To track down jobs in the advertised market, the following resources should be checked:

- *Classified Section of the Newspaper*...This is the best place to start because of the sheer volume of possible opportunities. A mailing list of all major newspapers in Florida is found in Chapter 22, "The Cities and Counties of Florida." I would advise you to subscribe to one or more papers for a few months prior to your move to learn about the job market and the area in general. A monthly subscription is about $7 or $8 if you just order the Sunday edition. It contains everything you'll need—jobs, real estate, local events, etc.

- *Job Service of Florida*...In Florida's major metropolitan areas, the Department of Labor and Employment Security maintains Job Service offices. Their services are free. You can set up an appointment with an interviewer, and discuss your needs and qualifications. They will show you a list of suitable job opportunities in that city as well as in other parts of the state. Naturally they are only aware of the jobs that have been brought to their attention by employers, but estimates are that they receive information on over 475,000 civilian jobs each year. Look in the phone book under government listings for "Job Services of Florida" (Department of Labor).

- *Employment Agencies/Professional Recruiters*...A good agency or recruiter will match your skills to the right job. Check your local library for Florida phone directories and look up the names of some larger firms.

- *State of Florida Employment Opportunities*...The state has 8 regional offices which house the Department of Labor and Employment Security. In addition, there are more than 100 local employment offices which can supply you with civil service job openings and opportunities. For more information about state employment, you can contact one of the regional offices listed below:

1770 Thomasville Rd.
Duval Plaza
Tallahassee, FL 32303
(904) 487-1795

215 Market St.
Room 300
Jacksonville, FL 32202-2885
(904) 359-6080

7925 N.W. 12th St.
Suite 126
Miami, FL 33126
(305) 591-3377

406 S. Florida Ave.
Suite 15
Lakeland, FL 33813
(813) 646-2908

555 N. Congress Ave.
Suite 202
Boynton Beach, FL 33426
(407) 737-0382

3830 Evans Ave.
Suite 2
P.O. Box 6946
Ft. Myers, FL 33911
(813) 278-7133

Kennedy Square
Suite 510
4950 W. Kennedy Blvd.
Tampa, FL 33609-1818
(813) 646-2908

- *College Placement Centers*...Many colleges and universities are willing to help with job searches for new residents, although their referrals are intended mainly for students.

- *Professional, Trade, or Union Associations*...Local chapters of national associations related to your profession or trade sometimes offer placement services for members. A list of openings may be available, or your resume can be placed on file for employers who may be seeking someone with your background and experience.

- *Realtors*...As part of their relocation services for corporate transferees, some realty companies offer help with job searches for employee's spouses.

- *Florida Job Directory*...Recently a small classified advertisement has been running in the *Wall Street Journal* for a directory of Florida's largest employers, as well as for a newsletter covering job openings across the state. While I don't know anything more about the firm, you might want to write or call for more information. *Job World, Inc. Dept. 3, Suite 2153, 499 St. Rd., Altamonte Springs, FL 32714. (407) 788-6232.*

As far as the "hidden" job market is concerned, digging is a little harder, but often more rewarding. When a job is available but not publicly announced, there is obviously going to be less competition for the position. Here are some ways to find out about these coveted positions:

- College Alumni Associations;
- Professional and Trade Organizations;
- Chamber of Commerce membership lists;
- Company and industry directories found at the library;
- Religious leaders or institutions;
- Your spouse's company.

Once you've selected some companies in which you are interested, the next step is to do some homework. Interviewers are impressed by prospective job candidates who have taken the time to familiarize themselves with their company. Here are a few ways you can track down information:

- Call the company's PR Department and request a copy of their annual report.
- Read the industry trade journals for newsworthy items about the company.
- Go to the library and look up firms in one or more of these business references: *Everybody's Business: An Almanac; Standard and Poor's Register of Corporations; Thomas Register of American Manufacturers; Value Line Investment Survey; Moody's Industrial Manual.*

Find out about current problems that are industry-wide, the company's key competitors, the company's growth pattern and reasons behind it, the number of branch offices and their locations, and the names of the key people in the organization.

Go!

It's time for the final step. The interview. For some people this is a real nerve-wracking, fingernail-biting time. The best way to alleviate the jitters is to be prepared. One way to accomplish this is to rehearse what you want to say, and just as important, what you want to ask. Here are some common interview questions you should be prepared to answer:

1. What are some of your most significant accomplishments in each of your previous jobs?

2. Why do you think you are qualified for the position?

3. What have you done about your personal skills development in the past few years?

4. Describe your relationships with your last two supervisors.

5. Tell me about yourself.

6. What are your career goals? (Where would you like to be in 5 years? 10 years?)

7. What do you know about our company?

8. What is the most difficult situation you encountered in your career, and how did you handle it?

9. What salary do you expect?

And, finally, you may be asked questions of a personal nature. What your spouse does, your marital status, questions about children and your childcare arrangements. However, it is illegal for a prospective employer to inquire about any factors which are potentially a basis for discrimination, including age, race, religion, etc. Therefore, you should not answer questions of this nature. To avoid an embarrassing moment, ask in a tactful way if that type of information is a prerequisite for the job. The interviewer should know to move on.

Part of any successful interview is the give and take. Often, the questions you ask are more revealing to the interviewer than your answers to their questions. That's why you should be equally prepared to take over the interview at the appropriate time, asking these questions:

1. What is the company's policy on promoting from within? What are the chances for advancement?

2. May I speak with someone who is doing what I would be doing?

3. How does the company feel about employees returning to school? Is any financial support provided?

4. What type of career development opportunities are there for me to better my job performance?

5. How and by whom will my performance be measured? How often can I expect a performance review?

6. How will the company and department help me achieve the goals we agree upon?

As for questions regarding job benefits, it pays to wait until a job offer has been made. Not only are these answers usually provided by the personnel department, you don't want to appear as though the benefits are more important than the job.

THE SALARY TRAP

The whole issue of salary, bonuses, and commissions is a tricky one. If you bring it up first, it may appear that money is your only consideration. If the interviewer brings it up first and asks what you hope to earn, you might sell yourself short. The best way to handle the situation is to wait and see if the interviewer broaches it during the first meeting. If he or she does not, and you are invited back for a second interview, then by all means ask. There's no point in pursuing a job if it turns out to pay well below your expectations. Following is a suggested response, should the subject arise during your first interview: "Through my research, I've found that a person with my background and experience should be earning $_____."

Starting Wages And Salaries In Florida

To give you a realistic sense of the earning potential for a particular job, you'll want to review this list of positions that were available between July 1, 1988 and June 30, 1989 across the state. The jobs are listed under their respective occupational category, such as professional/managerial, sales, services, etc. Then, next to each job is the average wage or salary as well as the highest wage or salary that was offered. Please remember that we're talking about salary ranges here and your experience may be different. Also, please note that salaries are based on a total of 2,088 hours worked per year. This takes into account a five day work week, sick days, vacation time and major holidays off. This information was provided by the Florida Department of Labor and Employment Security and should be extremely helpful as you map out the strategy for your job search.

Bear in mind that according to federal law, minimum wage is $3.35.

Job Openings and Wages Offered

Job Opening	Salary Offered	
	Average	Highest
Professional, Managerial and Technical		
Architect	$21,610	$33,303
Civil Engineer	$24,429	$39,776
Drafter, Mechanical	$22,049	$37,584
Financial Analyst	$20,160	$28,955
Psychologist	$ 8,769	$18,061
Dentist	$19,731	$37,145
Pharmacist	$21,442	$40,507
Nurse, General Duty	$16,599	$28,104
Nurse, Private Duty	$12,619	$18,228
Nurse, Licensed Practical	$15,889	$30,798
Psychiatric Social Worker	$12,006	$20,086
Recreational Therapist	$ 9,730	$19,355
Dental Hygenist	$17,376	$23,928
Medical Lab Technician	$16,328	$16,683
Emergency Medical Technician	$14,678	$23,594
Teacher, Elementary School	$16,662	$29,336
Teacher, High School	$14,750	$22,968
Lawyer	$19,272	$35,141
Paralegal	$15,764	$36,143
Accountant	$17,121	$40,152
Tax Auditor	$14,010	$35,141
Sales Manager	$15,513	$39,150
Claims Adjustor	$22,645	$37,312
Manager, Retail Store	$11,713	$30,100
Office Manager	$19,585	$30,192
Management Trainee	$11,024	$23,093

	Hourly Wage Offered	
	Average	Highest
Clerical		
Legal Secretary	$6.05	$15.00
Medical Secretary	$5.40	$ 9.00
Secretary	$5.67	$14.42
Word Processing Supervisor	$5.99	$10.00
Keypunch Operator	$5.88	$ 7.35
Bookkeeper	$5.45	$12.02

Job Openings and Wages Offered (continued)

Job Opening	Hourly Wage Offered	
	Average	Highest
Clerical (continued)		
Payroll Clerk	$5.69	$18.75
Insurance Clerk	$4.92	$ 7.63
Shipping/Receiving Supervisor	$4.84	$15.00
Telephone Operator	$4.83	$ 7.50
Receptionist	$4.87	$10.00
Reservations Agent	$5.35	$ 7.69
Sales		
Telephone Sales	$7.65	$12.50
Advertising Rep	$5.10	$14.42
Printing Rep	$4.90	$ 9.13
Retail Sales: Women's Wear	$3.77	$ 4.25
Retail Sales: Shoes	$3.94	$ 9.62
Retail Sales: Cosmetics	$3.88	$ 6.00
Retail Sales: Furniture	$4.70	$15.63
Auto Sales	$5.94	$14.42
Computer Sales	$6.50	$12.50
Manufacturer's Representative	$5.19	$10.63
Services		
Hostess (restaurant)	$4.36	$ 6.50
Head Waiter/Waitress	$5.63	$ 8.75
Fast Food Worker	$3.78	$ 6.00
Bartender	$4.10	$ 9.31
Waiter/Waitress, Informal	$3.79	$10.00
Waiter/Waitress, Formal	$4.15	$ 8.65
Cook	$4.61	$10.49
Chef	$5.99	$16.83
Pizza Baker	$3.99	$ 7.00
Deli Cutter	$4.41	$ 7.72
Food Service Supervisor	$5.73	$10.08
Motel Manager	$5.69	$10.10
Bellhop	$3.83	$ 6.00
Hairstylist	$4.15	$ 6.25
Manicurist	$4.29	$20.00
Firefighter	$6.41	$13.22
Police Officer	$11.64	$12.94

Florida's Largest Employers

To further assist you with your job search, we've compiled the names, addresses and phone numbers of some of the largest employers across the state. In order to match job skills and professions with companies, we've listed them by category of business.

In reviewing the following lists, remember that we are identifying Florida based headquarters only. In many instances these firms will also have regional and district offices, store branches, divisions, subsidiaries, etc., located throughout the state. Contact the personnel department at headquarters for information about employment opportunities, qualifications and the locations of their other offices.

Accounting Firms

Arthur Andersen & Co.
1 Biscayne Tower 5959
Suite 2100
Miami, FL 33131
(305) 374-3700

Deloitte Haskin & Sells
1 S.E. Third Ave.
Miami, Fl 33131
(305) 358-4141

Grant Thornton
500 E. Broward Blvd.
Ft. Lauderdale, FL 33394
(305) 764-1235

Peat Marwick Main & Co.
1 Biscayne Tower
Suite 2800
Miami, FL. 33131
(305) 358-2300

Touche Ross
201 S. Biscayne Blvd.
Miami, FL 33131
(305) 377-4000

Coopers & Lybrand
Blue Lagoon Drive
Miami, FL 33126
(305) 263-8200

Ernst & Whinney
1 Biscayne Tower
Suite 2700
Miami, FL 33131
(305) 358-4111

Laventhol & Horvath
777 S. Flagler Dr.
West Tower/Suite 900
West Palm Beach, FL 33401
(407) 833-5800

Price Waterhouse
Southeast Financial Center
Suite 3000
Miami, FL 33131
(305)381-9400

Arthur Young & Co.
1 E. Broward Blvd.
Ft. Lauderdale, FL 33301
(305) 523-8300

Advertising, Media and Publishing

Beber Silverstein & Partners
3361 S.W. Third Ave.
Miami, FL 33145
(305) 856-9800

Robinson, Yesawich & Pepperdine
555 Winderly Place
Suite 300
Maitland, FL 32751
(407) 875-1111

McFarland & Drier, Inc.
99 E. Fifth St.
Miami, FL 33131
(305) 358-0108

The Ad Team
15251 N.E. 18th Ave.
North Miami Beach, FL 33162
(305) 949-8326

Harris & Drury Advertising
6360 N.W. Fifth Way
Suite 300
Ft. Lauderdale, FL 33309
(305) 771-1800

SCI Holdings (Cable Communications)
P.O. Box 61-8000
Miami, FL 33261-8000
(305) 899-1000

Benito Advertising
600 N. Westshore Blvd.
Tampa, FL 33609
(813) 287-8200

Tinsley Advertising
2660 Brickell Ave.
Miami, FL 33129
(305) 856-6060

Market Development Group
1053 Maitland Center Common
Maitland, FL 32751
(407) 875-1770

West & Company Marketing
3201 Independent Square
Jacksonville, FL 32202
(904) 354-5601

Knight-Ridder Newspapers
One Herald Plaza
Miami, FL 33132
(305) 376-3800

Times Publishing Co.
P.O. Box 1121
St. Petersburg, FL 33731-1121
(813) 893-8111

Law Firms

Holland & Knight
1916 S. Central Ave.
Lakeland, FL 33803
(813) 682-1161

Steel Hector & Davis
4000 Southeast Financial Center
200 S. Biscayne Blvd.
Miami, FL 33131
(305) 577-2800

Carlton, Fieldes, Ward, Emmanuel,
Smith & Cutler, P.A.
One Harbour Place
Tampa, FL 33602
(813) 223-7000

Greenberg, Traurig, Hoffman, Lipoff,
Rosen & Quentel, P.A.
1221 Brickell Ave.
Miami, FL 33131
(305) 579-0500

Ruden, Barnett, McClosky, Smith,
Schuster, & Rusell, P.A.
110 E. Broward Blvd.
Penthouse B
Ft. Lauderdale, FL 33301
(306) 764-6000

Shutts & Brown
1500 Edward Ball Bldg.
100 Chopin Plaza
Miami, FL 33131
(305) 358-6300

Tew, Jorden, Schulte & Beasley
701 Brickell Ave.
Miami, FL 33131
(305) 371-2600

Flowler, White, Gillen, Boggs,
Villareal & Banker, P.A.
501 E. Kennedy Blvd.
Suite 1700
Tampa, FL 33602
(813) 228-7411

Rumberger, Kirk, Caldwell, Cabaniss,
Burke & Wechsler, P.A.
11 E. Pine St.
Orlando, FL 32801
(407) 425-1802

Mershon, Sawyer, Johnston,
Dunwody & Cole
4500 Southeast Financial Center
200 S. Biscayne Blvd.
Miami, FL 33131
(305) 358-5100

Architectural And Engineering Companies

Post, Buckley, Schuh and Jernigan
8600 N.W. 36th St.
Miami, FL 33166
(305) 592-7275

Dyer Riddle Mills & Precourt
1505 E. Colonial Drive
Orlando, FL 32803
(407) 896-0594

Ardaman & Associates
P.O. Box 13003
Orlando, FL 32809
(407) 855-3860

Gee & Jenson
One Harvard Circle
West Palm Beach, FL 33409
(407) 683-3301

Keith & Schnars
6500 N. Andrews Ave.
Ft. Lauderdale, FL 33309
(305) 776-1616

Spillis Candela & Partners, Inc.
800 Douglas Entrance
Coral Gables, FL 33134
(305) 444-4691

Insurance And Banking

John Alden Financial Corp.
P.O. Box 020270
Miami, FL 33102
(305) 470-3100

Barnett Bank of Florida
100 Laura St.
Jacksonville, FL 32202
(904) 791-7720

First Union National Corp.
200 W. Forsyth St.
Jacksonville, FL 32202
(904) 361-2265

NCNB National Bank of Florida
P.O. Box 25900
Tampa, FL 33630
(813) 224-5805

Southeast Banking Corp.
One Southeast Financial Center
Miami, FL 33131
(305) 375-7500

Sun Banks, Inc.
200 S. Orange Ave.
Orlando, FL 32801
(407) 237-4141

Citizens and Southern Florida Corp.
One Financial Plaza
Ft. Lauderdale, FL 33310
(305) 765-2000

First Florida Banks, Inc.
111 Madison St.
Tampa, FL 33602
(813) 224-1111

Retail Firms

Jack Eckerd Corp.
P.O. Box 4689
Clearwater, FL 34618
(813) 397-7461

Kash N'Karry Food Stores
6422 Harvey Rd.
Tampa, FL 33610
(813) 621-0200

Levitz Furniture Corp.
6111 Broken Sound Pkwy., N.W.
Boca Raton, FL 33487
(407) 994-6006

Publix Supermarkets
1936 George Jenkins Blvd.
Lakeland, FL 33801
(813) 688-1188

Winn Dixie Stores, Inc.
P.O. Box B
Jacksonville, FL 32203
(904) 783-5000

J. Byrons
15600 Northwest 15th Ave.
Miami, FL 33169
(305) 620-3000

Burdines Dept. Stores*
P.O. Box 2350
Miami, FL 33131
(305) 577-1913

Maas Brothers/Jordan Marsh Co.*
P.O. Box 311
Tampa, Fl 33601
(813) 223-7525

Claire's Stores, Inc.
6095 N.W. 167th St.
Miami, FL 33015
(305) 558-2577

National Merchandise Co., Inc.
Pic N' Save Stores
2321 Liberty St.
Jacksonville, FL 32206
(904) 350-9500

* Apply here for executive/management positions only. Inquiries for all other positions should be made through the personnel department at any of their branch stores.

Other Major Employers In Florida

Utilities

Florida Power & Light Co.
P.O. Box 029100
Miami, FL 33102
(305)552-3552

Florida Power Corp.
P.O. Box 14042
St. Petersburg, FL 33733
(813)866-5151

Home Building Products

The Worldmark Corp.
1208 U.S. Highway 1
North Palm Beach, FL 33408
(407)626-3116

Real Estate/Home Builder

General Development Corp.
111 S. Bayshore Dr.
Miami, FL 33131
(305)350-1200

Arthur Rutenberg Corp.
15351 Roosevelt Blvd.
Clearwater, FL 34620
(813)530-1691

Trucking

P-I-E Nationwide, Inc.
P.O. Box 2408
Jacksonville, FL 32203
(904)798-2225

Health Care

Care Plus, Inc.
6700 N. Andrews Ave.
Suite 700
Ft. Lauderdale, FL 33309
(305)493-6464

Beverage Importer

Bacardi Imports, Inc.
2100 Biscayne Blvd.
Miami, FL 33137
(305)573-8511

Medical Instruments

Coulter Electronics, Inc.
600 W. 20th St.
Hialeah, FL 33010
(305)885-0131

Building Materials Manufacturer

Jim Walter Corp.
P.O. Box 31075
Tampa, FL 33631-3075
(813)871-4811

Homebuilding and Financing

Hillsborough Holdings Corp.
1500 N. Dale Mabry Hwy.
Tampa, FL 33607
(813)871-4811

Food Wholesale/Distribution

Associated Grocers of Florida, Inc.
P.O. Box 520695
Miami, FL 33152
(305)696-0080

Affiliated of Florida, Inc.
P.O. Box 31667
Tampa, FL 33631-3667
(813)248-5781

Publishing/Family Entertainment

Harcourt Brace Jovanovich
Orlando, FL 32887
(407)345-2000

Entertainment

Walt Disney Company
The Casting Center
1515 Buenva Vista Drive
Lake Buena Vista, FL 32830
(407)828-2850

Universal Studios Florida
1000 Universal Studios Plaza
Orlando, FL 32819
(407)363-8400

Citrus Processor

Lykes Family Holdings
P.O. Box 1690
Tampa, FL 33601
(813)223-3981

Citrus World, Inc.
P.O. Box 1111
Lake Wales, FL 33859
(813)676-1411

Remember that while these are some of the largest Florida-based corporate employers, there are hundreds of out-of-state corporations that have offices, stores or divisions in Florida. This would include K-Mart, J.C. Penney Co., Southern Bell Telephone & Telegraph, IBM and others. For the names and addresses of corporations, whether they are Florida-based or not, write to the Florida Department of Commerce, Bureau of Economic Analysis, Tallahassee, FL 32399-2000. (904) 487-2971. Request a copy of "Florida Facts: Florida's Fifty Largest Employers."

If your background is manufacturing, here is a ranking of the largest industries in Florida, based on the total number of companies and employees in the state.

1. Fabricated Metal Products
2. Electrical and Electronic Machinery
3. Transportation Equipment
4. Food and Kindred Products
5. Machinery (except Electrical)
6. Printing, Publishing and Allied Products

In the above 6 industry categories, more than 5200 companies are doing business in Florida, employing close to three-quarters-of-a-million residents. Among these, the printing and publishing field is the fastest growing segment of the manufacturing sector. Between 1982 and 1987, this industry created 18,000 jobs in the state. And in just the first half of 1987, they added another 3300 positions, or 31% of all the goods-producing jobs in the state. Experts attribute this paper boom to being in an ever-expanding Information Age. It has apparently resulted in a tremendous demand for forms, direct mail pieces and other printed matter.

Coming Out Of Retirement

If your move to Florida is going to precipitate the urge or the need to come out of retirement, you'll probably take comfort in knowing that you are not alone in returning to work. Apparently 25% of all retirees make the decision to return to a workplace, either on a full- or part-time basis. They realize that they need a job to feel mentally and physically fit again, and the financial rewards guarantee a better lifestyle than they may be experiencing in retirement. Whatever your reasons, here are some suggestions on how to rejoin the legions of gainfully employed:

1. Emphasize your years of experience to help you win an interview.

2. Remind the employer that mature workers are usually reliable, dependable, responsible workers. Don't forget to mention your good attendance record at your last job.

3. It never hurts to try something new, such as working with computers. You may discover you're a natural.

4. Even though it is illegal to discriminate against a job applicant due to age, be prepared to discuss the issue in an indirect way. Point out your good health, your ability to drive and get around, and anything else that reassures the interviewer you are still able to perform the job.

5. If you are between the ages of 40 and 70 and feel you have been discriminated against due to your age, the Equal Employment Opportunity Commission will assist you in re-evaluating your application.

6. Look into employment agencies that specialize in working with seniors. They could be an excellent source of appropriate jobs.

7. If your gut feeling tells you that a job is going to be too demanding for you, don't try to alter the job to meet your needs. Just move on.

SOCIAL SECURITY

Obviously Social Security benefits are an important part of your retirement plan. If you are already receiving them and want to return to work, here are some facts you should know:

1. There *is* a ceiling on earned income over and above your Social Security benefits. While the sum is increased every year, you need to check with your nearest Social Security office to find out the top salary you can earn the first year.

2. Understand that two different limits are set. One amount is for those aged 65-69; the other for those under 65. At present, there is no limit on earnings for people who are 70 and older. Apparently the government feels that if these seniors still want to earn a living, God bless them.

3. If your additional earned income exceeds the annual exempt amount, for every $2 over that limit $1 will be deducted from your monthly Social Security check. Dependents' checks will be reduced as well as yours if they are collecting on your work record. Notify the Social Security office, not the IRS, if you have exceeded the limit. Any overpaid benefits will have to be returned to Social Security.

4. If you are self-employed, all of the rules regarding earned income limits apply to you as well.

The important thing is to confirm that taking a job will increase your income, not decrease it by jeopardizing your benefits. Check with your Social Security office—before you go back to work.

A Few Words Of Caution

As exciting as the volume of job opportunities is in Florida, statistics have not yet begun to reflect the current slow contraction of Florida industries which expanded in the 80s. They are shrinking in staff size due to changes in their industries, fluctuating economies and a realization that demand for their products and services may have hit a peak. Due to increased competition, labor strikes and other factors, such giants as IBM and Eastern Air Lines have implemented major cutbacks involving the release of thousands of employees. Hi-tech companies have implemented hiring freezes, and so on. This by no means indicates that the boom is over. Nothing could be farther from the truth. However, it's the nature of the beast for even the most prominent, successful companies to grow and expand, then experience some downward trends, then surge once again.

That's why I urge you to make a careful check of companies that are of interest to you before you jump in. Talk to employees, business competitors, the local Chamber of Commerce, employment agencies and executive search firms—anyone who might have a sense of what's on the horizon. It could save you from making a commitment to a company that won't be able to keep its commitment to you.

CHAPTER 12

The Business Of Starting A Business In Florida

I t used to be that owning a home was the great American dream. Today, it's owning a business. It seems that everyone from 6 to 66 has caught the entrepreneurial bug and stands ready to cash in. It's not terribly surprising when you consider that our country's most inspiring heroes were explorers, inventors, scientists, businessmen—people who worked tirelessly to create their own destinies. Imagine the course of this nation's history if Albert Einstein had to sell his "theory of relativity" to a bunch of empty suits in upper management. Suppose Lewis and Clark needed to obtain a budget approval before they set off to explore? It's impossible to imagine... because what America stands for is the opportunity to strike out on your own.

Looking at the state's aggressive efforts to attract new businesses, it appears that Florida has become the country's unofficial keeper of dreams. Market Force Corp., a Longwood, FL-based business research firm, estimates that 932 new businesses open every week within Florida's metro areas. That translates to almost 50,000 new businesses a year. No wonder Florida is to entrepreneurs what California was to the golddiggers... minus the hills.

If you are seriously considering moving to Florida and starting a business, you couldn't be making the decision at a better time. Florida is the 2nd fastest-growing state in the nation in terms of population, and it appears that 1989 will be the seventh straight year for business expansion. The economy is strong, and local government agencies, universities and private enterprise are practically tripping over each other trying to help newcomers put their business ideas into action.

This chapter will explore all the fundamentals of new business development—creating a business plan, securing financing, small business trends, partnerships *vs.* sole proprietorships, etc. We'll even consider some ideas for those who anticipate selling their business up north. Equally important, we'll cover the Florida factor—fast-growing regions, where to go to for help, rules and regulations—all the key pieces of information to help launch your new enterprise.

INVALUABLE INFORMATION TO SEND FOR
FROM FLORIDA'S DIVISION OF ECONOMIC DEVELOPMENT...

Before we begin, I recommend that you order a copy of a valuable booklet offered free of charge to anyone interested in opening a business in Florida. Entitled "Florida's New Business Guide and Checklist," it's a clear, concise handbook containing an enormous amount of reference material. While volumes have already been published on how to be a successful entrepreneur, this booklet will lead you through the myriad of resources and regulations specific to Florida. *Write or call: Florida Department of Commerce, Div. of Economic Development, 107 W. Gaines Street, Tallahassee, FL 32399-2000, (904) 488-9357.*

If you are visiting Florida, call their toll-free number, 1-800-342-0771.

Are You Boss Material?

Before doing anything else in the pursuit of your business, find a quiet place in which you can have an intimate conversation with yourself. It's time to confront the most important issue of any business—are you the right person to run it? Independent of your dreams, hopes and desires, do you have the energy, guts, steel nerves, and determination it will take to make a success of your idea? Do you honestly know why you want to strike out on your own, other than the obvious prospects of having complete freedom and financial rewards? As exciting as the whole idea is, not to mention the status, you must ask yourself these and other soul-searching questions. Below is an outline for this important talk with yourself. And please, knowing that there's an almost 50% chance of a business failing within the first two years, "To thine own self be true."

PERSONALITY SPEAKING...

1. Are you by nature aggressive, ambitious and persistent?

2. Do you plan ahead—are you organized, detail-oriented, careful, and accurate?

3. Do you genuinely enjoy and care about people? Will you be good to your employees and customers, or are they just a means to an end?

4. What is your stress tolerance? Are you someone who already relies heavily on drink, drugs and other escapist activities when the going gets tough, or are you known for your iron stomach?

5. Are you a creative person who trusts your instincts, or are you a methodical person who requires every "t" to be crossed and "i" dotted before taking action?

6. Are you known to become easily bored with projects, or do you have the tenacity to follow through to the end, no matter how difficult?

7. Do you have the courage to stand up to abusive customers, undependable suppliers, angry bankers, ungrateful employees, etc.? Could you fire someone if you had to?

8. Can your ego accept help, criticism, and other "blows" from anyone without falling apart?

9. Are you a total "do it yourselfer" or can you easily delegate authority?

10. Do you trust other people by nature, or are you convinced that most people would swindle you given the opportunity?

FINANCIALLY SPEAKING...

1. Are you prepared to put in long hours at the beginning without getting a paycheck? Will you be able to "stomach" handing employees their pay while you wait for yours?

2. Do you and your family have the means to survive while the business is growing, or will you need an immediate income?

3. Do you know how much capital you'll need to get started?

4. Have you calculated how much you'll be investing personally, and how much will come from outside sources?

5. Do you know how much bank credit will be available to you, and will you have this or other sources to turn to in emergencies?

6. Can you accurately project your annual net income for the first, second and third years? Will it take a miracle to reach the numbers you want, or are they within realistic reach?

7. Have you totaled the income you and your family will be sacrific-

ing in order to start the business? How long will it take you to make it back, and then some?

8. How is your personal credit rating? Are there any loan defaults, bankruptcies, or other financial crises lurking in your past?

9. When you create your first annual operating budget, will you factor in a salary for yourself, or are you going to assume you'll go without a paycheck until the business can afford it?

10. What is your timetable for success? How long are you willing to hold out for the business to be considered a financial success?

EXPERIENCE SPEAKING...

1. Are you knowledgeable about the business you want to start? Are you currently working in the same business?

2. Have you personally run this type of business, or have you observed the owner/manager run it?

3. Does your business idea evolve from previous work experience, or does it represent a departure from what you know?

4. Do you absolutely love the nature of this work, or are you pretty non-committal about it ("Business is business")?

5. Do you know your market and how to reach it, or will you be experimenting to find out at the beginning?

6. Will you be able to get the business running in a reasonable amount of time, or will you be walking in the dark for a while as you figure out the day-to-day operation?

7. Are you prepared with contingency plans for business slumps, poor advertising results, lack of traffic and other nightmares? Or would your lack of experience put you in a total panic?

8. Have you met with a lawyer and an accountant familiar with your kind of business? Do they have confidence in your concepts?

9. Do you know what to look for in a business location?

10. Do you know the local zoning and licensing requirements of the business you want to start?

There are no perfect answers to any of these questions, nor is there a scoring system to define your category of readiness. Ponder these subjects and decide for yourself if you've got what it takes.

If you're still looking for an indicator, however, I'd say that if these questions and your answers don't absolutely scare the living cajeebies out of you, it's OK to collect your $200 and pass "go."

What's The Big Idea?

More questions. What kind of business will it be? Will you open a store or restaurant? Start a daycare center or a cleaning business? Act as a management or data processing consultant? Open a professional accounting or legal practice? Will you be involved in direct sales or direct marketing? Will you be catering to business people or consumers? Will you be launching an entirely new idea based on a demand only you are aware of? The field is wide open! But that's where many novices' problems begin. They have the itch, they just don't know where to scratch!

Every expert will tell you to stick with something you know and love. Bucking that advice only increases the odds of failure. No matter how smart you are, how well educated, and how good your instincts, starting a business in unfamiliar territory is a pretty sure road to night terrors. That is not to say you shouldn't consider an entirely new business idea, but it should be based on one you know intimately. For example, if you are in a business that encounters chronic quality, service and delivery problems—your idea could germinate from these observations. This is, of course, provided you have solutions to these problems.

If your business idea centers around an already-existing category of business such as a restaurant, shoe store or data processing service, can you zero in on a special niche in that field? Would there be a demand in the market for a special cuisine, based on the increasing influx of newcomers from a particular part of the country or world? Could your shoe store specialize in seniors if their needs were not currently being met? Could your data processing business develop special services catering to the legal and accounting professions? Look for places where demand exceeds supply and go for it.

There are other telltale signs. Does a certain business seem to have endlessly-long lines (the bank doesn't count)? Do you find it difficult to obtain a particular product because it's always out of stock? Is it hard to get an appointment or reservation at a particular place of business—a hair salon, restaurant, optical store, etc? Why are their services in such great demand? Is it because they're the only ones in town? Or, are they doing something unique? What is it? Remember one other thing as you formulate your ideas—if a business is so easy to get into and so simple to copy, you may not be alone in the field very long. Fledgling businesses that have to contend with stiff competition never have a chance to build customer or distributor loyalty.

Finally, if you decide to start a new type of business, think about protecting your idea as long as you can. Be cautious about the persons with whom you share your idea. A little paranoia never hurt anyone. Also, keep a diary of when and how you conceived the concept, what steps you took to launch the business and when. Include sketches, blueprints...anything that could prove useful in the unlikely event of litigation. It might even help to ask witnesses to co-sign your entries.

BUSINESSES THAT ARE "HOT"

We all know the expression, "there's nothing new under the sun." I'm not so sure about that. There seems to be plenty of innovation going on under Florida's hot sun. Sylvia Porter's *Personal Finance* magazine (April, 1988) reported on some of the business ideas that were cropping up *and* succeeding in Florida as well as the rest of the country. Perhaps their list confirms your hunches:

- *Medical Facilities* (particularly for geriatrics).

- *Personal Health Facilities:* diet centers, health spas, etc. The jury is still out on tanning salons, but early indicators are not good.

- *Specialty Foods:* cooked and uncooked; fresh or frozen; experimental cuisine or good old American apple pie; gift items, etc.

- *Trash and Recycling:* private garbage disposal will be in tremendous demand as landfills fill up and close.

- *Computer Technology:* data processing, programming, repairs, consulting, word processing, you name it.

- *Financial Services:* especially those directed toward baby boomers who are becoming more affluent and need help.

- *Travel:* tours to exotic places; group travel; trips for grandparents and grandkids.

My personal observation is that furniture rental businesses are practically a can't-miss proposition, if well executed. When you add the number of snowbirds who migrate to their condominiums for the winter, with the thousand families a day who are making Florida a permanent home, that's a lot of beds. Many people come down and rent for a while until they find a place to settle permanently, leaving their furniture in storage. Others find their old, large pieces inappropriate for small condos, and decide to start over. In both cases, until they buy new furniture, they rent it.

According to Geoffrey Kessler, a small business consultant, there are many other solid ideas for the 1990s based on increasing consumer demands. For example, he observes that people are saying "Help me cope." You can translate that as a need for services locating childcare, housekeepers and private duty nurses for people, or that conduct stress-reduction classes. People are also saying, "I need to earn or save more money." That calls for budget and financial counseling services, job counseling, business consulting, used-equipment exchanges or other cost-cutting services. You get the idea. Now put your ear to the ground and listen to what people are saying.

Incidentally, if you are interested in more ideas for small businesses, you might want to subscribe to "The Kessler Letter." Write to Kessler and Associates, 11661 San Vincente Blvd., Los Angeles, CA 90049. Or call (213) 826-7835.

Partnership vs. Sole Proprietorship?

One of the most important decisions you will make after deciding the nature of your business, is deciding whether you will fly solo or form a partnership. Obviously if you are moving to Florida and don't know anyone well enough to join forces with, your decision is probably made. On the other hand if you work with a business broker, or read the classifieds under "Business Opportunities," you might be able to find someone whose interests and needs are similar. Before you decide, you should size up the pros and cons of each.

SOLE PROPRIETORSHIPS

The biggest advantage of owning a business in its entirety is that it's the least costly way to open. Sure, you'll also incur all expenses, but at least you won't need to worry about supporting more than one family at the beginning. Following are other advantages and disadvantages:

Advantages	*Disadvantages*
• It's the easiest way to start.	• There is unlimited liability.
• It offers complete freedom of action.	• Death/illness can endanger the business.
• You have total authority.	• Growth is limited to personal energy and knowledge/capabilities.
• Small firms have income tax advantages.	• Personal affairs are easily mixed with business.

PARTNERSHIPS

Partnerships are like marriages. They can be absolutely wonderful, or a disaster at any point in the game. Unfortunately, no matter how long you know your prospective partner, you don't *really* know him/her until you go into business together. If you decide to align yourself with one or more partners, don't make any sudden moves without consulting a trusted attorney and an accountant. You might

123

even ask them to meet your partner(s)-to-be for second opinions about this person's capabilities, compatibilities, etc.

The most important task in forming a business partnership is ironing out all the major details in writing—everything from hours, pay and responsibilities, to buy and sell agreements in the event of an untimely death or dissolution of the partnership. Your lawyers will hammer out the details. Just be sure you know what you're signing. For comparison's sake, following are the pros and cons of a partnership:

Advantages	*Disadvantages*
• Two heads are better than one.	• A partner can die, become ill, go bankrupt, or divorce—all of which will affect you.
• It's an additional source of capital.	• It's difficult to get rid of a bad partner.
• You can obtain a better credit rating than a one-person corporation	• There's a hazy line of authority.
• Different strengths will enhance the business.	• Conflicts with regard to business direction can impede growth.

CORPORATIONS

Another decision to make is whether or not to incorporate. Setting up a corporation represents a host of possible opportunities and problems. Again, you should consult with your lawyer and get his or her recommendation based on the type of business you're instituting. The biggest drawback for a new business is the up-front expense—attorney's fees, registration, etc. However, it's possible that incorporating will save you from a lot of legal grief later on. Following are the pros and cons:

Advantages	*Disadvantages*
• Stockholders have limited liability.	• Corporations have a heavier tax burden.
• Corporations have continuity.	• Their power is limited by charter.
• Transfer of shares	• Therefore less freedom of activity.
• Change in owners need not affect management	• There are more legal formalities.
• It is easier to raise capital.	• They are expensive to launch.

S CORPORATIONS

Finally, there is always the option of forming an S corporation (known as a Subchapter S). This legal provision allows the shareholders to absorb all of the corporate income or losses as partners, but report it as individual taxpayers. In effect, the S corporation is not affected by corporate income taxes, thereby eliminating the double taxation (personal and business) of standard corporations. Besides being treated as a partnership from a tax standpoint, the S corporation and standard corporation share most of the same pros and cons. However, the S corporation must meet certain requirements before one can be formed:

1. It must be a U.S. corporation.

2. There can only be one class of stock.

3. Only individuals or estates can be shareholders.

4. The corporation cannot be part of another organization.

5. A maximum number of shareholders is allowed.

6. No shareholder can be a nonresident alien.

7. 20% or more of the revenue must be generated in the US.

8. Dividends, interests, royalties, rents, annuities and securities transactions cannot account for more than 20% of the total revenue.

It Pays To Write A Business Plan

Whether you go it alone or with a partner, incorporate or not, every new business needs a road map.

Anyone who has ever attempted to write a formal business plan likens it to a marathon. If you do nothing more than finish, you're a winner! Creating a business plan is enormously time-consuming and guarantees nothing at all. Still, conventional wisdom holds that money solves most business problems, and business plans raise money. Therefore, you write a business plan to raise money.

The biggest misconception about business plans is that they're set in cement. At best, they're just ideas for getting started. After a year the plan may have nothing to do with reality, but by then it will have served its purpose. Secondly, many people believe that once they raise money their troubles are over. When you evaluate the majority of business failures, however, you discover, more times than not, that under-capitalization was *not solely to blame*. Central to the failure was the inability to attract the right management with the right skills and attitudes and with the same amount of commitment to getting the job done.

WHAT'S IN A BUSINESS PLAN

Business plans take many forms. Check with the library for numerous books which can guide you through the development process. It's important that all bases be covered. Following is an outline of the basic information found in more conventional plans:

- *Summary Statement*...Name and location; product or service your business offers; short- and long-term goals; amount of capital requested and return on investment; equity structure (total ownership divided by total capitalization—a one-to-one ratio, or 50% equity, is desirable).

- *Uses and Sources of Funds*...A list of initial costs including land, rent, equipment, operating costs for the first six months; a list of initial funding sources (the SBA, venture capital, banks, outside investors, etc.).

- *Personal Data*...Resumes of all major investors/owners; personal monthly budgets; current balance sheets of owners including assets and liabilities (within 60 days); copies of the past three years' income tax returns. Highlight any previous experiences in business ownership.

- *Management Team*...Copy of legal form of ownership (partnership agreement, corporate charter, etc.); resumes and job descriptions of key personnel; an organizational chart.

- *Legal Documents*...Lease or purchase agreements; franchise agreements; buy-sell agreements; life insurance policies; copies of licenses, zoning changes, trade names, current credit reports on owners, etc.

- *Market Analysis*...Projected revenues for the first 3 years; description of customer base; market size; competition and their strengths and weaknesses; future trends.

- *Product or Service*...Physical description of product or service and how it differs from the competitors'; brief history of the product, including patents or copyrights; list of suppliers and vendors.

- *Physical Plant*...Map of area and site location; building layout showing product or customer flow; manufacturing process; list of raw materials, components, etc.

- *Marketing Strategies*...General marketing philosophy; product features to be emphasized; methods for prospecting; pricing and credit policies; distribution policies; promotion and advertising strategies.

- *Financial Feasibility*...Cash flow projections for the first 12 months and then for the first two years; key business ratios; break-even charts; major capital investments within the first three years; a capitalization statement of worth-of-business based on net income rate-of-return.

Source: *Small Business Management Principles*, Stanley R. Sondeno

Money, Money, Money

"It takes money to make money," so the saying goes. But whose money and how do you get it? Unless you are already independently wealthy, raising the necessary capital to go into business is still the biggest challenge for any entrepreneur. Conventional sources such as the local savings and loan still say "no" more than they say "yes." With an almost 50/50 chance of a business failing within two years, you can't blame them.

As one banker friend told me, "Even if the business has nothing to do with football, you never know if it will end up in the hands of a receiver." Yet new businesses are springing up at a dizzying pace. Money must be available somewhere. The truth is, there are more ways to raise capital than ever before, and Florida is one state that will hold your hand through the process. As an entrepreneur myself, I'll tell you one thing about raising capital—all it takes is getting turned down to realize that you need less money than you thought to get started!

Let's explore the best ways to raise seed money and where to go in the state for further assistance. These first sources are the more conventional routes to take:

1. *THE BANK*...Sometimes they actually say yes. It helps to have an already proven relationship with them—either through a mortgage or installment loan you've never paid late, or a previous venture that was financially successful. Your chances are further improved by putting up collateral and/or getting someone of means to guarantee the loan. Remember, banks almost always want to see a well-thought-out business plan.

2. *THE SMALL BUSINESS ADMINISTRATION*...By the time you finish the paperwork, your idea could have gone out of style. Still, the SBA is there to guarantee loans to businesses that meet their specific requirements. If you want to pursue this avenue, call their toll-free number for more information. (800) 368-5855. In Florida call (305) 536-5521 for South Florida locations, and (904) 791-3782 for North Florida locations.

3. *CHARGE IT*...If your business idea needs only a few thousand dollars and the available funds have already been approved on your credit cards and/or overdraft checking, it's a quick way to start a

127

business. But it's an expensive way—averaging 17% interest a year. However, it eliminates the need to peddle your idea for approval. The downside is that you take 100% of the risk.

4. *HOME EQUITY LOANS*...Again, here's a way to capitalize relatively quickly without needing the bank's approval for your idea. However, please don't forget that if you lose the business and are unable to repay the loan, you'll lose the roof over your head, too.

5. *EMPLOYERS AND SUPPLIERS*...If your concept has the potential to serve your industry well, perhaps you can convince your current employer and/or suppliers to underwrite the seed money. Or perhaps the larger suppliers would arrange to give you generous and extended credit. They may be willing to get you started in return for a piece of the action. A word of caution—be careful about dealing with ex-employers. They could, in the future, claim you developed the idea on company time, used company resources, and then sue you for a piece of the action. Talk to your lawyer before approaching them.

6. *VENTURE CAPITAL*...Ironically, this is the most difficult route to take, yet the reason for their existence is to help new businesses get started. You'll need lots of endurance and sophistication to play in their league. Should you succeed at their game, it might be good news or bad news. The good news: the venture capital firm will work to bring your company public, which could make playing the lottery a complete bore. The bad: you're probably going to lose control of the company. Don't even bother to approach a venture capitalist unless your idea has the potential to make big bucks.

7. *PRIVATE HELPERS*...Got any rich uncles? Basically the ability to borrow from wealthy family and friends is still the most common source of raising seed money. The terms are more flexible than with banks or venture capitalists. Most "angels" don't want to be involved in the operation, usually the money they put up doesn't affect their life. However, let's not be naive. Businesses that flop using a family's or friend's money can mean the end of a pleasant relationship. Weigh the value of the loan *vs.* the value of the relationship before you borrow.

8. *VENTURE CLUBS*...If you can't approach anyone you know personally, there are a growing number of organizations that link entrepreneurs with private capital—doctors, lawyers, industrialists and other successful business people who are looking for ideas to invest in. Write to: Association of Venture Clubs, 19 W. South Temple St., Salt Lake City, UT 84101; The International Venture

Capital Institute, P.O. Box 1333, Stamford, CT 06902; and Venture Capital Network, P.O. Box 882, Durham, NH 03824.

Following are some of the more unconventional methods for raising capital that might be more appropriate for you:

1. *CASH UP FRONT*...If your idea is to provide a service to another business, sell the idea, get an order, and ask for payment up front. Tell them it's the only way you'll be able to get started—and if you are forced to borrow money from a bank, costs will rise.

2. *DISTRIBUTION AGREEMENTS*...If your idea is for a product requiring a network of distributors to market it, agree to give non-competing distributors exclusive sales rights if they lend you seed money.

3. *TURN ORDERS INTO CAPITAL*...If you're not prepared to offer your house as collateral, try to generate enough orders for your product or service and bring them to the bank. Tell the loan officer you'll put the income from those orders up as collateral if they approve the loan. You can go through the same process with outside investors, distributors, suppliers, friends, etc.

4. *TAKE IN WORKING PARTNERS*...If you can put together a small group of colleagues, friends, family, etc., all of whom have capital to invest and who would be assets to the business, form a joint venture. Have your attorneys spell out all the details, as they would with any partnership agreement.

5. *BORROW EXPERTISE*...If your network of family, friends, colleagues, etc. has expertise in areas that would be a big asset to your fledgling business, but they're a little short on cash, "borrow" their skills. You can offer them a small part interest in the business or a promissory note for payment when the business turns a profit.

6. *BARTER FOR PRODUCT AND SERVICES*...Not all new businesses need cash to get started. They may need office or store space, equipment, supplies, etc. In these instances, try to barter with the "investors" for payment. Offer to perform a service or give them "X" amount of product in exchange for their help.

7. *FIND SOMEONE WITH A NICE SIGNATURE*...In other words, ask someone who is well collateralized to co-sign your bank loan. Offer to repay that person with an up-front fee or stock in your company.

129

Tips For Selling Your Business Up North

For many of you, starting a business in Florida will not be your first venture. Some of you may have been in business for so long you were called peddlers when you started. In any event, if your plans to relocate to Florida mean selling your current business, you'll probably have a number of special concerns—starting with, "Is this a good time to sell?"

TIMING IS EVERYTHING

There are two issues to consider when an established business is about to be sold: 1) is the business fiscally fit? and, 2) are you emotionally ready to sell? The first question can be answered by your accountant. The second can only be answered by you and your spouse. In either case, timing is critical.

From the financial perspective, the ideal time to pass on the torch is when your product or service is growing. Once a business begins to slide the prospects for getting top dollar diminish. Also, it's best to try to sell when you are on the upside of the profit curve. In other words, the time to sell is when you've had a few bad years followed by a good one. Not the other way around.

Emotionally, you can tell if you're ready when you are legitimately willing to start negotiating with a buyer. If you find yourself asking an unreasonably high price and refusing to budge from it, you may be unconsciously trying to blow the deal.

Following are six good reasons to sell a business. Do you relate to any of them?

1. Boredom and burnout;
2. Slowdown in operating and capital growth;
3. No family or friends to take over the business;
4. A need for liquidity;
5. Aging and health;
6. Need to pursue other interests.

If you are ready to sell, you'll be more likely to get the best possible price by following these important "clean-up" steps:

- *Clean Up Your Records*...You need to be able to support your performance claims. The best way to do that is through complete, accurate, up-to-date record keeping.

- *Clean Up the Premises*...A store or business site that looks shabby and in need of repair is an automatic invitation for the prospective buyer to offer a much lower price. People who are in the market for an established business choose this route because the start-up costs, over and above the purchase price, are presumably minimal.

- *Clean Up Your Debts*...The less indebted the business is, the greater the number of interested prospective buyers. Let's face it, business buyers are already putting themselves in hock; they're not looking to finance any more debt than they have to.

- *Clean Up Your Payroll...* Get rid of excesses that show up on the books, i.e. children on the payroll; one or more luxury cars leased to the business. Even if the flab is legitimate, it can work against you at the bargaining table.

- *Clean Up the Capital...* Show enough capital to carry the business but not so much that it appears the business has peaked. Buyers are anxious to see excess cash and receivables reinvested in the business, proving to them the business is growing and demand is strong for the product or service.

SHOULD YOU WORK WITH A BUSINESS BROKER?

By definition, business brokers are matchmakers. Their aim is to put buyers and sellers together, assist with negotiations, and consummate a sale... presumably leaving everyone happy. In concept, they serve an important function, particularly to the inexperienced seller. However, the field is a growing one, and developing a reputation for attracting unsavory characters. You hear stories about enormous fees being charged resulting in a great deal for the broker, and no deal for the seller. This is unfortunate because as with any profession, all it takes is a few bad apples.

On a grander scale, there are M&A (Mergers and Acquisitions) firms. They provide the same service as brokerage firms, but generally represent businesses that are selling for a half-million or higher.

If you feel your interests can best be served by working with a broker since you have neither the time nor the expertise to sell your business, then by all means, check it out. In doing so, however, I urge you to follow these precautions:

- *Never Hit the First Pitch...* This old batting advice works wonders. Interview as many brokers as you can tolerate, insisting on proof that they sell at least 50% of the businesses they list. Next, you want them to prove they sell them within 20% of the average listing price.

- *No Double Teaming...* The only arrangement you'll find acceptable is one where the broker represents you, and not the prospective buyers as well. The potential conflict of interest is enormous, not to mention that some brokers expect to be paid from both sides of the bargaining table.

- *Ask for an Appraisal...* Ask the broker for an assessment of how much your business is worth. If the only response is, "How much do you want for it?"—move on. The asking price will determine the saleability of your business. It should be based on careful, educated calculations, not wishful thinking.

- *Confirm the Broker's Fees*...Some brokers charge an initial fee for "marketing" your business. The average price for this service is $1000 to $1500, and can go as high as $20,000 if you let it. For this fee you might get a business valuation and financial history. Both of these will supposedly help expedite a sale. Once a sale is consummated, a typical commission is between 8% and 12% of the selling price.

FINDING A BUYER ON YOUR OWN

Business brokerage firms are proliferating because the sale of a business is a very delicate matter. How do you communicate to potential buyers without alerting your competitors that you are vulnerable to being raided?

The first suggestion is never to identify your business in a newspaper or trade ad. Describe your operation in general terms and indicate a P.O. Box for inquiries. If you are planning to network through your lawyer and accountant, understand that confidentiality is pretty difficult. Be prepared for the news filtering out to the wrong people. But who knows? Maybe your biggest competitor will make you an offer you can't refuse.

Two other sources of business buyers are: liquidation officers at the SBA; and loan officers of local banks. They are usually aware of who is looking and the nature of the businesses in which buyers are interested.

This is not to say that you must sell only to neighborhood buyers. Increasingly, businesses are being sold to out-of-state and foreign investors (due to the weak dollar). To reach this market, place ads in the business opportunity sections of major metropolitan newspapers across the U.S., such as: the *Chicago Tribune*; the *Los Angeles Times*; etc. If you feel you have something to offer the international market, place your ads in foreign publications such as the *Financial Times of London*, and other major daily papers. Be sure to request replies in English.

WHEN IT'S TIME TO MAKE THE DEAL

There are no magic formulas for determining the value of a privately-held business. Much of it depends on location site, the regional growth pattern, and the potential of an industry. If you're in a business that's booming, obviously you can command more.

However, the tendency to over-inflate an asking price based on future profits will only hamper dialogue. Any sharp business person would rightfully assume that increased profitability occurring after a takeover had to do with their entrepreneurial strengths and capital infusion.

If you need assistance in establishing the current market value of your business, contact the American Society of Appraisers at 800-ASA-VALU. They will direct you to a business appraiser in your area.

With regard to the actual deal, you need to determine your personal and financial needs in advance. Do you need a large down payment in order to start your new business in Florida, or are you more interested in maintaining a small interest in the business after the sale? Decide what is negotiable and what is not. The structure of the deal is usually worked out on a contractual basis, with a 20- to 30-percent down payment and the balance paid out over ten years. As with real estate, the smaller the down payment, the higher the price—to the tune of 50% more than a cash sale.

Naturally, allowing the buyer to finance involves some risk. The only way to assure yourself that the new owner has the "right stuff" is to check him or her out as extensively as possible. Examine their credit rating and any other personal data that will reveal the person's backbone. Then insist on being able to review the books on a quarterly basis for as long as you are owed money. If you start to see some negative indicators, you can jump in before it's too late. Finally, you should secure the note with a lien against all assets in the business and a separate lien on the buyer's home or other major assets.

What Is The Value Of The Business You Want To Buy?

What about buying an existing business in Florida, rather than starting from scratch? Not everyone has the head for creating and building an operation from the ground up. It's understandable that would-be entrepreneurs presumably don't have the capital or patience to wait out the profit potential of a start-up situation. Thus, it's a logical step to look at business opportunities which are already in progress. While there are numerous advantages to taking over an operation having a loyal customer following, existing fixtures and inventory, a proven sales track record, etc., it can be a very risky proposition. Conventional wisdom holds that only 10% of businesses that are for sale at any given time are worth buying. What's wrong with the other 90%?

The problem is, you won't know until you're the proud owner. Even if every last detail is spelled out in the purchase agreement with the guidance of the best lawyer and accountant, it can be difficult to size up a business's hidden problems. This could include excessive staff turnover, outdated inventory, inadequate parking, changing trends, insufficient walk-in traffic, minimal street traffic, stiff competition and a host of other obstacles. Some things aren't obvious when you're in the heat of negotiations.

Does this mean you should never buy an existing business? No, but it does mean you should "shop 'till you drop" for the right property. It also means you should be diligent about negotiating a fair price based on the age and size of the business, the location, the assets and liabilities, and other critical factors.

ANALYZING THE VALUE OF A SMALL BUSINESS

To give you a sense of the fair market value of existing businesses, following is an overview of parameters for establishing a purchase price.

Business: Apparel Store
Purchase Price: .75 to 1.5 times net, plus equipment and inventory
Important Conditions: Location, competition, reputation, specialization
Cautions: Shortage of parking, old inventory, rapid turnover

Business: Beauty Salon
Purchase Price: .25 to .75 times gross, plus equipment and inventory
Important Conditions: Location, reputation, boutique image
Cautions: Excessive staff turnover, inadequate parking, outdated image

Business: Insurance Agency
Purchase Price: 1- to 2-times annual renewal commissions
Important Conditions: Client demographics and transferability, carrier characteristics
Cautions: Agent turnover, account mix

Business: Manufacturer
Purchase Price: 1.5 to 2.5 times net with equipment, plus inventory
Conditions: Distributor relations, market position, industry trends
Cautions: Single major customer, foreign competition

Business: Restaurant
Purchase Price: .25 to .5 times gross, equipment included
Conditions: Competition, location, reputation
Cautions: Predecessor failures

Business: Travel Agency
Purchase Price: .04 to .1 times gross, equipment included
Conditions: Revenue mix, location, reputation, lease terms
Cautions: Negative climate for international travel, insufficient street traffic

Business: Video Store
Purchase Price: 1- to 2-times net, plus equipment
Conditions: Location, competition, inventory
Cautions: Obsolete tapes, match of tapes to customers

Florida Is Ready And Waiting To Help

As has been mentioned, Florida is unusually cooperative in helping new businesses get started. Not that someone sits in Tallahassee with an unlimited bank account and a giant approval stamp, but the state government is very pro-business and can direct people to an unusually large number of capital resources.

Additionally, Florida's Small Business Administration has set up a network of Small Business Development Centers throughout the state to coordinate federal, state, local, private and university resources. These centers distribute literature as well as provide assistance in the areas of accounting, financial management, personnel management, purchasing, advertising, market research, competitive strategy and business plan development.

For a complete list of Florida's Small Business Development Centers (more than 20 Centers and Subcenters) contact:

Florida's Small Business Development Centers, State Coordinator's Office
University of West Florida
11,000 University Boulevard, Building 38
Pensacola, FL 32514
(904) 474-3016

For information on new business funding, Florida's Department of Commerce offers a comprehensive fact sheet entitled, "Sources of Business Finance." Write or call for your free copy:

Florida Department of Commerce, Department of Economic Development
434 Fletcher Building
Tallahassee, FL 32399-2000
(904) 487-2971

For information on various sources of financing, refer to this directory:

Conventional Debt Financing

Florida Bankers Association
P.O. Box 538847
Orlando, FL 32853-8847
(407) 896-6511

Information on commercial banks, savings and loan associations, and credit unions with pools of investment capital.

Conventional Equity Financing

Director, Division of Securities
Florida Department of Banking and Finance
Tallahassee, FL 32399-0350
(904) 488-9805

Information on filing private stock placements or public offerings.

Limited Partnerships

Division of Corporations
Limited Partnership Section
Florida Department of State
Tallahassee, FL 32399-0300
(904) 487-6050

Information on filing limited partnerships

Venture Capital

Florida Department of Commerce
Bureau of Business Assistance
G-26 Collins Building
Tallahassee, FL 32399-2000
(904) 488-9357

Ask for "The Florida Venture Finance Directory." Information is also available on local venture capital clubs located throughout the state.

Florida Economic Development Center
325 College of Business
Tallahassee, FL 32306-1007
(904) 644-1044

Maintains data base on venture capital firms across the country that are interested in investing in certain types of businesses.

The State of Florida also operates and supports sources of capital for businesses having special needs, or gaps in financing, that private sources generally do not cover. Here is a brief description of the State Debt Financing sources:

Long-Term Fixed-Asset Financing

Florida First Capital Finance Corp (FFCFC)
Florida Department of Commerce
G-26 Collins Building
Tallahassee, FL 32399-2000
(904) 487-0466

The FFCFC is a non-profit corporation that utilizes the SBA 504 loan program to give small businesses long-term financing.

Industrial Development Bonds

Florida Department of Commerce
Bureau of Business Assistance
G-26 Collins Building
Tallahassee, FL 32399-2000
(904) 488-0463

Information on private activity bonds available through state and local governments for the development of new industries in Florida.

Black-Owned Businesses

Director
Black Business Investment Board
519 East Park Avenue
Tallahassee, FL 32301
(904) 487-4850

Information on the $5 million trust fund which provides financing for black-owned businesses.

Low Interest Loans for Low-Income Areas

Administrator
Community Development Corporation
Support and Assistance Program
Florida Department of Community Affairs
2740 Centerview Drive
Tallahassee, FL 32399-2100
(904) 488-3581

Information on low-interest loans for businesses opening in low-income areas of the state.

Local Government's Loans and Grants

Florida Department of Commerce
Bureau of Business Assistance
G-26 Collins Building
Tallahassee, FL 32399-2000
(904) 488-9357

Information on a variety of federal and state loans and grants which can be used to finance a business development project or the construction of an infrastructure.

Information is also available on Florida's Enterprise Zone Program which offers tax incentives to businesses opening in designated declining areas or hiring employees from designated areas.

Florida Small Business Administration

Small Business Administration Office
1320 South Dixie Highway
Suite 501
Coral Gables, FL 33146
(305) 350-5521

or:

Small Business Administration
400 West Bay Street
Jacksonville, FL 32202
(904) 791-3782

Information on loans for the acquisition of buildings, equipment and working capital. Loans are available to creditworthy businesses that can't obtain conventional debt financing.

Research and Development Loans

Florida Department of Commerce
Bureau of Business Assistance
G-26 Collins Building
Tallahassee, FL 32399-2000
(904) 488-9357

Information on the Small Business Innovation Research Program (SBIR) which provides financing for businesses conducting research and development leading to the commercialization of products needed by a variety of federal agencies.

The following organizations are prepared to help you with quick answers about other possible sources of financing:

Florida First Capital Finance Corp.	(904) 487-0466
Bureau of Business Assistance	(904) 488-9357
Florida Economic Development Center	(904) 644-1044

Starting A Business In Florida

As one would expect, a number of regulations must be adhered to in order to run a business in the state.

EMPLOYER IDs

All businesses need an employer ID number issued by the Federal Internal Revenue Service. For information and applications phone 1-800-241-3860 (in state) or write to the IRS, Public Affairs Office, P.O. Box 35045, Jacksonville, FL 32202.

CITY AND COUNTY LICENSES

Many businesses and occupations are required to have a city and/or county license. Information on local requirements can be obtained from the office of the County Tax Collector. If you are seeking a professional license, contact the Department of Professional Regulations, Old Courthouse Square Building, 130 N. Monroe, Tallahassee, FL 32399-0750, (904) 488-0041.

ZONING REQUIREMENTS

Most cities and counties have occupancy requirements. Information on complying with zoning regulations is available from the city and county governments.

SALES TAX NUMBERS

Any business which makes retail sales, purchases materials for resale or offers goods or property for rent, must register with the Department of Revenue and be issued a Sales Tax Number. Contact the Department of Revenue, Office of Taxpayers Assistance, Carlton Building, Tallahassee, FL 32399-1000, (904) 488-9000.

FICTITIOUS TRADE NAMES

Businesses which use a name other than that of the owner must register the business name in accordance with the Fictitious Name Act. For additional information contact the County Clerk of the Circuit Court.

Florida Hot Spots

Some experts say that the whole state of Florida is hot, and they're not just talking about the balmy 70° climate. They're referring to the non-stop proliferation of population and business. Still, a number of regions are attracting more growth than others. However, the experts can't seem to agree on which ones.

A recent study by NPA Data Services, a Washington-based forecasting firm, predicts that the following areas of Florida will experience the greatest population increase by the year 2000:

AREA	POP. INCREASE
Tampa/St. Pete/Clearwater	473,000
Ft. Lauderdale/Hollywood/ Pompano Beach	339,000
W. Palm Beach/Boca Raton/ Delray Beach	305,000
Orlando	294,000
Miami/Hialeah	268,000
Fort Myers	139,000

Source: *Florida Trend*, January, 1989

The *Kiplinger Florida Letter* identifies Collier (Naples), Sarasota (Sarasota), Marion (Ocala), Lee (Ft. Myers/Cape Coral), and Seminole (Sanford) counties as the five fastest-growing areas, respectively, by 1998.

The University of Florida's Bureau of Economic and Business Research predicts that Hillsborough (Tampa Bay), Palm Beach (W. Palm Beach) Manatee (Bradenton), Lee (Ft. Myers), Brevard (Melbourne), Seminole (Sanford), Osceola (Kissimmee), and Volusia (Daytona Beach) counties will almost double in size by the end of the century.

The U.S. Census says that Hernando (Brooksville, Weeki/Watchee), Osceola (Kissimmee), and Flagler (Beverly Beach) Counties are among the top five fasting-growing counties in the whole country!

Did I hear anyone ask about Jacksonville? We couldn't possibly ignore this fast-growing neighbor to the north. Not when it's also on the verge of a population/business explosion. Housing starts rose by 200% between 1982 and 1987, with a 55% increase in total personal income during that same period. Retail sales were up 40% over that five year span, while unemployment kept to a minimum 5%. Jacksonville has a very aggressive private sector; some economists feel it's the one part of the state that's practically recession-proof.

Finally, let's not ignore the West Coast. The entire Southwest region including Sarasota, Ft. Myers, and Naples is one of Florida's best-kept secrets (residents are hopeful it will stay that way). Given its unparalleled scenic beauty and tranquil lifestyle, this area is fast emerging as a place to consider. Although it will grow at a slightly slower pace when compared to Central Florida and the East Coast, it will continue to attract an upscale audience. Currently, Sarasota county is one of the wealthiest in the state in *per capita* personal income; only Naples (the West Coast's Palm Beach) can giving it a run for the money.

Who's right about Florida's hot spots? It's really anyone's guess. The one thing everyone seems to agree on is that Florida has more momentum than a rubber ball shot out of a canon. There's no stopping it now!

WHERE IS THE BUSINESS HEADING?

As far as business formations are concerned, Pinellas County (St. Petersburg area) is jumping. It's a genuine magnet. It attracted 2,729 new enterprises during a single quarter (Spring, 1988), according to Market Force, a Longwood, FL-based business research firm that analyzes business starts. However, due to limited land masses, (lest we forget that this beautiful area borders the Gulf of Mexico) growth and expansion have become a double-edged sword. Property is already premium priced, forcing some companies to move due north to Pasco County (New Port Richey) or due south to Manatee County (Bradenton). Congestion and crowding are becoming commonplace; some experts worry that perhaps the area has overexpanded. Still, it's the eighth fastest growing area in the country and people are flocking there because of its lifestyle potential and pro-business arena.

One area that is an undisputed hot spot is Central Florida, including Orange, Osceola, Seminole, Volusia and Brevard Counties. You know these better as the Orlando, Kissimmee, Winter Springs, Daytona Beach and Melbourne areas.

Currently, Osceola and Seminole Counties are two of the fastest-growing counties in the state, population-wise, with new business formations trailing Pinellas County by only a fraction.

This region is attracting increasing attention because of its unlimited growth potential. What makes it so different from other regions? For one thing, it won't run out of land for a long time. Once viewed as a deterrent, the fact that it is not on the water now works to its advantage. Land developers and constructions companies think they've died and gone to heaven with so much building taking place. For example, *Florida Trend* magazine reported that a $375 million resort hotel and convention center at Disney World is in the works, as is a $1 billion "City of the Future," a brainstorm of the pizza man with all the dough, Jeno Paulucci. In addition, both Disney-MGM and Universal Pictures have built new motion picture sound stages outside Orlando, while two other Hollywood film studios are rumored to be on the verge of making land deals as well.

Forecasters are predicting a bit of a slowdown in tourism next year, but I wouldn't be surprised if it's due to the fact that so many people are moving there.

According to "Florida Outlook," the quarterly guide from the Bureau of Economic and Business Research, Tampa is also expanding. It will be No. 1 in population growth by 1991, anticipating more than 40,000 new residents, and close to 25,000 additional jobs.

What About Business Survival Rates?

While great attention has been paid to the positive aspects of owning a business in Florida, little is heard about the failures. In fact, the incidence of business failures in the state is fairly high. At least 15% of the retail businesses that open are gone within the first year, according to Market Force. A goodly percentage of general contracting firms are also out of business within the first 18 months. Service businesses seem to have a tendency to fold before you even knew they were around.

Much of this can be attributed to the typical reasons for lack of survival: under-capitalization; lack of experience; too much business, and not enough staff to handle it; and strategic errors, among other obstacles.

For an example, the business service sector is very volatile. Every year, thousands of one- and two-person companies get started with the intent of filling a recognized need in a particular industry. Given the founders' intimate knowledge of an industry, they are aware of the companies that are cutting staff, eliminating in-house services, selling off divisions, etc. That's when they hang up their shingles to pick up the slack for those companies. Unfortunately, these fledgling entrepreneurs may be experts in their field, but they can make incompetent business owners. After a while, they hang themselves by overpromising and/or underestimating their abilities...the result: they're out of business.

Other business failures can be attributed to Florida's growing pains. Retailers have been particularly hard hit, due to the fact that almost 70% of the available store space has been constructed in strip centers that were built without "anchors." An anchor is defined as a major drug, food or department store that can generate large and constant traffic flows. When a small independent store rents space in a strip, and only has other small independent businesses to count on for traffic, it's infinitely more difficult to survive.

Another problem for new retail businesses is that the only available and/or affordable land or rent is often located in "areas on the come." Unfortunately, they don't come fast enough. Either the small population can't support all the businesses, or there is already an overabundance of a particular business and demand hasn't kept up with supply. Video rental stores are a perfect example of this. When Goodkin Research studied the retail sector in Broward County, they discovered that 70% of tape stores that went into unanchored strip centers were out of business within nine months!

Which businesses do well in Florida? Statistically speaking, manufacturing and wholesale businesses have the best chance of survival, according to Market Force. Within the first 18 months of operation, 98% still answer the phones. The same is true for 96% of professional practices that have opened: doctors, lawyers, health care clinics, architects, etc. Finally, 94% of business and financial services are still plugging along after a year-and-a-half. The rule of thumb is that if a business can survive the first two years, it's on it's way!

High Growth With Low Business Costs

Business failures are hardly exclusive to Florida, and the truth is, the majority of new enterprises are thriving. The dynamics of this are as follows:

There is no other state as accommodating and eager to develop new businesses as Florida is, and beyond that, the state's enormous population growth and low cost of doing business make it a very opportunistic environment. The 5.5% corporate income tax, for example, is among the lowest in the nation. There's no unity tax, no inventory tax and sales tax is exempted on process machinery and equipment. Also, labor costs are lower than most areas of the country; less than 10% of the work force is unionized. Florida's average contribution rate to the state's unemployment compensation fund is lower than any other state in the country. The benefits to employed residents include Florida's lack of a personal income tax, the nation's seventh-lowest per capita state taxes, and overall, a lower cost of living.

Florida has one of the most abundant, educated labor forces in the country. More than 3,600 people are joining the work force *each week*, making Florida's labor pool the fastest growing among the ten largest states. There are more college graduates in Florida than anywhere else in the southeast. What's more, 80% of the workers are in their prime (between the ages of 18 and 44).

One more thing. The tourist influx in Florida represents the buying power of a permanent city of more than a million residents every year. The growing marketplace, a favorable tax structure, abundant qualified labor, and a low cost of doing business, are enough reasons to consider relocating to Florida. Add to that the high quality of life, and you should be running, not walking, to come down with your business idea.

CHAPTER 13

Franchise Row:

THE LANDSCAPE OF THE FUTURE

If you had been in the car the year we took our 4-year-old son to Sarasota, you would have appreciated the true impact that franchising has had on consumers. Barely out of diapers, and certainly unable to read as far as we knew, our son kept pointing out familiar signs as we drove from the airport to his grandparents' condo.

"There's McDonald's, Burger King, Wendy's, Kentucky Fried Chicken, Dunkin' Donuts, Pizza Hut, 7-Eleven, and Jiffy Lube (that one still baffles me)."

Was he a prodigy because he could identify so many different logos? Hardly. He was unwittingly showing me that he had spent more time in franchises than in nursery school. And when he wasn't at either, he was in front of the TV watching the franchises' commercials.

I suppose that the long-term implications of this are not relevant to this discussion, but it does point to the fact that franchises have evolved into the single-most-recognized business names in the country.

What is it about the concept of franchising that has taken so many enterprising Americans by storm? For one thing, franchises represent the opportunity to be in business for themselves—with a well-oiled company holding the net. For others it allows them to concentrate on the sales side of the business, leaving the more mysterious advertising and marketing aspects to the experts at headquarters. And still for others—a new franchise being introduced every day-and-a-half—there's that unspoken dream of getting in on the ground floor of another McDonald's.

As Ray Kroc himself, the infamous founder of McDonald's, was known to say, "Franchising means going into business *for* yourself, not *by* yourself."

For many people, franchises offer yet another advantage. They are turn-key operations. In concept that means people can come down, "buy" a job with unlimited potential, and start earning a decent living without missing a beat.

The consensus is that if they're going to uproot their entire life, it's got to be in exchange for a better lifestyle, not just to maintain the status quo.

The underlying viewpoint is that Florida's reputation for embarrassingly low wage scales scares people. And rightfully so. Many northerners move down after giving up high-paying jobs or successful businesses; they don't want to mess around trying to earn a comparable income. They want to jump in and start living the good life. So when weighing the prospects of starting a business from scratch *vs.* buying a franchise, people presume that there are less risks with a franchise. In their estimation, business formats with proven track records reduce the chances of making big mistakes, while offering the greatest potential for profits.

It's not a bad theory. By most definitions, franchises do offer well-developed business ideas that have confirmed their viability in the marketplace. Further, they have demonstrated that their products or services are equally successful when replicated.

To have confidence in a concept which has documented growth and profitability is reasonable. Nevertheless, *"caveat emptor"*—let the buyer beware. Franchising can be an extremely difficult, time consuming, and expensive route to owning a business. For these reasons, some franchisees contend that it is far riskier than owning your own business. Either way, if you have even the slightest notion that operating under a franchise umbrella is a quick road to financial success, think again.

There are an untold number of horror stories involving the most experienced, hard-working, well-capitalized entrepreneurs who fell flat on their behinds after they bought a franchise, leaving them in financial ruins to boot. Is this to say that franchises aren't good businesses? Not at all. Statistically speaking, the Department of Commerce estimates that only 3% to 4% of franchises fail per year, which means they have a much higher-than-average survival rate.

Also according to the Department of Commerce, they estimate more than half-a-million franchise outlets in the country generated over *$640 BILLION* dollars in retail sales in 1988, which is more than a third of the total U.S. retail economy. So obviously there have been more than a few success stories as well.

And therein lies the real reason people have so enthusiastically embraced franchises. When the formula works, the franchisor and the franchisee both make money. It's one giant win-win situation!

Unfortunately, what none of this takes into account is the number of years required to make a profit, or whether the profits are ever large enough to justify the years of struggle, limited income, and endless hours on the job.

When you begin to look at specific franchise opportunities, these are the factors you have to weigh: what is the profit potential of the business; and how long it will take to get there.

In the meantime, the intent of this chapter is to give you a basic overview of franchising by looking at both the positive and negative aspects. We'll cover the role of the franchisee, franchise trends, making sense of the UFOC (Uniform Franchise Offering Circular), and the necessary ingredients for a successful franchise venture.

OVERVIEW OF FRANCHISE OPPORTUNITIES

Let's first take a look at the franchise industry, if you can call it that. In actuality, franchises are *not* an industry, they span hundreds of different industries. Currently, there are more than 2,600 franchisors in the country operating more than a half-million outlets in the U.S. alone. Combined, they employ more than 7 million workers. By the year 2010, experts estimate that they will easily generate more than 50% of all retail revenue.

Future franchise opportunities appear to be in businesses that didn't exist a decade ago. This includes videotape rentals, home computer centers, mobile business services, specialty foods retailers, and financial planning firms. At the same time, there seems to be no stopping the already-successful categories: fast food and sit-down restaurants, apparel stores, auto maintenance shops, exercise and recreation clubs, etc.

THE DIFFERENCES BETWEEN FRANCHISES AND BUSINESS OPPORTUNITIES

You should be aware that there is another way to buy a business concept which is not a franchise, although there are many similarities. These are called *non-franchise business opportunities*.

In these offerings, owners purchase a business format, sometimes buying equipment from the company, or receiving some training, but they do not pay ongoing royalties. In effect, the owner buys the right to sell a licensed product, but can do business under a different name if he chooses. This obviously costs a lot less than buying into a franchise.

The biggest difference, however, is that business opportunities are generally less rigid than franchises in their operating requirements. The owner has more flexibility with respect to business philosophies and advertising and marketing strategies.

The most widely known example of a non-franchise business opportunity is Stride-Rite children's shoes. Although they offer many of the same services as a franchise, their agreement is different in principle. For a one-time, up-front fee of $65,000 to $75,000 for a neighborhood store ($160,000 for a major mall site), they license the Stride-Rite name and product. This entitles the local owner to hang the Stride-Rite sign in the window and carry their line of shoes. However, as a non-franchisee, they can also maintain a 20% inventory of other shoe brands. A true franchise would require its products to be sold exclusively.

Business opportunities are emerging as viable alternatives to buyers who don't have the deep pockets necessary for a franchise, but who still want to dovetail with the success of a particular business concept. Buyers are also comfortable with the idea of paving the way for themselves once they've opened their doors.

It's important to be aware of the differences between franchises and business opportunities so that you can determine which one is right for you before you begin talking with a variety of savvy business sellers.

The Ins And Outs Of Franchises

There are two categories of franchises available to prospective owners. The first is the traditional or "product and trade name" franchise. You know these as auto dealerships, gas stations, and authorized dealers who pay for the privilege of selling and distributing a manufacturer's product.

The second type is the "business format" franchise such as McDonald's, Century 21, Baskin-Robbins, and Kinney Shoes. In these cases, franchisees purchase an entire method of doing business and agree to follow all procedural aspects set forth by the franchisors. These dictates usually cover sales, marketing, advertising, merchandising, pricing, and other day-to-day operations.

WHAT'S IN IT FOR THE FRANCHISE PLAYERS?

Basically, companies develop franchise offerings as an efficient way to expand their businesses when that might not otherwise be possible. It allows them economies of scale with respect to purchasing power, and affords them the opportunity to move into new areas by using the infusion of capital and ongoing royalty revenues.

For franchisees, it provides the opportunity to go into business, with the strength of a successful operation behind them. The primary benefits include: comprehensive training programs; assistance with site selection; professional advertising support; established co-op advertising programs; marketing strategies and techniques that have already proven themselves; and continued support and guidance from the franchisor.

Franchisors are generally more interested in prospective owners who expect to be involved in the business on a day-to-day basis, instead of being an absentee owner who will check in periodically to look at the books. Obviously, the more the franchisees are tied to their operations, the more of a vested interest they have in assuring their success. That's why you may be told that the amount of experience you have in a particular industry is less important than being a motivated franchisee who is willing to invest years of hard work for a big payout. Disgruntled franchisees differ with the claim that success is at hand if you work for it. They report that knowing a particular business is critical to a successful venture.

THE FRANCHISE RELATIONSHIP

When franchisees and franchisors define their relationship under optimal conditions, they compare it to a marriage where the give and take of two committed partners build a strong and lasting foundation for success. Interestingly, most franchise agreements span 10 years (subject to renewals), which is longer than many real marriages last. In the most successful franchises, both parties recognize the need for each other. Without the franchisee, there is no revenue or growth. Without the franchisor, there is no product development, advertising support, volume discounts and long-term planning.

On the other hand, many franchisees have bailed out of the "marriage" mid-stream due to ongoing disagreements with a franchisor's policies and plans. Or he feels that the franchisor has grossly misrepresented the franchise program, or has outrightly lied about the services they provide. Friction mounts, particularly when the business is suffering and the franchisee is unable to implement ideas he feels will turn the situation around. Much to his dismay, he likens his circumstances to being a lowly employee whose boss runs the show and makes all the important decisions. This, in spite of the fact that he "owns" the business. So what may have started out as a marriage of convenience can sometimes evolve into a bitter partnership, resulting in a split.

UFOCs Tell The Story

One way to avoid any major disappointments or disagreements with the franchisor is by conducting an intensive investigation of the company before signing a contract. Franchise consultants have indicated that they are truly baffled by the number of intelligent business people who jump into a franchise agreement without really doing their homework. And then they can't figure out why they got burned.

The first step in learning about a franchise operation from top to bottom is through an important legal document called the *Uniform Franchise Circular Offering (UFOC)*. Required by the Federal Trade Commission (FTC), this important charter spells out the specific franchise program in great detail.

By law, the franchisor must give you this offering document at the first meeting in which a serious discussion about buying the franchise takes place, or no later than 10 days before you pay any money, or legally commit yourself to the franchise.

What's in the UFOC? Franchisors must disclose information regarding the background of the business as well as the personal history of its founders and owners. They must describe any previous, present or potential litigation in which the franchise has been involved, all up-front starting costs, a detailed listing of all other franchisees, and finally, the UFOC must spell out all terms of the franchise agreement.

A typical franchise agreement will make reference to the ten most offered services:

1. *Operations Training*...both classroom and on-site;

2. *Equipment*...in some instances the franchisor requires that it be purchased/leased from them;

147

3. *Corporate Identity*…registered trademarks, logos, corporate philosophies, etc.;

4. *Products*…and projections for inventory replacements, plans for new products, test marketing, etc.;

5. *Advertising and Promotion Plans*…many franchisors charge a separate but mandatory royalty for this (usually 1% to 2% a year);

6. *Field Support*…frequency and duration of visits, procedures for day-to-day contact, chain of command;

7. *Site Selection*…help in finding the best possible location for opening the franchise based on past experiences;

8. *Design of Store*…as well as recommendations on signage, merchandise placement, physical layouts, etc.;

9. *Grand Openings*…advertising and promotion strategies, collateral display material, merchandising and pricing, etc.;

10. *Networking*…contact with other franchisees who can pass along their advice, assistance, and support.

Make certain that you can distinguish between the franchisor's grand plans for service *vs.* what they have to specifically offer right now.

Most importantly, the franchise agreement must define the binding rights and obligations of both parties. The ideal agreement offers the right balance of control over uniformity while giving the franchisee enough leeway to meet local market conditions.

If a franchisor tells you that their "business opportunity" is not covered by FTC rulings, you should check that out with the FTC. Even if through some loophole they are exempt from disclosure, you should request a document providing the same details anyway. If they balk, you walk. You simply must make an informed investment!

One-To-One Dialogues

At the point where you are ready to begin serious conversations with a franchisor, in addition to the UFOC, be prepared to discuss the following in depth:

- Insurance requirements;
- The franchisor's first right of refusal on a transfer of the franchise or lease;
- Obligations of the franchisor before and after the grand opening;

- Conditions for renewal and termination of the franchise;
- Length of time allowed for finding a location and opening the store;
- Performance standards and quotas to be met;
- All obligations to purchase or lease products, equipment, collateral material (signs, flyers, etc.) from the franchisor or affiliated companies.

Other discussion points should concern the amount of experience realistically needed to effectively run the business. If you're told that they'll teach you everything you need to know, take heed. A franchise is like any other business. Nothing replaces hands-on experience, knowledge of the industry, and strong skills relating to the operation.

One franchise neophyte I read about explained that his inexperience in the commercial drapery cleaning business cost him dearly for the first two years. Although he had been promised as much support as he needed to learn the business, he found there was much he didn't know, causing some very costly mistakes. This resulted in investing good money after bad—considerably more than he was told to anticipate by the franchisor. Ironically, in his first business year, his sales were the second-highest in the franchise group. Unfortunately, he spent so much on advertising and marketing he couldn't turn a profit. In his second year, sales dropped when he cut back on advertising, but at least he broke even. The third year looks a little more promising, but he's still wondering if it's been worth the long hours and sleepless nights.

Finally, there are two other steps to take, and these are perhaps the most important. First, talk with other franchisees and visit their business sites. You want first-hand feedback as to whether the franchisor has met their expectations and lived up to agreements. How has the franchisor's product held up once it's been shipped to the store? What is the quality of the merchandising and equipment, and the general "look" of the store? Would you want to shop there, let alone own the place?

Second, your franchise contract should be meticulously examined by a lawyer experienced in franchise law. Does he/she approve of the agreement in principle? Are there any concerns regarding trademark infringements, antitrust laws, and the FTC's Franchise rules? Is your legal counsel satisfied that any previous or pending litigation is being handled properly? Can they confirm that the franchise is not currently operating under bankruptcy protection? Are there any concerns about third-party dealings? In other words, what roles do the landlords, bankers, shareholders, or local regulators play in determining how the franchise is run?

Attorney's fees could seem steep, but believe me, professional advice is a prudent investment that could save you tens-of-thousands down the road.

FRANCHISES AND THE FLORIDA STORY

Florida has always been a hotbed of franchise activity, now ranking third in the nation for franchise outlets, just slightly behind California and Texas. Andrew Kostecka, the franchise expert at the U.S. Department of Commerce, theorizes that the trend of franchise buying in Florida began when so many retirees moved down with money to invest and time on their hands.

In 1987, American Business Information, an Omaha-based business research firm, determined that there were a total of 10,103 franchise outlets operating in the state. And they're not owned just by retirees any more. These franchises spanned 15 of the most popular categories, including: automobile muffler repair shops; auto renting and leasing; service stations; restaurants; pizza parlors; ice cream shops; photo retailers; convenience stores; and shoe stores. This figure did not include any authorized dealerships, such as Lincoln/Mercury dealers, IBM computers, or other products with multiple distribution outlets.

In 1988, ABI determined that an additional 425 units opened in the state, representing a 4% increase. Each category grew in number of units sold, with the exception of auto renting/leasing franchises and photo shops. They showed slight declines in the number of existing franchises, which could be an indication of over-saturation of these services and/or decreased demand.

When *Florida Trend* magazine studied franchising in the state (March 1986), they found that Florida was home to more franchised hotels, motels, campgrounds, and laundry establishments than anywhere else in the country. The state also ranked near the top nationally in real estate, temporary employment agencies, accounting and credit collection firms.

FLORIDA LAWS

The state of Florida does not make a distinction between franchise and non-franchise business opportunities, insofar as the legalities are concerned. To this end, they have laws governing all business opportunities. Each year, they require every business to file a declaration statement with the Florida Department of Agriculture's Department of Consumer Services.

In this document, the business must: disclose the name of the company and the nature of their business; describe the history of the business and any promises that have been made regarding training, assistance and prior sales; refer to any bankruptcy proceedings or litigation the firm has been involved in; enclose a financial statement which is no more than 13 months old; and provide a copy of any contracts they use as the "seller" of a business opportunity or franchise.

Florida law also stipulates that a minimum $50,000 surety bond be posted if a seller makes any of the following promises to the buyers: 1) income from their investment will exceed its selling price; 2) the purchaser is entitled to a partial or complete refund; or 3) the seller will repurchase from the buyer if he is dissatisfied with the franchise or business opportunity.

Before you buy a franchise in Florida, I urge you to obtain the franchisor's filing and be certain that it is consistent with what you've been told or that which you've read in the franchise agreement.

For more details on Florida laws for business opportunities and franchises, order your free copy of "Florida's 1988-9 New Business Guide and Checklist." Contact the Florida Department of Commerce, Div. of Economic Development, 107 W. Gaines St., Tallahassee, FL 32399-2000. Or call (904) 488-9357 to request a copy of this important booklet.

Extra, Extra, Read All About It!

If you're ready to do your homework, you'll find an endless stream of books, magazines and directories dedicated to educating, and hopefully convincing, prospective franchise owners to pursue the franchise route. I urge interested parties to seek out these publications and read them from cover to cover (a suggested reading list is found below). Attend seminars and Franchise Expos. Talk to franchisees. Consult with franchise consultants. Only then will you be ready to start the process of researching specific offerings. In other words, this has to be one of the most carefully checked-out and thought-out investments you've ever made.

SUGGESTED READING MATERIAL

1. *Entrepreneur* magazine's "Guide to Franchise and Business Opportunities—1,851 Opportunities" and "1989 Annual Report";
2. *Enterprise* magazine's "The Franchise Handbook";
3. "What You Need To Know When You Buy a Franchise" and "Investigate Before Investing," published by the International Franchise Association in Washington, DC.;
4. "Franchise Opportunities Handbook," compiled by the U.S. Commerce Department's International Trade Administration office. Call (202) 377-0342 for your free copy.

The Big Scoop

Burton Baskin fell in love with and married Irvine Robbins' sister in 1946. After that successful merger, Baskin decided to continue his good luck by consolidating his Burton's Ice Cream Store with Robbins' Snowbird Ice Cream Store. In 1947 they opened the first Baskin-Robbins in Glendale, CA. Their aim was to make $75 a week and have fun offering the public more ice cream flavors than anyone else. In spite of their modest goals, they opened seven more locations within a year's time. They were so pleased with their burgeoning business, they became anxious to open more shops. The problem was, they were tapped out and didn't have the means of expanding.

That's when they came up with the idea of selling preselected locations to individual investors instead of funding each store themselves. That very concept, as you can well guess, was the start of franchising as we know it today. I suppose you could say it solved their cash flow problem handily. Now serving more than 1.5 million customers a week in over 3300 locations worldwide, the rest is history.

If you're uncertain whether you'd be happy as a franchisee, perhaps you should go into a Baskin-Robbins and order a double scoop of Rocky Road and French Vanilla. There's no guarantee the answer will be any clearer, but at least you can say you pondered the decision while doing an on-site inspection of a franchise operation.

SECTION
III

The Real Estate Trap And How To Avoid It

CHAPTER 14

Selling Your Home Up North...

WOULD YOU, COULD YOU, SHOULD YOU?

I have never met anyone who enjoyed the process of selling their home. It makes even the most self-assured people feel anxious ("Why didn't she go crazy over my new wallpaper?"), defensive ("What do you mean he thinks skylights are dumb?"), cautious ("Oh that? It's just a little water spot...") and leery ("Are these people just casing the joint?"). The only thing that could possibly be more of a stomach-turner would be having Robin Leach drop over unexpectedly. With a camera crew.

That's why I'd like to point out steps you can take to generate the greatest possible profits when you sell your house, even in a down market. If you have to suffer the aggravation and inconvenience of having complete strangers sift through your closets, you have every right to want a maximum return on your investment.

I'd also like to touch on whether you *should* sell the house. Although many of you will be counting on the profits from the sale in order to buy a house or condo in Florida, you might want to review the checklist of reasons NOT to sell. Believe it or not, there are several sound financial arguments for holding on to your house, at least for the time being.

SMALL FIX-UPS THAT MAKE A BIG DIFFERENCE

First, let's take a look at sprucing up the place before a "For Sale" sign ever gets staked into the grass. The key to selling property at top dollar is putting it on the market when it's in marketable condition. Never mind that it's been good enough for you all these years. You're not buying it this time.

If you resist the idea of making improvements, it's possible that buyers will resist your home...in droves. Or they'll find countless reasons to bargain the price down. It would be a shame to let them reduce the profits of your largest and most important investment.

Now don't go feeling badly about the condition of your home. Every house can benefit from a cosmetic face lift, no matter its age or how well it's been maintained. This might involve cleaning the draperies and rugs, replacing the carpeting on the stairs, throwing a fresh coat of paint on the dining room walls, installing an attractive new storm door and hiring a heavy duty cleaning service to tackle the windows, walls and fireplace.

Other inexpensive but worthwhile fix-ups include:

In the Bathrooms:
- Replacing worn or broken fixtures;
- Caulking the bathroom tiles;
- Installing a new vanity to hide a worn sink;
- Putting up a pretty new shower curtain and new towels to brighten up a dull powder room;
- Installing a modern light fixture to add soft, flattering illumination.

In the Bedrooms:
- Creating the illusion of space by getting rid of large, odd-sized pieces of furniture;
- Buying a new quilt and matching accessories (and don't forget to make the bed so you can show them off);
- Disposing of the accumulated clutter—the books, magazines, toiletries, etc.;
- Cleaning the carpeting and rugs or replacing them with ones in soft neutral colors;
- Putting up artwork to give the room a more romantic, comfortable feel.

In the Living Room, Dining Room and Den:
- Cleaning out the fireplace and adding a handsome set of implements;
- Putting up pretty but inexpensive fixtures;
- Having the draperies and carpeting steam cleaned;
- As with the bedrooms, disposing of anything that clutters up the rooms: large outdated furniture, trinkets, oversized chairs that are losing their insides, etc.

In the Kitchen:
- Giving the cabinets a good cleaning. Painting them to help give them a more modern appearance;
- Putting away the occasionally used appliances that take up valuable counter space;
- Buying new curtains, or better yet, putting up vertical blinds.

There are even some people who swear by putting vanilla extract on light bulbs and baking fresh bread just to make the house smell good on the days it's being shown. Who am I to argue?

SOMETIMES YOU HAVE TO GO FOR BIG BUCKS

In other cases, the only way to command top dollar is by replacing the leaky roof, renovating a dilapidated bathroom and getting rid of the speckled linoleum in the kitchen. If the thought of sinking money into your house at a point when you won't be able to personally enjoy the improvements is too unsettling, keep this in mind. Updating the look of your home and correcting some of the more obvious flaws before you sell can be an investment in future profits. It's possible that if you put $5,000 into all the right places, you could up the asking price by twice that amount, maybe more. It's pure and simple bottom—line thinking.

WHO DOES YOUR HOME APPEAL TO?

Before you make decisions about which major improvements will result in the greatest return on investments, try to figure out which segment of the home buyers market is most likely to be interested in your neighborhood and your home. Whether it's first time buyers, homeowners who are trading up or down, or empty nesters, various renovations and improvements will only appeal to a certain type of buyer. You can't entice everyone, nor should you try. That's why you need to have a sense of who is most likely to be looking at the house. You can then direct your efforts accordingly.

For example, if your home is priced appropriately for first time buyers, know thy market. The overwhelming majority are young couples who plan to have a family once they own a home or who already have one in diapers and another on the way. Since staying within a budget is priority number one, don't expect them to be willing to pay extra for features that are of little interest. Like the expensive mahogany paneling in the den. Or the custom velvet print wallpaper in the master bedroom. Or the elaborate burglar alarm system. The things that young buyers care about are light, cheerful rooms. That means vertical blinds in the kitchen to let the sun pour in. Fresh white or beige paint in the hallways. Even mirrors to give the house the image of being larger than it is. Young families also prefer thick carpeting in the bedrooms and modern fixtures in the bathrooms so the rooms don't look like they date back to Beaver Cleaver.

To appeal to this group, keep your selling price realistic and do everything possible to make the house look bright, cozy and airy.

If you know that your large house is going to attract second and third time buyers, people who are trading up, you can count on their expectations being far greater. They're more aware of what they want in a home and are determined to get the features that show everyone they've moved up in the world. They want large formal dining rooms, endless closet space, big pantries, and impressive foyers, and, they're willing to pay a premium for updated kitchens and baths, decks and patios, room additions, etc. What's interesting is that the actual selling price is less impor-

157

tant to these buyers than knowing that they can keep up with the mortgage payments. They'll pay top dollar provided they can cover the monthly nut *and* get the features they're looking for.

If you own a more modest home in a quiet middle class neighborhood, then your target market may very well be the empty-nesters. 15% of all home buyers fit this description: couple's whose kids are grown and out of the house. These people care about lower taxes, reduced maintenance costs, easy upkeep, safety and having close access to shopping. They don't want big back yards or houses on four levels. They need a more a casual environment now, with combined kitchen and dining space, a few bedrooms and bathrooms (in case the kids visit). If your house fits this description, you should be able to sell quickly with a minimum of refurbishing.

Finally, the other predominant market is a less fortunate group. These are the divorcees, widows and other financially strapped people who can no longer afford their homes and must step down to more modest living arrangements. For obvious reasons, this is a tough crowd to please. Still, they make excellent prospects because they *must* buy something soon. What appeals to them? Probably some illusions of prosperity—anything new and modern, but mostly comfortable, affordable living quarters. Again, similar to first time buyers, they won't be in a position to pay for extravagant features such as an inground pool or central vacuuming. Point out the features that they can't live without—a new dishwasher, a built-in microwave, extra bathrooms. Also, if your home is set up to accommodate a tenant arrangement, this could be a tremendous selling feature.

To review, before putting your home up for sale, take an objective look at the cosmetic changes you can make to enhance the look and feel of the house. Then decide, based on the particular features of the home, which type of buyer is most likely to respond to it. Finally, you need to decide if there are any major improvements to be made that could possibly result in selling at a higher price.

Major Improvements That Pay For Themselves

What kind of improvements result in a payback? The home improvement industry would have you believe that just about anything you do will come back to you through a higher selling price. Although that may be true in some instances, the question is how high is up? Will you get another $20,000 to $40,000? That sounds great. But what if that means your new asking price will price you right out of the neighborhood?

Another consideration is if you have to contract out for the improvements, they may not be worth the expense. Especially if they only represent an extra few thousand in profits. For example, a new kitchen floor might look great, but will it allow you to increase the sale price enough to put up with the stress and mess you'll go through first? And what about the delays it will cause before you can put the house on the market? And horror of horrors, it's entirely possible to pick a replacement tile that the new owners find dreadful. Ouch!

Before you pick up a hammer or start rifling through the yellow pages for general contractors, it's at least helpful to know the difference between the improvements that typically command a higher selling price and those which do nothing at all to increase the value of your home.

Here are some of the major improvements which home buyers are willing to pay a premium for (up to a certain point, of course):

- *Remodeled Kitchens:* vinyl or ceramic flooring, new appliances, new cabinets and counters, vertical blinds, and ample counterspace;

- *Renovated Bathrooms:* Fresh paint or unoffensive wallpaper (mylar, velvet, and other loud styles are usually a turn-off), contemporary cabinets, attractive tiles and fixtures, shower doors and lots of mirrors;

- *Outdoor Entertaining:* Decks, patios, sliding glass doors, built-in gas grills, gazebos, and other features that people can show off;

- *Room Additions or Enlargements:* Extra or expanded bedrooms and bathrooms, a large family room, and a garage (two car is best);

- *Exterior Painting:* If you do nothing else, at least paint the outside of the house. Some buyers make their decisions without ever stepping foot inside. If the general first impression of your home is shabby and tired looking, you're out of the ball game before it starts.

Does this mean that you should run out and hire a general contractor? Probably not. Rumor has it that the only reason God built the world in six days was he did it without one!

Seriously, the first step is to evaluate the cost of these improvements and consult with respected realtors to determine how much they will realistically increase your asking price. If they concur that a $10,000 kitchen renovation in your $200,000 home will increase the odds of getting closer to $250,000, then that's a smart move.

The second step is to determine if you can perform any of these tasks either by yourself or with the help of family and friends. Paying for materials without the labor will be a much more profitable undertaking.

Finally, it might be a smart idea to show the house and wait for feedback from prospective buyers. If no one seems to point out the areas of the house you thought you'd have to improve, you can probably forget it. Or perhaps you'll be alerted to things you never considered important which are actually keeping people away. Taking action based on a little research could be a life saver!

You might be surprised to discover that there are other improvements which will only result in marginal profits. These include adding a fireplace, doing special landscaping, adding air conditioning and replacing windows and doors. Most people are willing to forgo these improvements because they can see a time when they'll be able to afford them on their own, unlike a major renovation. From their vantage point, it's better to pay a lower price and do without.

Similarly, adding a swimming pool or converting an attic or basement into living space are not likely to add to the value of a house at all. For some buyers, these improvements are deterrents because of small children or because they don't want to heat and cool more rooms. Changing the heating system from gas to oil or oil to electric is also a waste of money. Most people just care that the house stays warm; they don't care how it gets that way.

Important Tax Considerations

Before you sell the house, be aware that there are two important tax considerations. The first is that if you buy a less expensive home in Florida than the one you sold up north at a profit (which just about everyone does), you will be subject to taxes on the profits that don't get rolled over into the new house. The only way to offset the taxes on the profits would be through losses from the sale of other assets, such as the sale of stocks and bonds, or investment properties.

An entirely different strategy is to buy a home of equal or greater value in Florida so that the purchase qualifies as your principal residence within the required 24-month period. By doing so, you can defer paying taxes on the profits by taking advantage of the 1034 rollover provision in the IRS code.

But Wait...Should You Sell The House At All?

It's a reasonable assumption that if you're going to relocate, part of the process involves selling the house. And in most instances, that's fine.

For example, if you can clear a nice profit which enables you to invest in a new home and/or business, then great. If many of your family and friends are already down there and you're certain you would never come back to live up north no matter what, then maybe psychologically it's important to cut your ties. And, if you know that you aren't the type to rent your house, then maybe the financial gains are less significant to you. It's no great sin not to want to hear from a tenant calling collect to tell you that the hot water heater is leaking.

But what if you're moving to Florida at a time when the real estate market is very flat? The bids you get on the house will probably be lower than you expected or needed.

In real estate, the name of the game is timing and cycles. It's a given that at some point the market will make a comeback, perhaps the greatest one ever. If you hold on and rent the house instead of selling it, you're bound to clear a greater profit when the market heats up again.

Or what if you're the least bit hesitant about becoming a permanent resident of Florida? Not *everyone* goes down there totally assured. Would you feel better knowing you had an escape valve if you changed your mind?

Finally, many real estate experts suggest that you ask yourself the following questions before putting a house up for sale:

1. Do you have substantial equity in your house?
2. Is your neighborhood very desirable?
3. Is demand greater than supply?

160

If you said "Yes" each time and you don't need the profits from the sale in order to live comfortably in Florida, you can probably improve your financial picture considerably by *renting* your house instead of selling.

Here's how this would work. Let's say your home was worth $175,000 and you owed $40,000 on the mortgage. If you rented it out instead of selling it, your monthly mortgage payments could easily be covered by the tenant. For the next year or two, the house, which would then be considered a real estate investment, would continue to escalate in value (perhaps by as much as another $20,000 to $40,000). In the meantime, you would have taken the equity out of the house, which would have given you ready cash to start a business, make a down payment on a house in Florida or simply to reinvest. You would then have two investments increasing in value for the price of one: your old home and your new home or business.

Keep in mind, however, that this scenario works best when your home is situated in a desirable neighborhood where there is a continued demand for housing, and when you have built up enough equity in the house to remove a sizeable sum. Finally, you must be able to charge adequate rent in order to break even on the expenses, at a minimum. If average rental prices in your area won't allow you to cover your mortgage, utilities and maintenance, then it probably *is* wise to sell.

IF YOU'RE NOT YET 55 . . .

Another important reason to postpone the sale of your house would be if you or your spouse are close in age to being eligible for the capital gains exclusion. This is the once-in-a-lifetime opportunity you have to sell your home without paying taxes on the first $125,000 of profit. In order to take advantage of this tax break, the IRS stipulates that one of the spouses be 55 or older before the house is sold. Another important provision is the stipulation that you must live in your principal residence for three out of the five years before you sell it. Thus, you could rent your home for up to two years and then decide to sell.

Let me repeat this last point, because a word of caution about renting for more than two years is important if you are counting on taking advantage of the gains exclusion. If you rent out your home for three or more years, that means you will not have lived in that home for three out of the past five years. The IRS takes that to mean this home is no longer your principal residence, it is rental property, and therefore is not eligible for the $125,000 exclusion when you sell the home.

I recommend that if you and/or your spouse are only a few years from turning 55, and your home is located in an area that's hot or on the verge of making a big comeback, you should hold off on selling. You could still move down to Florida, rent or buy (using equity from the house), sell the house up north up to two years later and possibly increase your profits by 20% to 30%. Then with the capital gains exclusion, you would have realized a big gain in profits without paying the larger tax liability.

SELLING THE HOUSE BEFORE 55 DOESN'T MEAN
YOU'LL LOSE THE EXCLUSION FOREVER

I mentioned earlier that this $125,000 exclusion is a once-in-a-lifetime opportunity. That confuses many people because they think if they sell their home before turning 55, they'll forever lose the chance to exclude the capital gains. That is not the case.

If you do decide to sell your home up north before age 55 and then buy a place in Florida, you have not lost out on this once-in-a-lifetime exclusion. You could take the break when you eventually sold the Florida house (assuming you were older than 55 at that time). The only reason it would not be as advantageous then is that you would presumably be retired, your earned income would be less and the tax bite wouldn't be as big as when you were working and had a larger, more valuable house.

Incidentally, there are numerous other provisions for the $125,000 capital gains exclusion, but unless the age and residency requirements are met first, you are not eligible.

Renting vs. Selling—The Bottom Line

If you are still unsure of whether it's better to sell your home up north or rent it out for a while, why not take a look at the hard numbers. Maybe the solution will be clearer to you when you fill out the worksheet on the next page and compare bottom lines.

DECISIONS, DECISIONS

While this worksheet is a guide, remember that it's possible for some uncontrollable problems to alter even the most positive looking figures. What this step-by-step analysis can't possibly do is take some realities into consideration.

For example, what would happen if your home were vacant for several months because your tenant was transferred unexpectedly? You'd still have all the expenses of the house, but without the income. What if the house required a major repair such as a new roof? The expense could possibly wipe out your profits for the year. Yes, there would be tax advantages to offset the losses, and your home would have continued to escalate in value, but that wouldn't be much solace if you were counting on a monthly income.

Another subject for discussion is how you feel about being a landlord. Some people are just not cut out to deal with the two T's, toilets and tenants, no matter how profitable the set-up. You and your spouse need to iron that out before you rent the house and decide which one of you is going to take responsibility for the accounting, maintenance and repairs, emergencies, etc.

Finally, if you convert your home to a rental property, there will be certain tax breaks you won't be able to take full advantage of should you sell at a later time. This may be offset by the fact that in the meantime you will have been able to deduct management fees, property taxes, and other expenses on your income tax; and although depreciation is also deductible, it must be added back to your tax basis at the point that you do sell the house.

Lord knows it's not a perfect world out there, but the more factors you weigh into your decision, and the more contingencies you plan for, the better off you will be.

Present Home

Mortgage Payment $_____ × 12 = $_____
Property Taxes   _____
Homeowners' Insurance   _____
Repairs and Maintenance   _____
Electric Bills $_____   × 12 = $_____
Gas/Fuel Oil $_____   × 12 = $_____
Other Costs   _____
TOTAL CARRYING COSTS $_____

If You Rent Your Home

Income
Monthly Rental $_____   × 11 = $_____
(Use 11 months to allow for tenant changes)
Expenses
Mortgage Payments   _____
Property Taxes   _____
Repairs and Maintenance   _____
Liability Insurance   _____
Management Fees or Collection Expenses   _____
Other Costs   _____
TOTAL COSTS $_____

If You Sell Your Home

Income
Estimated Selling Price $_____
Expenses
Real Estate Commission   _____
Painting/Other Spruce Ups & Repairs   _____
Mortgage Balance   _____
Attorney's Fees   _____
Potential Taxes   _____
Miscellaneous Costs   _____
TOTAL COSTS $_____

Net Benefits

Rental Income Minus Expenses $_____
Selling Price Minus Expenses $_____

When You're Ready To Sell, "Don't Worry, Be Happy"

I have many clients who can't wait to get down to Florida and start their lives over. It's something they've wanted to do for a long time, and although it's an emotional time, they're happy.

If you know that it's the right time to sell, even if the market is soft, follow these suggestions:

- *Price Your Home Fairly*...Everything about your home is tied to 1001 fond recollections—of first steps, Thanksgiving dinners, slumber parties, weddings, etc. Memories are wonderful, but they add nothing to the value of your house on the open market. When you're deciding on an asking price, leave your emotions out of it and concentrate on the reality of what the market will bear. Homes that are priced appropriately are the always the first to be sold in either an up *or* down market.

- *Choose an Aggressive Broker*..."Sounds easy," you say. "They're all barracudas." Perhaps, but not all of them have the savvy to market a house during a soft period. Look for one who will go right to the multiple listings service, will pursue more unusual ways of finding buyers, such as relocation services and companies that are transferring employees, and will commit to a solid advertising effort for you. If you find such a broker, don't haggle over their 6% commission. If the market is flat and they find qualified buyers who can meet your price, they certainly deserve their compensation.

- *Think about Creative Financing*...Any type of financial incentive you can offer will make your house that much more marketable. Lower your asking price to someone who can close right away. Or agree to pay for the buyer's points at closing. Or, the more common tactic is to help finance the mortgage itself. This is not as risky as you might think. If the new owner does default (it's very rare), the house, which has escalated in value, is yours again to keep or sell at an increased price.

- *Don't Forget the Home Improvements*...As we've already discussed, a home that gives the appearance of being well-cared-for is the one that people want to own. So fix up, touch up, get rid of, repair, renovate...whatever it takes, within reason, to make your home the kind of place a new family will want to start making memories in.

- *Be Ready with the Facts*...Compile answers to the most-asked questions such as the room dimensions, the square footage of the property, heating systems (water, kitchen and house), average monthly utility costs, boundaries of the property, distances between the house and shopping, schools, houses of worship, recreation facilities, etc. (preferably in minutes, not miles). You should also prepare a list of recent home improvements and their costs, a list of household appliances that are still under warranty, and the results of any recent termite, or other, inspections. Ask yourself what else you would want to know if you were buying the house and be prepared with the answers.

Selling your home doesn't have to be a nightmare. If you are fortunate enough to find buyers who feel they'll enjoy the house as much as you do, that's a great feeling. If you'll just take the necessary steps to make the house as marketable as possible, and price it fairly, the whole thing could be over in a few months. Then it's "Good-bye snow, hello sunny Florida!"

CHAPTER 15

To Buy Or To Rent In Florida:

THAT IS THE QUESTION

I f you thrive on the prospect of having endless choices, then the decisions to buy or rent a home in Florida, and/or rent or your sell your home up north probably won't faze you. On the other hand, if you're not certain of which direction to take at either end, this chapter is for you.

Actually, even if you *think* you're certain, read this anyway. I'll tell you why.

I know of a couple who bought a condominium in Sunrise seven years ago. They intended to make it their permanent retirement home. They started out being very enthusiastic about relocating and saw no reason to hang on to their Bayside, New York co-op. What they didn't anticipate was that they wouldn't like spending summers in Florida, or that Arnie would miss working a few days a week in his business in Manhattan.

Every summer for the past seven, they've been coming back to New York and renting an apartment in their old neighborhood. And every summer the price for returning goes up. They're disheartened. They'd like to buy another co-op in New York, but the prices are prohibitive. They considered taking equity out of their Florida home as a way to raise cash, but their current appraisal was low, and nothing times nothing is nothing. Without a substantial amount to put down on a new co-op, taking a new mortgage would be unaffordable. It's quite a bind, but hardly an unusual one.

That's why we'll start our discussion with the question of what to do with your home up north, since from a financial planning standpoint, it will pretty much dictate the chain of events in Florida.

Renting Your Home Up North Instead Of Selling

As we discussed in the chapter, "Selling Your Home Up North...Would You, Could You, Should You?," there can be numerous good reasons for holding on to your home, in spite of the fact that you are relocating to Florida on a permanent basis. Please review this chapter if the decision is a complicated or difficult one for you. In the meantime, here are just a few good reasons it might pay *not* to sell:

- If you are currently a homeowner and are not absolutely, positively certain that Florida is going to be your cup of tea, you'll always have an escape valve if you don't sell your home up north. The couple I just mentioned would give anything to have their co-op back. 7 years ago they sold it for $30,000. Today it's worth four times that.

- Secondly, by delaying the sale of your home, you also defer the decision on what to do with the capital gains. Perhaps the upcoming tax year would be a better time to sell because your move to Florida will result in being in a lower tax bracket.

- Should you be in the lucky position of owning your home outright, you could decide to rent it, using the monthly rental income you receive to pay for your Florida rent or mortgage, probably with money left over.

Renting Your Home Up North Even Though You Want To Buy In Florida

Should you decide that it makes sense to rent your home, but you still want to buy something in Florida, you might be wondering how you could afford to do this. Many people assume that without the proceeds from the sale of their home, they won't be able to purchase a new house or condo. You can if you consider either refinancing your mortgage or taking out a home equity loan. How do these work?

Basically, if you refinance, you are using the increased value of your home to apply for a larger mortgage. In other words, if your home is currently valued at $150,000, and you only owe $50,000, you could refinance and take out up to 80% of the house's value, which in this case would be additional $70,000. That would give you the needed money to buy in Florida. Then you could rent your home in New York and use the rental income to pay back the higher mortgage. With this new mortgage, you'd receive a lump sum and immediately begin paying interest on the total amount owed.

Remember, if you take a home equity loan, again, you are borrowing against your property's appreciation, but this time you're taking out an additional loan on top of your current mortgage commitment. Unlike refinancing, you don't surrender the first mortgage. Typically you can borrow up to 75%-80% of your equity. This gives you a ready amount of cash, as much as you like at a time, up to the limit of the loan. In other words, home equity loans are like buying a line of credit. You can borrow from it at any time and then pay interest only on what you borrow.

Although these tactics obligate you to higher monthly payments, or two payments instead of one, you might feel that these advantages are worth the added expense:

- You'll still own your home in case you want to come back

- Even if you don't live there, your home will have continued to appreciate in value

- In the meantime, you'll have had the necessary cash to buy a place in Florida or put down a sizeable down payment.

If you pursue the home equity route, there are several important things to know. First, as of December, 1987 Congress instituted new laws. Unless you are borrowing to buy, build or improve a home, the loan is considered home equity debt, which means that there is a limit on its deductibility. However, the new laws have eased up on the restrictions over the amount of interest you can deduct. Basically, the loan is fully deductible up to $100,000. If the loan exceeds $100,000 and that is less than the homeowner's equity and improvements, no further interest deductions are allowed.

In English, here is an example of how this works: Bob and Anne bought their home ten years ago for $100,000. They put down 20% and have subsequently made $25,000 worth of improvements. Together with their $15,000 of principal payments, they now have a $60,000 cost basis (original investment). However, between the improvements and the increased real estate values in their community, they could sell their house in the $300,000 range. Because their income and net worth have risen steadily during this ten year period, they would qualify for a $200,000 home equity loan. Interest on $160,000 of it ($60,000 equity + the first $100,000) would be deductible. Interest on the remaining $40,000 would not be. It would be treated as a personal loan without a tax benefit. However, if Bob and Ann decide to purchase a vacation home in Florida, they could avoid the tax bite by borrowing $40,000 in financing, enabling them to deduct the interest on that amount. Secondly, closing costs could be high, although the banks are getting so competitive that they may be negotiable. Finally, and most importantly, never forget that if you default on a home equity loan, you'll lose the house, no "ifs, ands, or buts," just as you would with a primary mortgage.

When shopping for financing, start with the bank that is holding your current mortgage. It's possible that they will waive certain fees, or offer you an "insiders" deal because they would love to renegotiate an old mortgage, which may be fixed at 6%. That's a great incentive for them to sit down with you and give you a new interest rate you can *both* live with.

QUESTIONS YOU WANT ANSWERED
BEFORE YOU TAKE A HOME EQUITY LOAN

Shopping for a home equity loan is like shopping for a first mortgage. There are hundreds of deals out there, and they may all look and sound the same until you investigate further. We're talking about putting your home up as collateral,

169

so you want to be sure you know precisely the terms of the agreement. Here is a list of questions you should ask each lender.

1. What does it cost to apply for the loan, and is the fee refundable if you change your mind or don't qualify?
2. How long will it take the bank to approve the loan? One month should be enough time.
3. What are the minimum and maximum allowable loans? Determine in advance how much you think you'll need for your move to Florida.
4. If you're borrowing, let's say, $50,000, what are the terms? What will be the monthly payments and for how many months? Is there a large balloon payment at the end of the loan?
5. Is there a penalty for pre-payment? Is there an annual maintenance fee, even if you owe nothing on the loan?
6. Which index is your variable interest rate tied to? How often will rates change, and therefore how often will you have increased costs passed along to you?
7. What is the annual ceiling, or "cap," on the interest rates?
8. What portion of each payment will be tax deductible?
9. When you add up the monthly payments along with the up-front fees, how does the total compare with the amount you'd pay if you took out a second mortgage or used some other sort of financing arrangement?
10. Finally, what are the closing costs? How many points will you be paying for the privilege of using this bank's money?

Remember that in today's competitive home financing market, there are plenty of fish in the sea. If you're dissatisfied with the deal at one place, keep shopping.

Selling The House Instead Of Renting

If you know that you want to sell your home, or need to in order to buy in Florida because refinancing doesn't appeal to you, it's obviously very important to assess the value of your home before the "For Sale" sign goes up. It is also important to anticipate how much profit will be left after you pay a broker's commission, pay for repairs and renovations, etc.

If indicators point to a potentially small profit, don't be discouraged. It will probably still be enough to buy something quite suitable in Florida. Even if it forces you to buy something smaller than you'd like at first, at least your taxes and maintenance costs will be reduced, and virtually all your living expenses in Florida will be much less. From that vantage point, the move would be worthwhile on that basis alone.

If you expect that the profits will be sizeable, sit down with your financial planner to map out how you will invest the funds in order to generate the greatest amount of income with the smallest tax bite.

If you are currently in a soft real estate market but are still anxious to sell, consider the idea of being a lender to a buyer. Home buyers, particularly first timers, are known to pay top dollar for a house if seller financing is part of the package. The risks are minimal, since you'll insist on a 20% down payment to protect your principal. In addition, you'll still have the property, which will continue to escalate in value, in the unlikely event that the buyers default on the loan. Further, the interest payments you receive on the loan will exceed the income you would have received if you'd sold the house for cash and invested the proceeds in five-year treasury notes or other conservative vehicles. These are paying around 8% to 9%, while mortgage rates are a full 2 points higher.

Renting In Florida Instead Of Buying

Our discussion about selling your home up north vs. renting has centered around being able to roll over the profits in order to buy in Florida. However, this is not a mandatory requisite. Should you choose to, you can rent a place in Florida and reinvest 100% of your profits. Just be aware that with respect to tax breaks, you have 24 months from the time of the sale to buy or build another property. If you have not rolled over the profits from the sale into a new home by then, you will be taxed on the profits. As with everything else, renting has its good and bad points.

THE ADVANTAGES OF RENTING

On the upside, if you rent a home or apartment, you'll certainly have a lot of leeway when it comes to the use of your money. Being liquid will enable you to travel and enjoy other freedoms associated with having cash on hand. You'll also have a great deal more flexibility if you decide to move again.

It is not unusual for newcomers to settle in an area of Florida, only to discover months later that they would have been happier in another development, another town or even another part of the state. As a renter, you won't have to be concerned if the real estate market has gone soft or if you'll be able to get your money out of the house. You just wait for the lease to expire or somehow maneuver your way out of it. In either case, it will be a whole lot easier to make a move.

Finally, on a month-to-month basis, renting is cheaper than owning. There are no property taxes, no homeowners' insurance (although you should still purchase renters' insurance), no maintenance and repair costs. It's a hassle free existence. If you're unhappy, you complain to the landlord. If there are problems that can't be resolved, you move!

THE DISADVANTAGES OF RENTING

The problem with renting, on the other hand, is that there are no financial rewards. You'll have no tax deductions, no hedge against inflation, and less control over rising rental costs. You are basically at the mercy of the marketplace. From a financial planning perspective, I'll always vote in favor of owning property because it can be the single best investment you make in terms of a return on the dollar. And unless the market is soft, a home or condominium will generally be a reliable source of income should you need to sell or tap into the equity at some point.

The one aspect I do like of renting is that it can be a lifesaver when you first move to Florida. It can be very advantageous *not* to make a major commitment to an area until you are absolutely certain it's right for you. No matter how much your friends and family may rave about Pompano Beach or Ft. Myers, you won't know if it's for you until you actually put down stakes.

Besides, when you do decide to buy, why should you have to settle? Often people go to closing just to have something to move into when they arrive. That's silly. If you find that the move is happening quicker than expected and you're rushing to buy, slow down. There will still be more than enough homes and condos to choose from six months from now. Yes, I know that means moving again, but it won't be anywhere near as massive an undertaking as the first time because you'll have less things to move. More importantly, it could mean the difference between being very unhappy in your new surroundings or extremely satisfied.

If You Buy, Should You Take A Mortgage Or Pay Cash?

There are pros and cons to buying your Florida house outright, as there are for taking out a new mortgage. The way to decide which is right for you is by asking yourself the following questions:

1. Are you still in a high tax bracket and need deductions to offset it?
2. Do you have a predictable cash flow, or would monthly mortgage payments eventually be a problem?
3. Can you get a mortgage at a rate cheaper than the money could earn for you? It's unlikely. Mortgage rates in Florida are between 9 and 11% while conservative investments are yielding an average of 8%.
4. How important is liquidity to you? With a mortgage your cash will be tied up in a non-income-producing asset until such time when there's considerable equity again.
5. Do you anticipate having any difficulty getting a mortgage due to previous financial problems or other factors that banks frown upon?
6. If you or your spouse dies, will there still be the means to keep paying on the mortgage? If not, paying cash for the new house guarantees it will always be yours.

If you are still undecided about the best road to take when it comes to the matter of your home up north and a new place to live in Florida, I would encourage you to rent on both ends. It offers the course of least resistance and more importantly, when you finally do know what will be best, you can immediately put a mid-course correction into effect. Whatever expenses are incurred for the delay in your decision, the cost of breaking a lease, increased asking prices, etc., it will be well worth it. Being able to make a decision when your back is not up against the wall will always work in your best interest.

CHAPTER 16

How Much House Can You Afford In Florida?

As soon as you buy a house or condominium in Florida, your investment will appreciate immediately. The electrician will appreciate it, the furniture stores will appreciate it, and your relatives will absolutely love it! But if it's a rapid appreciation in value you're counting on, forget it. Houses don't jump in value on an hourly basis anymore. Today's low inflation rates have taken care of that! Maybe that's a good thing. If houses *had* continued to escalate in value by 10% to 12% a year, not only would most of us been unable to trade up, but the asking prices of our own homes would have been so high, they would been unaffordable even to us!

As a result of the slower growth rates, lenders rarely give buyers the option of burying themselves in debt to buy their dream home, as they did in the late 70s and early 80s. What's interesting is that consumers are not resisting the banks' more conservative stand.

Despite the fact that the American dream is to own the biggest house possible, it appears that buyers are less inclined to be "house-poor." Without spiraling inflation rates to increase their annual earnings, their comfort zones have changed with regard to housing affordability.

A case in point is the 1987 study conducted by the U.S. League of Savings Institutions, which found that of the 11,000 home buyers surveyed, less than a third were planning to spend more than 25% of their pre-tax household income on housing (*Changing Times*, Feb., 1988). Compare that to 1981, when 45% said that they would spend at least a quarter of their earnings on housing costs.

THE OLD FORMULA FOR BEING HOUSE-POOR

Back in the early 1980s, when people were prepared to offer their first-born as collateral in order to obtain mortgage approval, people were told to calculate a house's affordability by doubling their gross income. It was a simple formula. If you were earning $40,000, you could spend $80,000. If you were bringing in $100,000, you could afford a $200,000 home. Today, figuring out what's affordable and sensible is slightly more complex. You must consider the ever-fluctuating mortgage rates and the size of your down payment. More importantly, the variety of available mortgage arrangements greatly affects the size of your monthly payments. If you select an ARM (adjustable rate mortgage), you could ultimately pay more than if you'd applied for a conventional 30-year fixed mortgage. A balloon mortgage will not cost the same as an FHA- or VA-backed mortgage, insofar as monthly payments are concerned.

Since moving to Florida will put many of you back into the housing market, let's try to address the question of affordability before you commit to a house or condominium. Here's today's conventional wisdom on mortgage debt.

WHAT'S AFFORDABLE IN 1989?

The new acceptable industry standard, according to Fannie Mae (the Federal National Mortgage Association), is a 28%/36% income-to-expense ratio on fixed-rate mortgages. What does this mean? Simply that the nation's largest investor in American home mortgages (Fannie Mae) has determined that consumers should be able to spend 28% of their gross income on house payments, and up to 36% on their total obligations—without jeopardizing their financial stability.

House payments include principal and interest on the loan repayment, plus property taxes and homeowners' insurance. Total obligations include house payments plus all other outstanding debts with 10 or more monthly payments remaining. Thus, if your total family income is $75,000, you should be able to spend $21,000 a year on the house, or $1750 a month. Your total financial obligations, including the house, should not exceed $27,000 a year, or $2250 a month.

If you apply for an adjustable rate mortgage, the ratio drops to 26%/33%. The rationale here is that because interest payments could go up by 2% a year, and up to 6% over the life of the loan, Fannie Mae contends that there is less risk if the total mortgage obligations are slightly lower to begin with. In other words, even if ARM borrowers get hit with an increase, they would presumably still be in a comfort zone because they had bought "less house" up front.

Regardless of whether you agree with these formulas, they are the basis upon which virtually all lenders evaluate mortgage applications. Why? Because most banks, savings and loans and credit unions sell their mortgage commitments to Fannie Mae, which subsequently repackages them and sells them as securities to private investors. Banks that don't conform to the Fannie Mae formula risk not being able to resell the loans. This leaves them holding the obligation for 30 years or finding other investors, which is exactly what they want to avoid.

Another Fannie Mae stipulation that will impact your mortgage costs is their $187,600 ceiling. If you are borrowing this amount or less, you will have a "conforming" mortgage, which means Fannie Mae will agree to buy it back from the bank. If you borrow more than $187,600, you'll have what's called a "jumbo" mortgage and will pay a higher interest rate because the bank will have to turn to other investors. The reason that interest rates increase is that the higher the mortgage, presumably the higher the risk to the lender. Therefore they want to build-in greater return up front in the event of defaults, which they achieve by charging more interest.

Here are some random examples of interest rates and points charged by South Florida lenders for conforming ($187,600 and less) and jumbo ($187,600 and up) mortgages. These rates were based on 30-year fixed-rate mortgages in Dade, Broward and Palm Beach Counties as of January 12, 1989.

30-Year Fixed Income Mortgage Rates

	Conforming		Jumbo	
	%	Total Points	%	Total Points
AmeriFirst Mort.	10.75	2.5	11.50	2.75
First Florida Mtg. Co.	10.50	2.8	11.00	2.5
Gold Coast S & L	11.50	0	12.00	0
Lincoln S & L	10.87	2.25	11.50	2.25

Source: The Peeke Report, 1/12/89

	Rate of Interest			
Annual Income	9%	10%	11%	12%
$ 30,000	$ 77,676	$ 71,219	$ 65,629	$ 60,761
$ 40,000	$103,568	$ 94,959	$ 87,505	$ 81,015
$ 50,000	$129,460	$118,699	$109,382	$101,269
$ 60,000	$155,352	$142,439	$131,258	$121,522
$ 75,000	$194,190	$178,048	$164,132	$151,903
$100,000	$258,920	$237,398	$218,764	$202,538

Source: National Association of Home Builders Mortgage Finance Dept.

A Quick Look At Affordable Mortgages

Before you start your search for the perfect new home in Florida, refer to the chart at the bottom of page 175 to gauge approximately how much of a mortgage you can apply for, based on current interest rates. Although these figures are based on 25% of gross income, it's close enough to the current Fannie Mae standard to get a feel for what ballpark you'll be in. If your particular income level is greater than $100,000, simply add any two columns that equal your income to arrive at an approximate mortgage figure. For example, if your total annual earnings are $150,000 and you can lock in a mortgage at 10% interest, you could feasibly borrow $356,697. Whether you'd want to is another story.

CALCULATING MORTGAGE PAYMENTS

Ultimately, your exact monthly payments will be dependent upon numerous factors. These include the size of the down payment, type of mortgage (fixed or adjustable), total amount borrowed, and rate of interest. After you determine the amount of your down payment, you can estimate the amount of principal and interest you'll be charged by referring to the next chart. Figures are based on 30-year fixed-rate mortgages.

Monthly Payment Factors

Instructions: Select the interest rate closest to the one you're applying for. Multiply its corresponding factor by the first 3 digits of your loan amount. For example, if your rate is 10.5%, and you are borrowing $150,000, then multiply 9.15 (the factor) by 150. That equals $1372.50 (your approximate principal and interest).

Interest Rate/Factor

Rate	Factor	Rate	Factor
9.0%	8.05	11.0%	9.52
9.5%	8.50	11.5%	9.90
10.0%	8.78	12.0%	10.29
10.5%	9.15	12.5%	10.67

Keep in mind that if the figure you arrive at doesn't equal 28% of your gross income, it doesn't mean you can afford a more expensive house. You still have property taxes and homeowners' insurance to add to this number. When you've done that, you'll probably be at the 28% ceiling.

IS THIS WHAT YOU CAN REALLY AFFORD?

It can be very discomforting when the message in a newspaper ad or TV commercial tells you that you afford something and you say to yourself, "Who are you kidding?" Well the same may be true with the formula for calculating how much of a mortgage you should be able to handle based on your income. It's nice if the figures and charts tell you it's affordable, but the only real way to find out if that's true is by doing some quick addition and subtraction using *your figures*.

To assure both you and the lender that you're not getting in over your head, turn back to our budgeting section at the beginning of the book. To start with, refer to the pages where you worked up your current income and expenses and divide by 12 so that these represent monthly figures. Now, fill in the blanks on the facing page.

Now that you've calculated the bottom line and can see from a mathematical perspective if a house or condominium is affordable, there's one last thing to consider. It's called your own personal "comfort level." If the figures conclude that you've got $1500 a month for housing expenses, do you want to pay that much?

People's views on acceptable comfort levels vary greatly. Not everyone wants to spend their last dime on their house. They'd rather live comfortably and have money for other interests and needs. Others feel that being house-poor is perfectly all right because a beautiful living environment is what makes them happy.

Ellen Niewold, Vice President of American Pioneer Savings Bank in Orlando and Senior Officer of the Florida Home Builders Association, says that banks also have varying attitudes regarding their comfort-lending levels, often based on the customer's mortgage history. In other words, two people with the same income could apply for the same mortgage amount. If Customer "A" had historically paid a high percentage of his gross income for a mortgage, then he's already built a lifestyle around a large monthly payment and would probably be able to handle it again. If Customer "B," however, has never been house-poor before but would be if the pending mortgage application was approved, the bank takes this into consideration and weighs the risk factor.

Before you start your house and bank shopping expeditions, my advice to you is to forget that you know anything about Fannie Mae and bank loan officers' lending limits. After you've worked up the figures and know the approximate amount available for housing, you should then determine your personal comfort level. What is the magic number you're willing to spend on monthly house payments? Only you really know the percentage of income you're prepared to allocate. And ultimately, you're the one who's got to come up with it every month, so for your sake don't choke yourself. It's only a house. It might feel like a castle on the first of the month, but it's only a house.

What's Left for Housing Expenses Each Month

1. **Average Household Monthly Income**
   Take home pay (gross pay less taxes)   _____
   Interest, dividends, rents   _____
   Other income   _____
   Net Average Household Monthly Income $_____

2. **Average Monthly Non-Housing Expenses**
   Food, household supplies   _____
   Clothing   _____
   Medical costs and insurance   _____
   Life and casualty insurance   _____
   Car, insurance, and repairs   _____
   Commuting   _____
   Installment payments/interest   _____
   Recreation/hobbies   _____
   Telephone   _____
   Contributions, dues, fees, etc.   _____
   Personal (dry cleaning, hair styling)   _____
   Savings/investment programs   _____
   Entertainment   _____
   Miscellaneous expenses   _____
   Total Average Monthly Non-Housing Expenses $_____

3. **Monthly Income Available for Housing**
   Net average monthly income (1)   _____
   Minus total non-housing expenses (2)   −_____
   Average Monthly Income Available for $_____
   Housing Costs (3)

4. **Average Monthly Expenses of Home You Wish To Purchase**
   Principal and interest on mortgage   _____
   Insurance (fire, theft and flood)   _____
   Property taxes   _____
   Utilities (water, AC, electric, gas)   _____
   Maintenance & repairs (allow 1% of the home per year) _____
   Condo or co-op fees/dues   _____
   Other expenses for the house   _____
   Average Monthly Housing Expenses (4) $_____

5. **Can You Afford This House?**
   Average monthly income available for housing (3)   _____
   Minus average monthly housing expenses (4)   −_____
   Surplus/Shortfall After Paying Housing Expenses $_____

Source: National Association of Home Builders

CHAPTER 17

The Florida Home Buyer's Checklist:

WHAT TO LOOK FOR IN RESALES AND NEW-BUILDS

I recently asked a representative of the Florida Association of Realtors what advice she might offer those who were buying their first house in Florida. She immediately replied, "If the house has a basement and the asking price is surprisingly low, don't buy it!"

You can't argue with that! The water tables in Florida are so high that basements can end up looking like inground pools. But underneath the humor is a more subtle message which is "DON'T BUY ON IMPULSE!" Don't get so swept off your feet with the beautiful environment that you forget to look for other important features such as being in close proximity to schools or medical care. Apparently, we quick-talking northerners have reputations among realtors for making fast deals. We come down with money in our pockets, we're totally enthralled with the clean, modern houses that we can get for a song (relative to home), and we're so afraid that all the opportunities will dissipate by the morning that we go to contract on the spot.

Slow down, my friends. Florida is still the south, and nothing happens overnight there. Nothing. There will be plenty of great houses for sale tomorrow and next week. Even next month. Florida has one of the strongest housing markets in the country and estimates are that close to 90,000 new single-family homes and 55,000 multiple houses (duplexes, townhouses, etc.) will be built in the state in 1989 alone. As far as resales are concerned, Betty Loth, the Relocation Director at Coldwell Banker says that "given the tremendous expansion and continuous development of new areas of the state, there is plentiful supply of available homes at competitive prices at any given time."

Over and over again I have heard from clients who have said that the biggest mistake they made when moving to Florida was that they bought something too quickly. They didn't check out the developer as thoroughly as they should have. They didn't shop around enough to compare floor plans and prices. They didn't look at enough communities or regions. They settled where their friends and family settled without really knowing if it was for them. They didn't shop for financing; they took what the developer offered. The net result is that a lot of people have become completely disenchanted with Florida, when the only problem was a bad match. Haste makes waste. Spare yourself the aggravation, time and expense. If you are considering a move to Florida and plan to buy a home right away, give yourself the luxury of time to make the best possible choice for you and your family.

WHAT KIND OF HOME HAS YOUR NAME ON IT?

When you start looking at homes in Florida, your first impression will be that they're certainly not like the ones you're used to. You won't find musty attics, damp basements or cold garages. You won't find the traditional brick two-story center hall colonials, split-levels, and mother-daughter arrangements. And you won't see houses with lots of little compartmentalized rooms to cut down on drafts. Instead, you'll find a more contemporary casual living environment, with large open spaces, light, and jumbo plants.

What else is different? Sliding glass doors in the master bedroom that lead to an enclosed pool. Screened-in porches or "lanai's" for year-round enjoyment. 25 varieties of grass (none of which will look familiar to you). Lakes, canals, and other water views. Vaulted and cathedral ceilings. Fruit trees and vegetable gardens. And don't forget the ubiquitous ceiling fans. These are the hallmarks of a Florida home. Looking at the exterior the vast majority of home exteriors are of cinderblock construction. And with good reason. Florida's tropical climate is vulnerable to hurricanes and storms, as well as termites and other insects. To withstand these quirks of mother nature requires the strongest-available materials: concrete or cinderblock. For variety, finishing touches include stucco, wood (now that lumber is treated), and shingles.

In terms of architecture, you'll notice immediately that Mediterranean and Spanish styles dot the landscape as do the "California contemporaries." Tile roofs, picture-perfect arches, wrought iron gates and the greenest of palm trees complement many homes. Single-story, or ranch styles are the most predominant design choice, in part because they epitomize the casual living that Floridians demand. However, the absence of two-story houses probably has just as much to do with the fact that Florida started out as a retirement haven...and retirees wanted nothing to do with climbing staircases.

For many people, the best news is that maintenance costs are minimal in comparison to the regions of the country which go through a change of seasons. With cinderblock and wood trim, there's no need to paint every few years. With asphalt tile roofs to protect against ultraviolet rays, the need for replacement tiles occurs every 10 to 15 years. Heating and air conditioning systems are not used on a year-round basis, and subsequently require less repair and maintenance. Overall, houses don't demand the same level of attention or expense you're accustomed to.

ADVICE FROM THE EXPERTS

Chris DeMaio, Sr. is both a veteran licensed building contractor and a licensed real estate agent. For the past 13 years he has helped thousands of newcomers buy and build homes in the greater Pinellas area. In addition, he is widely respected for teaching courses to hundreds of other brokers about home construction in Florida.

His background, knowledge and expertise are unparalleled in the industry. He has worked with newcomers for years so you can believe him when he tells you that there is a predictable course of events that takes place when people buy their first house in Florida. And all too often that pattern spells trouble. Here is a summary of our interview with Mr. DeMaio, Sr.

Q. What is the biggest mistake that people make when buying their first home in Florida?

A. It seems that a lot of people take an immediate dislike to the look of cinderblock and tell the brokers to show them homes made mostly of wood. I agree that wood can be very attractive and it's a more contemporary look, but what they don't understand is that our weather conditions are vastly different than the north. And that means that our building materials must have certain standards and meet certain functions. Treated wood is not cinderblock and it can't be expected to hold up as well. I am very concerned about the homes that are being designed for beauty rather than practicality.

Q. Describe Florida's climate and how that affects the construction of a house.

A. First of all, we get more rain in a day than some places get in a month, and we get more rain in a month than some places get in a year. Last Labor Day our area got hit with 18″ of rain in just four days. June through November is hurricane season, which can mean torrential downpours every afternoon for weeks at a time. The Panhandle area even gets snow in the winter. Between the intensity of the heat all year (moist air) plus the rain, that's a tremendous amount of moisture month in and month out. When does the wood get a chance to dry out? It doesn't.

You see, people don't really consider that homes up north have to contend with the cold, which means dry air. The lumber can dry out, so it's not as likely to rot. That's not the case in Florida.

Q. What do you recommend that people do look for in construction?

A. I tell them to stay away from the homes that have California-style roofs and sheered windows, which in my opinion are unsafe in the areas most prone to hurricanes. What you do want is a home built with masonry tile roofs, cinderblock, and any materials that are not heat-conductive. Remember up north you want to keep the heat in; here we want to keep it out. Look for overhangs, landscaping that provides shading, and features that keep the ultraviolet rays out of the house.

181

Q. What is the biggest change in home building in the last ten years?

A. That would probably have to be what's happened to home design as a result of land availability. With the huge influx of people, desirable property is getting more sparse, the lots being divvied up are narrower but are also more expensive. Since they can't build out, they're building up. So for the first time we're seeing a surge of two-story homes. While this is not necessarily an efficient-style home down here, it's what people are asking for.

It's interesting that everyone comes down and wants to build their Taj Mahal. They want a large modern house and they don't care about sacrificing practicality for design. They're not buying construction, they're buying a monthly payment, like they do with a car. If they can swing the monthly mortgage, they go for it. And builders are very happy to build whatever customers demand.

Q. Does that mean construction is not of sound quality?

A. Not at all. In fact, I think by and large the construction is far superior to homes I've seen built in Long Island and other areas up north. We have strict building codes, we take a lot of precautions because of the climate and many of the builders are very experienced.

Incidentally, just because a home is inexpensive doesn't mean it's not well built. In Florida, the asking price sometimes has more to do with the land values of the area.

Q. What advice do you have for building a home?

A. First, you should avoid buying a spot-lot. That's an empty lot in an established neighborhood that never got built up. The reason is that most people end up building a $250,000 home there but it's situated in an older, more modest area. When they try to sell for $300,000 they don't understand that they're in a $100,000 neighborhood and it will be very difficult to command a high price.

Secondly, you must find out how long the builder has been licensed in Florida, how many homes he's *completed*, and then talk to his customers to see if they were satisfied. If you have any doubts about the builder, contact the Department of Professional Regulation in Tallahassee to check out his credentials. Call (904) 487-1395.

Q. Are there any problems with buying an older home in Florida?

A. Not quality-wise. The older homes are as solid as a rock because we used a lot more materials back then. What you do have to look out for is "functional obsolescence." The layouts in the older homes are not always conducive to today's lifestyles. For example, the split plan is very popular in newer homes down here. That's where the Master bedroom is on one side of the house, the kitchen and family area are in the middle and the other bedrooms opposite that. Also, people like kitchens that are in the back of the house today because we live in our backyards. That's where the pool and lanai are, where we entertain, the kids play, etc. It's just easier. Most of the older homes are not designed like this.

If you plan to relocate to the greater Pinellas area and would like to talk to Mr. DeMaio, Sr. about buying or building a home, contact him at DeMaio & Sons, 214 A Howard Drive, Belleair Beach, FL 34634. Or call him at (813) 595-2744.

WHAT'S BEST? NEW OR USED?

After you've read through the chapter, "How Much House Can You Afford," the next decision to make is how much house do you need? If you have small children, do you need a playroom plus a den? What about frequent out-of-town guests (count on it!)? Is three bedrooms enough, or is four the minimum? How about bathrooms? Do you want a pool? What's more important, a water view or being in close proximity to schools and recreation?

Furthermore, you need to figure out if you're interested in a brand-new home vs. a resale. There are merits to both.

The biggest advantage of a new-build is generally greater land values and more house for the money. Also, you'll probably be privy to more financing deals, including no points at closing. With a new home, there's flexibility with respect to colors, tiles, carpeting, appliances, etc. In many cases, the builder will present you with a long list of options. Anyone who has ever moved into a used home will appreciate not having to live with someone else's idea of beautiful wallpaper. However, buying into a new development and/or new part of town can mean buying into isolation for a while. That can mean a longer commute to work, traffic build-ups around the main shopping areas and other inconveniences. Additionally, you should anticipate slower appreciation and difficulty in selling within the first few years. With so much development going on in your neighborhood, the later buyers are bound to want to buy new *vs.* used, just as you did.

The biggest advantage of a resale can be the beauty of an older neighborhood. The landscaping is mature, not barren. There may be greater privacy. And inside the home, it's possible that the owners will have added some beautiful features—things you couldn't have done yourself right away. Also, the built-ins will be up—the shelves, hooks, storage areas, etc. Everything will have a place, making for a quicker adjustment.

FLORIDA IS THE LAND OF PLANNED COMMUNITIES

If you're unfamiliar with the term "planned community," you'll become very familiar with it once you start looking at Florida real estate. There are thousands of these "microwave towns" across the state. Zap and they're there in an instant.

What are planned communities exactly? They are pockets of land that have been bought up and built up as self-contained communities by developers, corporations and other financial investors. By self-contained I mean that they offer a variety of housing choices, public schools and parks, recreational facilities, shopping, all in the same locale.

Historically speaking, planned communities served a very important function when the great expansion boom started in the 60s and 70s. Developers were buying land in what was considered "God's country", or the hinterlands. To attract buyers and to assure them that they wouldn't have to travel long distances for schools, shopping, etc. they "planned" the development of commercial and public facilities that would serve the community, in addition to building housing. Coral Springs, a planned community 20 miles northwest of Ft. Lauderdale started by Westinghouse Corp., is probably one of the best known.

SHOULD YOU WORK WITH A REAL ESTATE AGENT?

Yes, yes, yes. A major relocation such as this cries out for the guidance and direction a professional real estate broker can offer. Remember, they come to the party with more than just the knowledge of homes for sale. They know everything about the local communities: taxes, school systems, houses of worship, recreation—they know where it's at. They may also be equipped to help you with financing arrangements. And if you are honest about your needs, your price range, and your preferences, most will do a bang-up job for you.

Lani Prilliman of Mike Prilliman Realty in Zephyrhills is an experienced broker as well as the vice president of the Florida Board of Realtors. She offers several suggestions for working with a broker.

First, she feels strongly that you should interview several real estate agents. Then select one that you really get along with and feel confident has the greatest resources to help you. The more loyal you are to an agent, the more devoted they will be to you in turn. If the broker knows that every competitor on the block is looking for you, there is very little incentive for them to work hard on your behalf. Ms. Prilliman says that there is no need to worry about missing out on a house because the Multiple Listing Service (MLS) assures that every realty office has access to the same information and the same homes.

As far as the shopping process is concerned, Ms. Prilliman suggests that if time permits, you limit yourself to looking at no more than four different houses in one day. After that, everything will become blurred in your mind. Which one had the blue bathrooms with skylights? Was that the one that where the kitchen had no eating area? Or was that the one with the huge walk-in closets in every bedroom? Even if you think you're committing a house to memory, all it takes is one similar-looking home to make you forget. Another tactic she recommends is to play the "Game of Elimination" so that you are never comparing more than two houses at a time. Here's how this works:

Let's say you tour House "A" and House "B" in the morning. You loved House "A" but thought House "B" was dreadful. Thus, you completely eliminate House "B" from your list of possibilities. In the afternoon, you visit House "C." You compare it to House "A," since that is still on the list, and you decide that House "C" has a better location and has that extra half-bath. Now you eliminate House "A." Finally, you visit House "D" and compare it to House "C." House "D" is really beautiful but has been vacant and neglected for a year. It would need too much work to be suitable for a fast relocation. Thus House "C" wins out for the day. The next day you start over again if necessary, and keep eliminating so that you are never comparing more than two houses at a time. This should keep the process from getting overwhelming.

THE RELOCATION EXPERT

Because of the tremendous migration to Florida each year by tens of thousands of newcomers, you'll find a new breed of professional to work with. They are called relocation specialists. And although their primary function is to work with corporate transferees, many local realtors employ trained counselors whose job it is to provide professional assistance to any "out of town" buyer.

First and foremost they are there to help you speed up the process of finding the right home for you, or finding the right rental until you are ready to buy. Often they are responsible for assisting transferees who have three days to buy, so they know their market extremely well. These certified specialists can also provide job placement information for spouses, commuting information, and numerous other details that can make a complicated relocation into a positive experience. Incidentally, most have been through a major relocation themselves and understand the anxieties, and social and psychological needs of incoming families.

Virtually all of the large real estate brokerage firms and developers in Florida have a staff of trained relocation counselors or specialists, including Coldwell Banker, Century 21, Better Homes and Gardens, Don Gallagher Realtors, Tam-Bay Realty, Merrill Lynch Realty, Jeanne Baker, Inc., Watson Realty, Arvida Realty Sales, and others. Even Sun Bank and Barnett Bank have mortgage hotlines, relocation experts and other newcomers' services.

Betty Loth of Coldwell Banker urges out of town buyers to seek the help of a professionally-trained relocation counselor. She says that in the state of Florida there are close to 350,000 licensed real estate brokers—more than any other state in the country.

"Unfortunately, many work at it part time and don't have the proper dedication or commitment to the job that a full-time, trained person will. People who have a made a career out of helping newcomers relocate can provide service and information that is unparalleled in our industry. Because they spend so much time working on behalf of this segment of the market, they are very familiar with their special needs and questions. You can't find this level of professionalism just anywhere."

INTRODUCING "FLORIDA BOUND"

To find out how to be in touch with the realty companies and relocation counselors that specialize in out of town buyers, I urge you to get a hold of a copy of a most impressive publication. It will provide you with virtually everything you'll want to know about the current Florida real estate market. It's called "Florida Bound," and it's a beautiful magazine full of relevant information, tips from the experts, and gorgeous color photos of houses. You'll also find comprehensive descriptions of the different regions in the state, including recreation facilities, cultural opportunities, schools, medical care and, of course, real estate. You'll find the names and toll free telephone numbers of many of the key players in the state—those relocation specialists and realty agents who can be such a big help to you.

To order your copy of "Florida Bound," call this toll-free number: 1-800-US-BOUND (872-6863). The cover price is $6.95, plus $2.00 for postage and handling (it's tax deductible). The magazine is published annually with a new issue put out each fall.

So You Want To Build A House

If you discover that your dream house is under construction, or that plans call for it to be built in the near future, you should move with extreme caution. Working with builders and developers can bring on a whole host of questions and concerns. And unfortunately, on top of this, there are still problems with fly-by-night operations in Florida. That's not to say their hearts aren't in the right place; they just may be slightly undercapitalized.

TIPS FOR WORKING WITH BUILDERS

Discussion point number one with any builder you talk to is how long they've been around as home builders. Secondly, how many homes have they built and sold. To confirm that a builder is solvent, you should insist on reviewing current financial reports. You should check with the Better Business Bureau to see if complaints have been lodged by previous customers. You should contact the Florida Home Builders Association in Tallahassee to determine if they have information on the developer. Check with the local Chamber of Commerce, the local Board of Realtors—any credible organization that will help you confirm that you're working with a legitimate builder.

The key is not to be overly influenced by the glossy brochures and impressive models. If the developer is financed only up to that point, you'd better find out before you buy.

The Home Buyer's Guide To H.O.W.

If you are leaning towards new construction, you should be aware of a warranty program that ensures over 300,000 new homes across the state. It's called H.O.W., "Home Owners Warranty", and basically if your builder is an affiliated member, you've got one less thing to worry about.

Every H.O.W. builder agrees to provide written warranties on their work and has also been evaluated for their performance in three areas:

- *Construction Competence*
- *Financial Stability*
- *Customer Service*

If the builder is found to be lacking in any one of these basics, they are deemed ineligible to participate. If they pass muster, you can be reasonably assured that you will have a means of recourse, other than litigation, if there are subsequent problems with the builder's work.

Further, if for some reason the builder's work requires repairs and the builder is no longer around, this is when the H.O.W. program can be a life saver. Through their insurance program, repairs will be paid for if the builder cannot meet his obligations after a $250 deductible has been met.

According to Ken Kanline at H.O.W. headquarters in Washington, D.C., the biggest problem with Florida builders today is insolvency. "Florida is such an active and lucrative market, developers come from all over to try their luck. Unfortunately they come to the party with varying degrees of financial support, and the average customer really has no way of determining that."

Rarely is there a problem with a house falling down, as you might find in some parts of the country. It's quite the contrary. Florida builders are some of the best. Further, the state has very strong building codes and even better, they have excellent code enforcement, but the state can't guarantee that a builder will be around in five years.

The H.O.W. insurance policy is paid for by the builder, and if you sell your home within 10 years of purchasing it, the left-over portion of the program is transferrable.

If you are seriously considering buying a new home from a builder who is not a registered H.O.W. builder, you should find out if they offer a comparable warranty program. If not, you should find out why, and more importantly who does.

For more information on H.O.W. builders in Florida, call their toll-free number, 1-800-241-9260.

Another Buyer Warranty Program

If you want your new home protected from roof to floor, you should be aware of an insurance policy that covers the mechanical components of the house. The Homeowners Association of America sells an inexpensive package that covers everything in your newly-built home from the electrical system to the plumbing to the major appliances, right down to the door bell and chime. You purchase the policy directly from one of the 1800 realtors in Florida who are affiliated with the Homeowner's group. The cost to insure a new single-family home is $420, with a $100 deductible per claim.

For more information, call their national toll-free number, 1-800-327-9787. In Florida, call 1-800-432-1033.

The Major Home Builders In Florida

Given how important it is to work with a reputable builder, it might help to know who the major players are across the state. Recently the Professional Builder's Association came out with their 21st report on "Housing Giants"—a listing of the top 400 builders in the country. 35 of those are Florida builders. Eight out of the country's top ten builders, such as Pulte Home and U.S. Home, work in Florida.

Being on this list does not guarantee quality that is acceptable to you, that they'll deliver on time, or that your contractual arrangements will run smoothly. All it indicates is that at least these developers are known entities in the state and you can assume that they have a good track record, or they would never have achieved this status.

Florida's Big Home Builders

AmeriFirst Development Corp.	Arthur Rutenberg Corp.
Arvida/JMB Partners L.P.	Avatar Holdings
Beacon United	Beverly Hills Development
Blosam Contractors	Burg & DiVosta
Cenvill Development Corp.	Chrisdon Communities
Dimcas	Engle Group
Epoch Properties	General Development Corp.
Graham Cos.	Gulfstream Land & Devel.
Homes of Merit	Kimmins Corp.
Landstar Homes	Lennar Corp.
Levitt Homes	Mahaffey Co.
Orange Blossom Hills	Oriole Homes Corp.
Palm Coast Construction	Regency Communities
Savill/Sanderlin	Stokes & Co.
Sun City Center Corp.	Tompkins Heritage Homes
Trafalgar Developers	Weitzer Communities LTD
Wynne Building Corp.	Yusem Homes

Purchase And Sale Agreements

If you've bought a home previously, then you know all about going to contract. This is the step where you iron out every single term of an agreement with the seller before you officially purchase their property. In Florida, this important document is called the Purchase and Sale contract. What's different in Florida is that it is not unusual for the real estate broker to draw up this initial contract, unlike New York where an attorney handles the entire matter. It happens that the Florida Association of Realtors and The Florida Bar jointly developed a contract form that can be used by the brokers to expedite the purchase agreement.

Nevertheless, the Florida Bar Association recommends that you have an attorney draw up the contract if the purchase involves any unusual or complex details, such as seller financing.

Every Purchase and Sale contract should address the following issues:

1. Precisely what land, buildings and furnishings are included in the offer, i.e., appliances, light fixtures, etc.

2. All details pertaining to payments.
3. Exact date you can take possession.
4. Which kind of deed the seller will be giving.
5. Whether the seller will be giving you a good, marketable title.
6. Who pays for the examination of the title and who for the abstract of the title and title insurance.
7. Whether it is necessary for a survey to be done to confirm that improvements were done on the property, and who will pay for the survey.
8. If the seller gives the mortgage, who pays Florida's intangible tax?
9. If the buyer lends from an outside source, who pays the closing costs?
10. If termite damage is found, will the seller be the one to pay for repairs?
11. What are the zoning regulations or restrictions on the property?
12. How much time can elapse before the purchase is accepted or refused?
13. If the offer is accepted, what steps are to be taken to insure that all improvements and other promises will be made before the final closing?
14. Are boundary lines properly specified?
15. Who is responsible for the paying of taxes?
16. What is the recourse if either the buyer or seller defaults?
17. Will the purchase agreement be contingent on the buyer getting financing approved and/or the sale of the buyer's house being sold first?
18. Whose responsibility it is to pay for governmental special assessments that arise prior to closing?

Here are examples of who is typically responsible for what's in a closing.

House Closings In New York And Florida

Action	Florida	New York
Closing By	Title Insurance Co.	Attorneys
Termite Inspec.	Buyer or seller pays	Buyer pays
Title Insurance	Required. Seller pays	Buyer pays
Property Taxes	County and local paid at year's end	Paid in advance
Possession	On closing	On closing but negotiable

189

Obviously depending on the particular house you are buying, there may be other issues to be decided. Unless this is a very black and white case, it's probably advisable to retain a lawyer to help you through the purchase process.

This may seem to be an unnecessary suggestion, since those coming from the north and midwest are accustomed to working with attorneys when buying or selling a home. However, in Florida, a house closing is handled very differently. Some people say that it's so simple, they can't believe they own the house!

Closing costs are typically less in Florida than they are in the east. They average about three percent of the mortgage amount, plus whatever points the bank charges. In New York, closing costs can be triple that.

YOU'RE GOING TO LOVE YOUR FLORIDA HOME

Most people who end up buying a house in Florida, whether it's brand new or 10 years old, say that it's the best home they've ever owned. The layouts are designed to accommodate a casual lifestyle, the rooms are bright and cheerful if not larger than they're accustomed to, and the amenities are beautiful. A built in pool, a screened in patio, water views, skylights...it's no wonder so many newcomers liken their Florida lifestyle to a vacation that never ends.

CHAPTER 18

The Buyer's Guide To Florida Condominiums

Are condominiums popular in Florida? Is the Pope popular in Rome on Sunday? To say that condominium living is synonymous with Florida is an understatement. The Bureau of Condominiums in Tallahassee estimates that more than 2.5 million people live part or full time in the more than 1 million units across the state. That's practically a quarter of the population. Last year there were more than 20,000 Condominium Associations registered in Florida, and there's no end in sight to an annual 5% to 10% growth rate in condominium building.

It goes without saying that if you are considering buying a condo, you're in very good company. But if you're moving from a private single family house or even a rented apartment, you should prepare yourself for some very significant changes with respect to decision-making about how you live.

Let's face it. The very foundation of condo ownership is communal living. Not that you'll be sharing the bathroom down the hall, but there will sharing of common grounds, facilities, and amenities. Absolutely nothing happens in a condominium complex without the direct vote of all the owners. If you and/or your spouse are the kind of people who insist on complete privacy, who don't appreciate having someone telling them what to do and simply won't put up with a laundry list of rules and regulations, condo life is probably not for you.

On the other hand, there are numerous advantages of owning a condominium, including tax benefits, equity build up, convenient locations, economical living conditions, impressive recreational facilities, and generally speaking, minor

191

maintenance or repair obligations for your unit.

In this chapter, we'll discuss more of the pros and cons of this housing choice as well as give you an understanding of what to expect as a condo owner in Florida. Even if you currently own one up north, read on. Florida condos march to the beat of a different drummer. Anyone who already owns there can attest to the fact that they are an entirely different breed.

THE CASE OF JAMIE SWARTZ

Many of you will recall a recent story in the news of a 9-year-old girl whose mother, a divorcee, lost her battle with cancer. As a result, Jamie Swartz had no choice but to move in to her father and step-mother's Adults-Only condominium in Margate, Florida.

It's certainly a tragedy for any child to be exposed to death and divorce at such an early age. But the crisis was further fueled when her move caused a furor among the other condo owners. Because of Viewpointe's adult-only status, the condo association felt they were well within their rights to order her to vacate. Whether right or wrong, this case illustrates what a volatile issue the adults-only concept is. Florida is notorious for age and other restrictions due to the fact that the state has always been a respite from children for millions of retirees.

You should be aware however, that as of March, 1989, *age discrimination is prohibited* except in subsidized facilities for the elderly or in complexes where all occupants are 62 or older or if 80% of units have one resident at least 55 years old.

Florida Laws Are Some Of The Toughest

Because so many Florida residents own and live in condos, the state has established strict legislation to ensure that owners will be kept informed, that they will be insulated from unscrupulous developers and that they will enjoy this type of living to the fullest. This has been accomplished through Chapter 718, Florida Statutes, the Condominium Act, one of the most comprehensive legislative acts for condo owners in the country.

For more information on the Florida Condominium Laws and protection for unit owners, write away for a free booklet entitled, "Condominium Living in Florida." This spells out the most important aspects of the law in a way that is easy to read and understand. I urge you to get a copy before you buy. Write to:

State of Florida Dept. of Business Regulation
Dept. of Land Sales, Condominiums, and Mobile Homes
The Johns Building
725 S. Bronough St.
Tallahassee, FL 32301-1927
Or call (904) 488-0725
In Florida, call (800) 342-8081.

THE CONDOMINIUM CONCEPT

True or false: Condominiums are high-rise buildings overlooking the ocean.

The answer (I hope you got this right) is false. The word condominium comes from the Latin, "common ownership or control." It has nothing to do with its physical form. Although the high-rise condo is the most well known in Florida, in the last decade there has been a tremendous surge of alternative condominium properties. These include low-rise buildings, garden apartments, detached or semi-detached townhouses, mobile homes, resort-like motels, camper sites, docking facilities, stables, and even a former luxury liner. Any real property can become a condominium.

By definition, a condominium is a form of property ownership in which someone owns a unit exclusively and owns the common elements jointly with the other owners. Common elements include roofs, exterior walls, the condominium grounds and recreation facilities. Legally they are attached to each unit and are automatically transferred with the sale of the unit.

CONDO ASSOCIATIONS

Living in a condo complex is like living in a miniature democratic society. Each owner has an equal vote in determining how the condo will be run, but majority rules. If you're not part of the consensus, so be it.

Every condominium has what's known as its Association, usually a non-profit corporation made up of all the owners. The Association is charged with managing and operating the condo community, providing common services and maintaining common elements. Each member, by purchasing a unit, is bound by its rules and regulations.

Condo associations are often compared to small city governments in that they collect condo dues and fees, pay for the expenses of the complex and are there to enforce the rules. In addition, they act as legislators of their community, amending laws to improve the use, maintenance and appearance of the complex.

THE BOARD OF DIRECTORS

Every association has a Board of Directors, all of whom are elected by the owners. Their primary function is to represent the owners in the ongoing management of the condominium. Some would say that their real function is to create as many committees as there are units as a way to control the affairs.

The typical Board will appoint people to head up the Rules Committee, the Finance Committee, the Election Committee, the Social Events Committee and so on. If you've ever dreamed of being a power broker, here's your chance. Because the Board has fiduciary responsibilities, it is hoped that they will act with the highest degree of good faith and will place the interests of the owners above their own. Just in case they don't, Florida law dictates that all owners have a voice in the operation through annual meetings, open board meetings, elections, recall of directors, voting, and personal access to condominium books and records.

After you hear a few horror stories about condo associations and Boards of Directors that use terrorist tactics to get compliance, you'll understand how Florida's condominium laws are there to protect owners from each other.

PERSONAL INVOLVEMENT IS THE KEY

Everyone will tell you that the key to a successfully-run condominium is the ongoing involvement and participation of its membership. And they are absolutely right. Apathy, or absentee ownership, or both, are the death knell of any condo. Without an active membership, only a few select people will determine the needs of the property and its owners. That can lead to dissention when the others wake up, but they will only have themselves to blame. After all, they have a mutual investment at stake.

The Condominium Documents

Every condominium developer in Florida must file documents with the Florida Division of Land Sales, Condominiums and Mobile Homes before a single unit can be sold. Information found within consists of the declaration of condominium, articles of incorporation of the association, the bylaws of the association and the plot and floor plans of your unit.

The developer is required to give each purchaser a copy of these documents for their inspection, and it will behoove you to not just leaf through them, but to study them carefully for your own protection. Often this information will be summarized in a prospectus, particularly if you're looking at a large development. This does not serve as a substitute for the Official Condominium Documents, but may make them more easily understood.

Remember, you are buying an expensive piece of property, going through the inconvenience and expense of shopping for a mortgage, moving all of your belongings and adjusting to a whole new life. If you discover afterwards that you find the developer's terms unacceptable, you'll be more than a day late and a dollar short. Have an attorney decipher the documents if you don't feel confident that you'll understand them.

Ask Before You Buy

As you are beginning to see, you will be buying into a great deal more than a 2-bedroom 2-bath apartment overlooking the golf course. You'll be buying into the shared philosophy of a group of otherwise unrelated peers, and their handling of matters could turn out to be more of a disappointment than the cancellation of Bingo Night.

Even after you've reviewed a condominium's documents, you'll undoubtedly have questions. And when shopping for condominiums, there is probably no such thing as asking too many questions. According to the Department of Business Regulation, Division of Land Sales, Condominiums and Mobile Homes and the Florida Bar Association, it's time to play the game of 20 questions (or more). Here is what they suggest you find out before you buy:

1. What are your ownership rights in the common elements, your voting rights in the association and your share in the common expenses?
2. How are the unit boundaries defined?
3. What are the restrictions on the use of the common elements and the unit itself?
4. Does the board of directors have the authority to set the monthly assessments, or do the unit owners set them? Are there restrictions on how much the board can spend without unit owner approval?
5. Does the board have the right to impose special assessments without approval?
6. Exactly which items will the unit owners be personally responsible for maintaining?
7. Are there clauses in the condo documents that owners automatically approve all actions of the developer? If so, do you understand and accept the developer's plans?
8. Is the condo a "Phase Condominium" (developers are not required by law to complete all proposed phases)? If so, how many units will eventually be added to the condominium and what impact will they have on the use of the common facilities? In what phases are the recreational facilities to be built? If the recreational facilities are planned for one of the first phases, what will be the assessments if later phases are not added? If the recreational facilities are in a latter phase and the developer fails to complete that phase, what recourse do owners have?
9. What is the scheduled timetable for the start and completion of each phase?
10. Do the expenses that are set forth in the estimated operating budget appear realistic? If they appear too low, will this mean an increase in the assessment when the developer turns control of the condo association over to the owners? The best way to gauge operating budgets is to compare those of the different condos you are looking at.
11. Is the condo being created from previously-occupied property, such as a resort hotel or motel? If so, what is the condition of the property, and is there a foreseeable need for major repairs? Is the developer providing written warranties?
12. Are you aware of the reputation of the developer and the quality of his previous work?
13. Is the condo one of several operated by a single association? If so, how are the various condos related? Will each condo be represented on the board?

14. Has the developer filed the condo documents with the Division of Florida Land Sales, Condominiums and Mobile Homes?
15. What are the restrictions on your right to sell, lease, and mortgage your apartment?
16. What are the restrictions on the age of children who may live in or visit the condo and use the pool, beach or other facilities?
17. Are there any restrictions on pets?
18. Are there restrictions on the parking of boats, vans or vehicles other than cars?
19. Are there any restrictions on the types of floor covering materials, drapes or window hangings, screening or glassing in open balconies, etc?
20. Are the club memberships or recreation facility leases mandatory?

Wait, there's more.

Florida's Impact Fees

If you are looking at a brand-new condominium development, you should be aware of another assessment you will be paying for, even if it's an indirect cost. In effect, we're talking about a new tax base called impact fees and they are Florida's way of grappling with the costs of providing roads and services to the tens of thousands of new residents that move in each year. In other words, each new resident has an "impact" on the infrastructure of the community where they choose to move. Infrastructure includes roads, water and sewers, parks, police and fire stations, schools and libraries—any physical service or facility that is shared by the residents. Thus, to ensure that the counties will be able to keep up with the growing population and the subsequent wear and tear on services and facilities, they have devised impact fees as a way to raise enough revenue to cover increased costs for building and maintenance. These impact fees are developed, assessed and collected by counties and are charged purely at the their discretion. Currently, 25 of Florida's 67 counties have elected to do so. Naturally these are the counties where all the action is happening.

In the view of the counties, it is unfair to penalize or tax current residents for the strain on services. Thus they assess the land developers of new condominiums and other private residential communities. Obviously it is through their housing that new residents will be attracted to the county, and if they're going to reap profits, they're going to have to toe the line by taking responsibility for the increased burden on the infrastructure.

Even though impact fees are not directly passed on to consumers, you can rest assured that the asking price of your new condo will reflect a portion of the impact fees that have been assessed. If you are seriously considering a new condominium development, here is what you should find out:

1. Does the county you are looking in charge impact fees to developers of new properties?

2. What is the specific impact fee that this developer has been assessed?
3. What portion of that will be passed along to you, the buyer?
4. Have the impact fees already been paid?

Although builders are not supposed to be able to receive their building permit until the impact fees have been paid, you should confirm that. The last thing you want is own a unit in a condominium complex that has a lien attached to it because the impact fees were never paid.

As for specific costs you might expect to pay, court rulings have held that impact fees must be the same whether you're buying a $50,000 one-bedroom condo or a $200,000 single-family home. If the fees were assessed based on the value of the homes, it would be considered a tax, not a fee. In 1989, over 700 million dollars in revenues will be raised among these 25 counties through impact fee programs. The average assessment per family seems to be in the $1500 range.

Here are the 10 counties whose residential impact fees are the highest in the state, in order starting from the single highest to the tenth highest: Indian River, Pasco, Brevard, St. Lucie, Monroe, Sarasota, Manatee, Alachua, Bay and Pinellas.

The Cost Of Ownership

The median purchase price of a condominium in Florida is $125,000. But keep in mind that your down payment and monthly mortgage costs only represent a portion of your living expenses, albeit the largest portion. As a condo owner, you have a continuing obligation to share in the expense of maintaining the common elements. And unlike a fixed mortgage in which payments remain stable throughout the life of the loan, you can expect that condo maintenance fees will go up every year. Also, these fees are *not* tax deductible.

One more thing. The larger the unit, or the higher the value, the greater the monthly maintenance. Thus, if the unit you have your heart set on is on one of the top floors overlooking the Gulf of Mexico, and if the terrace from your bedroom is in direct view of the golf course, you'll be paying a lot more in maintenance fees than the people who live downstairs and have a view of the parking lot.

TAXES AND INSURANCE

Condo owners receive their property tax bill every November, the same as those who own a private home. The assessment is based on the value of the unit and the undivided share of the land and common facilities.

As far as insurance is concerned, by law the condo association must purchase a policy covering all common property against fire, liability and other risks. As an owner, you will be responsible for insuring the contents of your unit and insuring against liability, similar to a homeowner's policy. At your option, you can also buy a unit-owner's policy that protects against any kind of losses not covered by the association's policy, such as living expenses incurred if the condominium is unusable due to fire or other damage. As a unit owner, you should be aware of what the association policy covers so that you can insulate yourself from high replacement costs in the event of a claim.

Comparison Shopping

While you are shopping the condo market, use this handy worksheet to price-compare.

Condominium Ownership Costs

Purchase Price	$_____
Square Feet	$_____
Cost Per Sq. Ft. (price divided by sq. ft.)	$_____
Initial Cash Investment	
Downpayment	$_____
Closing Costs	$_____
Initial Repairs	$_____
Moving Expenses	$_____
Total Initial Costs	$_____
Monthly Costs	
Mortgage Payment	$_____
Real Estate Taxes	$_____
Insurance	$_____
Association Dues	$_____
Unit Maintenance	$_____
Utilities	$_____
Total Monthly Cost	$_____

Pre-Construction Deposits

If you plan to buy a brand-new condominium, one that is not yet built, you should be aware of the types of agreements you'll be presented with.

The first is the *reservation deposit agreement*, which confirms your interest in purchasing a unit when the condominium is developed. Although this is not a binding contract, you will be asked to make a good faith deposit. You or the developer can back out of the agreement at any time, and it's possible that the actual purchase price will be different from the one stated in this reservation agreement. Since the money paid to the developer will be in an escrow account, you will not be at risk of losing your deposit should you change your mind.

If you are actually ready to purchase a condominium unit in which the construction, furnishings and landscaping are not substantially completed, your sales deposit here is only partially protected under the law. In pre-constructed condos, deposits of up to 10% of the purchase price must be put in escrow. Deposits in excess of 10% can be used by the developer for construction purposes.

If you are buying a unit that is almost complete, deposits are not required to be put in escrow. The only way to ensure that your deposit would be refundable should you decide to back out, would be if that provision was stipulated in your signed purchase agreement.

WHAT'S SO GREAT ABOUT CONDOS

With the limitations and restrictions we've discussed, maybe you're wondering how 2.5 million Florida residents can be wrong about condos. They're not. Condominium living has a lot of things going for it, particularly if you don't want the burden or expense of maintaining a private house. Condos are virtually hassle-free! In addition, because the greatest growth has taken place in the last decade, most Florida condos have new, modern appearances, complete with new appliances, new carpeting and cabinetry, etc. It's possible to move in and not need to put any money into the place, unless you *choose* to do so.

Then there's the purchase price of a condo. Theoretically speaking, you can buy a condo for less than a house because you aren't buying a large plot of land with your home. Thus, you can enjoy the same tax and equity benefits as a homeowner, with less of a financial commitment.

Here is one of the best reasons to own: having use of facilities you couldn't possibly afford on your own. So many of the condo complexes in Florida offer luxurious country club-like facilities. The tennis courts, golf courses, clubhouses, swimming pools, health clubs, and restaurants that may be on the premises can offer you a quality of life unlike anything else you've ever known.

Finally, many of my clients have commented about the ease of making new friends, given the conducive environment for meeting fellow owners. They simply can't imagine their lives without the neighbors who have become their Florida family.

SHOULD YOU BUY A CONDOMINIUM?

While condominiums do have numerous advantages, that doesn't mean they're right for everyone. For some people, the most unacceptable aspect is the lack of seclusion and privacy. If you couldn't handle the fact that your neighbors would know your business, condo living would be a challenge. Like it or not, your neighbors would be aware of when you come and go, when you have visitors, where you shop, etc. In such close quarters, it's difficult to expect complete privacy.

Secondly, there are the prospects of ever-increasing costs associated with condo living due to maintenance and upkeep. It's like any other property. The older it gets, the more it will need and therefore, the more you will need to cough up.

Finally, there is the question of a condominium's resale value. In Florida it's no secret that the number of available condos, both new and used, is exceeded only by the number of palmetto bugs in the swamps. They're everywhere! It's probably true when they say it's easier to get rid of a disease than it is a Florida condo. Thus, if your intent is to sell quickly (within a year or two), take the profits and buy a larger condo or private home, think again. It might be very difficult if not impossible to compete with the new and exciting deals offered by developers. What can you, as a single owner, offer that compares with their list of fringe benefits, financing arrangements, and "free" closings? The only real weapon in your arsenal is a lower asking price. And that could mean the end of the profits.

One other thing about selling. Before a sale can be consummated, the Directors of your association must approve the purchaser. You can probably rent the unit without their OK, but not sell it.

Is it impossible to make money on a condo? No, it can happen if you have a fabulous apartment that has been tastefully decorated, is desirably located and offers features that are not available for love or money anywhere else. But as a general rule, in today's competitive real estate market, Florida condos are for keeping.

CHAPTER 19

The Mortgage Maze:

HOW TO GET THROUGH IT SO IT DOESN'T COST AN "A.R.M." AND A LEG

Webster defines a maze as "a confusing, intricate network of winding pathways with one or more blinding alleys." When referring to today's mortgage market, I couldn't have said it better myself, Noah.

Trying to figure out what lenders are selling exactly, and how that compares with the neighborhood bank, baffles even the most educated among us. If you think about it, the banks are the new Baskin-Robbins of money. They offer at least 31 ways to borrow, many of which look and sound the same, but are not. No wonder many of us long for the good old days when you could walk into your local savings and loan, apply for a 30-year fixed mortgage, and walk out with a toaster and a deal!

You know what happened? Interest rates went through the roof in the late 1970's, hitting double digits and then an unthinkable 21% in many places around the country. Most banks were locked into 6% and 7% long-term mortgages and took a bath. Particularly when all those homeowners with low-interest, assumable mortgages sold their homes and passed the savings on to the new buyers. Not that you ever had to attend a charity ball for a banker, but you know what they say about being fooled once...

As a result, today's mortgage market is more like a supermarket. The bank's newspaper ads are as crowded and confusing as your favorite grocers, shouting out this week's specials. 1-year Adjustables with no income checks. Convertibles. 15 year. 30 year. No points mortgages.

What does it all mean? Before you start shopping for financing, you need to find out. Mortgages are usually the single-biggest personal debts incurred in a lifetime. It's the wrong time to leave the choice to "eenie meenie miney mo." A mere quarter percent difference in deals could cost you thousands and thousands of dollars over the life of the loan. After you've reviewed this chapter, decide which arrangement makes the most sense for your budget, your lifestyle and your nearness to retirement. Then, just as if you were planning a trip to the supermarket, make a list of what you've decided to buy. Maybe it's a 30-year fixed rate or a 5-year adjustable. Whatever your decision, write it down and bring your list with you. You all know what happens when you don't make up a shopping list—you end up spending a lot more than you need to and come home with things you don't want.

LESSON NUMBER ONE IN MORTGAGE SHOPPING

The place where most people run into trouble when comparison shopping is that they ignore the fine print in mortgage advertisements. I'm here to tell you that even if you have to invest in a new pair of reading glasses so you can see all the information in minuscule type, do it! Otherwise you won't have the slightest clue what you're really going to pay until after you've agreed to pay it.

You see, most consumers compare lenders by their advertised interest rates. But that's only half the story. There's a little asterisk at the bottom of most ads which indicates the APR, or Annual Percentage Rate. The APR equals the advertised interest rate plus all the extras: points, service charges, origination fees, mortgage insurance and other charges. Similar to unit prices you see on supermarket shelves, use the APR for comparison shopping. How can the banks get away with promoting what looks like a bargain basement interest rate when it's not the total cost? Marketers are very clever in claiming that these additional charges aren't interest payments *per se*. They are added expenses for the privilege of using the lender's money. Well they can call them whatever they like, but those fees are a very large part of the cost of borrowing money. And every month when you pay the APR, you'll be reminded of just how much.

SPEAKING OF POINTS...

Ah yes. The dreaded "P" word for mortgage shoppers is points—the prepayment of interest that buyers pay at the closing. Each point you pay is equivalent to 1% of the loan. Thus, if you're borrowing $100,000 and are being charged 2 points by the lender, you will pay an additional $2000 just for the privilege of doing business with the bank. Remember that this charge is separate from the down payment and other closing costs.

The big question in trying to figure out which bank is offering the best deal is which is better: a 9.75% interest rate with 1 point? Or, a 9.5% loan with 3 points? According to HSH Associates of Butler, NJ, the nation's largest publisher of mortgage information, it all depends on the prevailing interest rates and the length of the mortgage commitment. Here's a sample from their comparison chart of *effective interest rates*.

As the next chart indicates, it's slightly cheaper to borrow at 9.5%, paying 3 points at closing, than it is to pay 9.75% with 1 point at closing. This is particularly

30-Year Term

Interest Rates	Points			
	1%	2%	3%	4%
9.00%	9.11	9.23	9.34	9.46
9.25%	9.36	9.48	9.60	9.72
9.50%	9.62	9.73	9.85	9.98
9.75%	9.87	9.99	10.11	10.23

true if you plan to own the home over a long period of time.

What you should keep in mind, however, is that the average American stays in a house for around 7 years. If you are pretty certain that the first place you buy in Florida will only serve your needs for five years or less, then it's better to reverse strategies. You'll come out ahead if you opt to pay the higher interest rate with less points.

For more information on HSH's services and their other comparisons, refer to page 210.

Now let's move on to the different mortgage options.

FIXED RATE MORTGAGES

These are the granddaddies of the mortgage market—the conventional 15- or-30 year loans that remain constant insofar as interest rates and monthly payments are concerned. If you're paying $1250 a month in principal and interest in 1989, you'll be paying the same $1250 a month in 1999, and so on.

The biggest advantage of fixed-rate loans is that they protect consumers against rising interest rates. Of course, should they drop significantly, fixed-rate loans are not irrevocable. You can always opt to refinance. In the meantime, however, with a fixed-rate mortgage, you can't be asked to pay a sudden increase due to a fluctuating market index. In addition, once the loan is signed, you'll never have to go through the closing process again, unless you decide to. No more applications, approvals, points, closing costs, etc.

The difference between a 30-year and 15-year commitment is that with the shorter term loan, you'll pay a quarter to a half percent less in interest rates while saving 15 years' interest payments. Think of it as 180 big checks you won't have to write! On a $50,000 mortgage, that could amount to savings of over $80,000! Plus, you'll have been accruing equity in the home at a much faster pace, which is ideal for those who are nearing retirement age.

The interesting thing about 15-year mortgages is that most people assume that the monthly payments will be twice as high as a monthly payment on a 30-year loan. Surprisingly it doesn't work that way. Payments on a 15-year loan are usually only 10% to 20% higher. So on that same $50,000 loan, your payments would be another $70 a month. Most people drop that in a single night out!

15-year loans are great not just for people who are close to retirement, but for anyone who would like to surrender a 10%-13% loan. The obvious benefit is that you'll be paying off substantial debt at a much higher interest rate than you're earning on investments. If you're smart about it you'll sock away what would have gone towards reducing the mortgage debt and put the money in an investment that yields 8% or 9%. Then when you do retire, you'll be living free and clear (at least of mortgage payments), you'll have the accumulation of all those years of equity in the house and you'll have your additional investments. If more people had followed this strategy we wouldn't have millions retiring each year whose sole source of income was Social Security!

When shopping for fixed rates, there are two other features you should have on your list. You want a loan that does not penalize you for pre-payment after the first year. In the event that you inherit money, double your income, etc., you should have the choice of paying back the principal on your loan at a faster pace, or to pay off the loan in its entirety. Banks justify penalties for pre-payment because of the loss of potential income they were counting on over a long term period. Pre-payment penalties can run anywhere from several hundred to several thousand dollars, depending on the particular penalty clause and the size of the loan. Please note that Veterans Administration (VA) and Federal Housing Authority (FHA) loans have never had pre-payment penalties.

Secondly, the ideal set-up is to arrange for an assumable mortgage that has no pre-payment penalty clause. This way, should you decide to sell at some point, you'll have a tremendous benefit to pass along to the buyer, particularly if interest rates have risen since you took out the loan. With this kind of ace in your pocket, you'd be in a strong position to get your asking price.

I'm very much in favor of fixed-rate mortgages for all the reasons mentioned, and feel that although there are exceptions to the rule, for most people, they are still the best mortgage option around. Locking in a bank at a fair interest rate on a large loan offers not only ongoing tax benefits but the possibility of paying a lot less for the use of money, compared to the prevailing interest being charged in, say, 10 years.

ADJUSTABLE RATE MORTGAGES (ARMs)

Adjustables are the new kids in town, brought in by the banks as a way to prevent the severe losses they took when they were lending money at 6%-8% while paying 11% to 13% on CDs and money market accounts.

The way ARMs work is that the interest rate you pay, and therefore the monthly payment you make, is adjusted at regular intervals based on a fluctuating index. For example, a 1-year ARM index might be tied to the price of one-year U.S. Treasury Securities, or to Ginnie Maes. If the index moves up, so does the interest you pay. If they go down, you pay less—for that period only.

This is not to say that if interest rates go up by 5%, you'll suffer accordingly. In order to ensure consumer acceptance, adjustable mortgages do have caps on the interest rates that can be charged. There are usually two caps built in. The first is on the amount that can be adjusted annually; the second is the total adjustment that can be made over the life of the loan. A typical cap is 2% a year, with a 6% life cap. This means that interest rates can move either up or down by 2 points from the index in the contract year, and no more than 6 points up or down through the span of the loan. If you take out a 1-year Adjustable Rate Mortgage, your loan payments will fluctuate on the anniversary of the loan each year. Three-year ARMs adjust every three years at the anniversary of the loan, and so on. Some ARMs adjust every six months, others at 5-year intervals. Read the fine print.

The major selling point of the ARM loans is that their initial interest rates are 1% to 3% below a typical fixed rate loan. Often you'll see ads that promote a 7.25% 1st year guarantee, compared with a 9.5% rate for fixed mortgages. Lower interest rates and lower monthly payments make ARMs ideal for people in one of the following situations:

- You are certain that your income will rise steadily over the next 5 to 10 years and can easily keep pace with any subsequent rate increases. Professionals who are just starting their businesses or practices offer the best example of people who can count on making more money each year.

- You are certain that you'll sell the house within 5 years of buying it.

- You are in the process of selling off other real estate and will be able to use the proceeds from the sale to pay off this new mortgage early.

For many of you who are moving down to Florida, either of these situations might occur. For example, a lot of people relocate to an area of the state, buy a condo or home, but aren't positive they're going to like it. Maybe a year later they discover a different community, or a different region of the state that is better suited to them.

Or, maybe they've come down to Florida and have plans to start a business. Until such time when the business generates enough cash flow, a year or two later, they're going to need the lowest possible mortgage payments. With an adjustable rate mortgage, the odds are in their favor that they'll have paid less than they would have with a fixed rate during this short time period.

THE "DOWN" SIDE OF ADJUSTABLE RATE MORTGAGES

Many people are so excited about the prospect of paying less up front that they neglect to acknowledge many of the inherent risks with ARMs on a long-term basis. The best example is that they fail to consider what happens when interest rates do go up, and they most certainly will at some point in the life cycle of the loan. The monthly payments are going to come along for the ride, making things a little bumpier than you'd like.

There are a number of features of ARMs that you want to be aware of and compare. Any one of these could turn the monthly payments into problems.

The first is that different banks use different market indexes. I mentioned earlier that their interest rates could be tied to T-bills, treasury securities, etc. (it just has to be a public index that the lender doesn't control). Thus, when comparison shopping, the comparison is only relevant to the APR at the moment. In other words, on the loan's anniversary, if you didn't go with the bank whose mortgages were tied to the 6-month T-Bill, and their interest rates are now lowest, you'll pay more than those who chose the bank tied to 1-year T-Bills. From year to year, it's a horse race, but that's the name of the game.

Which index historically has allowed for the lowest interest rates? Again, according to HSH Associate's extensive studies, it appears that the 6-month T-Bill has been remarkably consistent in its good performance for borrowers in comparison to the index values of 1; 3; and 5-year Treasury Securities, and the NMCR index (National Mortgage Contract Rate). Ranked second in good performance would be the 1-year Treasury Securities.

When shopping for adjustables, another important comparison point is the bank's margins over index. Many people aren't aware that lenders adjust their rates not only against a financial index, but against a separate "profit" margin. This margin is extra interest charged by the lenders to cover their administrative "expenses." An example of this is a loan that starts out at 9%. At adjustment time, the lender's index might be at 7.87%. But an added 2.5% for "margins" could be tacked on, making your new interest rate 10.37%. What this means exactly is that *even if interest rates did not fluctuate by 2.5% by the anniversary date, you'll pay an increased amount anyway (or whatever the maximum cap is in your contract).* At a minimum, you can count on an annual cap of 2%, which in this case would have resulted in an interest rate of 9.87%.

Finally, one of the biggest down sides of *some* ARMs contracts is something called negative amortization. This occurs when your total monthly payment is insufficient to cover the amount of interest due because the bank is limited to a 2% cap per year. If the banks can't cover their costs for that year, they'll just make up the difference at the end of the loan. It's possible that your last payment could represent the entire difference between what you paid and what the bank had to pay for the money. That could be a whopper.

Lenders argue that negative amortization keeps the customer's monthly payments lower and more stable. This is true, but be aware that it increases your overall indebtedness. Make sure you understand how your bank handles this situation before you sign on the dotted line.

CAN THOUSANDS OF PEOPLE BE WRONG?

In spite of the numerous risks, consumers appear to be jumping on the ARM bandwagon in a big way. *Money Magazine* recently reported that 60% of all new mortgages approved are adjustable rate and that over the last four years, these borrowers have come out ahead of those with fixed-rate loans. They cite a $100,000, 30-year ARM tied to the one-year T-bill taken out in February, 1985. These mortgage holders have paid $37,500 in interest, compared with $50,700 paid by those with fixed-rate commitments at the then rate of 12.77% interest. It represents a savings of $13,200. (February, 1989).

To them and to you I say, the jury is still out. It's understandable that consumers have had a call to ARMS because of lower interest rates and lower monthly payments in the first years. And for the past few years, as *Money Magazine* pointed out, they legitimately have offered lower interest rates than fixed mortgages. But remember we could be talking about 30 years of payments here.

What people don't realize is that over the life of the loan, they will probably end up with several interest rate cycles which favor the bank in rising interest rate markets. The impact of those increased costs on the consumer could easily offset any savings achieved at the beginning of the loan. When an adjustable rate mortgage is paid off, it's possible that borrowers will have ended up paying an average of 11% or 12% for the use of the money. In comparison, at the time they might have been able to lock in a 10% rate with a fixed-rate mortgage.

Similar to that first bite of ice cream, let's see how good ARMs look after consumers get a taste of higher interest rates. As of this writing, Fannie Mae announced that the average interest rate on one-year adjustable mortgages had risen to the highest level in more than 2½ years. It was at a record 8.58% (January 20, 1989). Is this a trend? It's too difficult to say, and that's why for many people, ARMs are too risky to consider.

A good client of mine said to me, "Don't worry Lee. If interest rates get out of hand, I'll just refinance." When a client tells me not to worry, that's when I worry. Refinancing is a great expense both in time and money. It involves going through the shopping and application process, having a new appraisal done, going through a credit check, waiting and hoping for an approval, paying attorney's fees, plus paying the extra points and closing costs, etc.

More importantly if you have to refinance your ARM it's going to be because interest rates have risen steadily. Even if you respond quickly in arranging for refinancing, you're not going to lock in as good a rate as you would have if you'd taken a fixed rate mortgage when you were first in the market for money. In fact, the new rates you lock in could end up costing an "arm" and a leg. Obviously, the best time to refinance is when fixed rates are low so that you can lock in the least-costly interest payments. Again, however, if an adjustable mortgage bought you time, and gave you the chance to earn more money, you might feel that paying higher rates was worth it. But most of us don't own a crystal ball, and with ARMs, it's hard to predict exactly how much you'll pay in the end to pay less up front.

So who are adjustables good for? They're great for the banks, that's for sure. It means when interest rates rise, they can pass the increase along to the borrowers.

THE CONVERTIBLE ARM

Given the potential downsides of ARMs to those who *do* intend to stay in a home for the long haul, lenders have devised a less risky strategy for getting the best of both adjustables and fixed-rate mortgages. It's called Convertible Adjustable Rate Mortgages, and just as the name indicates, it allows borrowers to take advantage of lower interest rates at the start of the loan and then have the option to convert to a fixed rate mortgage, usually between the 13th and 60th month. The ability to straddle both sides of the fence not only buys you time but gives you a great deal more flexibility once you're situated and have had time to grow confident in your earnings in a new job or business.

The option costs the borrower approximately 1% of the loan plus a few hundred dollars in administrative fees for converting. This decision to go to a fixed rate is at the discretion of the borrower, not the lender. And 1% is a small price to pay for getting in and staying in the real estate market, where the potential for appreciation is greater than most other types of investments.

Other Mortgage Options

You may have heard about other mortgage offerings, including Balloon Payments, Graduated Payment Mortgages (GPMs), Growing Equity Mortgages (GEMs), Shared Equity Mortgages (SEMs) and Interest Rate Buydowns. Not all are available in every market and at every bank, so if you're interested, plan to let your fingers do a lot more walking when you make your comparison calls. Here is a brief overview of these specialized mortgage arrangements:

- *Balloon Payment Mortgages*...These are best for people who want very short-term mortgages at fixed rates. In a 3/30 balloon mortgage, for example, you'd pay the loan for three years, usually at the rate you'd be paying off a 30-year loan. But at the end of the third year, you'd have to pay off the entire balance of the mortgage. Some of you will recall Hollywood's references to balloon mortgages in the 1920s where the damsels in distress couldn't pay off the balance of their loans and had to contend with nasty villains as a result. Instead of tying you to the railroad tracks, many lenders today will opt to renew the mortgage at the prevailing rates. However, if it's very likely that you won't be able to pay off the balance at the end of the balloon, be sure that the lender *will* renew with a *rollover guarantee*, or don't sign. Typical balloon terms are 3, 5, 10, and 15 years based on a 30- or 40-year payout.

- *Graduated Payment Mortgages*...Basically this is a fixed-rate loan, but with lower monthly payments at first. Payments increase by a set amount each year, usually for up to 5 years, and then level off. Many of these loans have negative amortization built in, which in effect, defers a portion of the interest and recaptures it later in the form of principal. In the end, you do pay more, as well as having to pay a larger down payment. However, GPMs typically require lower incomes to qualify.

- *Growing Equity Mortgages (GEMs)*...This option allows the homeowner to build up equity in their home at an accelerated pace while paying less for the loan overall. This is accomplished by increasing monthly payments annually, either for the first few years or for the life of the loan. Similar to 15-year fixed-rate mortgages, it gives you greater investment flexibility when the loan is paid off, while being able to live "rent free" for however long you own the home.

- *Shared Equity Mortgages (SEMs)...* If you can't swing the down payment, a portion of the monthly payments, or both, many lenders will allow you to rely on an investor who will pay these for you. It's usually a close family member. You buy the house together, and the investor pays the agreed portion. The borrower then goes to pay property taxes, insurance, etc. In exchange for the investor's generosity, they get a share of the property (it might be 50%) as well as some of the tax benefits. The borrower also gets equity in the home, which otherwise would have been impossible. The contract usually allows you to buy out the investor at any time. The tax law implications of this arrangement are tricky, so be sure to get a good attorney who knows the ins and outs of SEMs.

- *Interest Rate Buydowns...* This method allows for lower mortgage payments for the first few years without negative amortization. The most common approach is to have the seller, the buyer or a third party deposit a certain amount of money into a non-interest-bearing account at the closing. Monthly payments are then made, with some of the payment coming from the buyer and the balance from the account. The interest rate increases around 1% a year for four years, or until the buydown account is empty. People can qualify for this type of loan with a lower income. This type of incentive is commonly offered by builders who need to give buyers an inducement to use their services.

TAKE THIS QUIZ AFTER EACH BANK COMPARISON

The National Home Builders Association suggests that you ask yourself the following questions each time you evaluate a bank's mortgage story:

1. Do I understand how it works?

2. Can I afford the monthly payments?

3. If the monthly payments change, are increases in my income likely to be large enough to cover the increased mortgage payments?

4. How often will payment changes occur?

5. If any of the interest payment can be deferred and added to the mortgage principal (negative amortization), will I be living in an area where property is likely to appreciate enough to cover the additional debt?

6. Do I understand how the annual and life time caps on the adjustable rate mortgage will effect my total costs?

WHAT ABOUT WORKING WITH MORTGAGE BROKERS?

Often after I've explained mortgage options to a client they throw up their hands and decide to let a mortgage broker deal with the shopping headaches. They feel that the process is too complicated and cumbersome, and besides, it's always nicer to have someone else to blame if the deal that's struck doesn't turn out so great.

Are mortgage brokers the answer to better, safer commitments? Unfortunately there is no black or white answer. It really depends on the particular broker, their reputation and staying power in the business, and the relationships they have with the local lenders. Many times if you apply for a mortgage at the bank where you are currently a depositor, it's possible to get an "insiders discount," which could be better than the deal a broker gets for you.

On the other hand, working with a professional who knows the intricacies of this complex aspect of financing could well work to your advantage. Nothing can compare with their previous experience with various lenders, their knowledge of mortgage trends, and perhaps the volume discount they can offer because of the amount of business they turn over to certain banks.

Therein lies the catch, however. You need to have confidence that you're not being turned on to a particular bank because of a relationship that benefits the broker. It's like anything else. You've got to do your homework. If you can find a broker who's been referred by family or friends and you think they can arrange for better financing than you could on your own, it could be a smart move.

If you'd like to check out a broker's background, check with the Mortgage Banker's Association of Florida. In Orlando, their number is (407) 423-9502. If they are a member in good standing, that should tell you something about their credibility.

Another option, if you'd like to do the shopping yourself but with some impressive weaponry in hand, is purchasing the *Homebuyer's Mortgage Kit* from HSH Associates. They will provide you a with a whole host of user-friendly tips on negotiating the best deal for yourself, along with updated comparisons of interest rates, terms, down payments, points, lender margins, indexes, application fees, number of days the bank will lock in quoted rates and much more information—on every major lender in the area of Florida you're interested in. Call them at (201) 838-3330 for more information. Or write to HSH Associates, 1200 Route 23, Butler, NJ 07405.

THE IMPORTANCE OF THE WRITTEN WORD

It's unfortunate today, but a handshake isn't enough to clinch a deal. After you've gone through the trouble of negotiating a satisfactory mortgage commitment, the most important step is getting everything confirmed in a letter: interest rates, points, the length of time they'll lock in the offer, etc. Also, you want to know what will happen if the lending rates go down by the time you're ready to close. Finally, make sure that letter is signed by a bank officer. A handshake is nice as long as the written commitment is in your other hand.

CHAPTER 20

Tax Breaks And
Tax Rates For
Florida Homeowners

F lorida offers a valuable tax break for homeowners called the Homestead Tax Exemption. It's a large deduction that entitles permanent residents to deduct the first $25,000 of their home's assessed value from their real property tax.

In order to qualify, you must be a permanent, legal resident. The emphasis here is on legal and permanent. This is not a break for snowbirds. Secondly, you must both purchase *and* occupy a home in Florida by January 1 of the year in which you are applying for the tax exemption.

To receive the exemption, homeowners must file an application with their county's Property Appraiser by March 1 of the tax year. This office can also let you know if you are eligible for the additional $500 homestead exemptions available to widowed, blind and disabled residents.

A new ruling for veterans has also gone into effect. If due to your connection in the armed services, you are a totally permanently disabled veteran, or a disabled veteran confined to a wheelchair, and you have been honorably discharged, you will be exempt from paying any property taxes at all.

PROPERTY TAX ASSESSMENTS

Property taxes are not assessed by the state, but by the cities, counties and special districts. Assessments are made on each individual property, with location and real value the basis on which total millage rates are calculated. "Millage" is the rate at which property is taxed for *ad valorem*, or valuation purposes. One mill equals one dollar of taxes for every one thousand dollars of value.

County taxes cover all government and school board operating expenses, as well as services provided in special districts. For example, if the total countywide millage rate for Broward County is 14.9142, as it was in 1988, then the property tax would be $14.91 for every thousand dollars of value. If your home in Broward County was valued at $175,000, you would deduct $25,000 of value for the homestead exemption and then calculate property taxes from there. Using the millage rate of 14.9142, annual property taxes for the county would amount to $2235. Additionally, most municipalities have their own property tax assessment.

For example, if this Broward County house was located in Ft. Lauderdale proper, there would be an extra millage rate of 4.4326, or approximately $665. In total that would equal $2900.

1988 County And City Millage Rates

Just as a means of comparison, here is a breakout of 1988 millage rates so that you can estimate your annual property tax liability. Obviously you should check with the county tax assessor and/or your real estate agent to confirm the most current rates before you buy.

To calculate property taxes of your permanent legal residence, first deduct $25,000 from the price of the home. Then take the county millage rate and divide by 1000. Multiply that amount times the appraised value of the home. For example:

1) $14.9142 \times 1000 = .0149$ or 14.9%
2) 14.9% $\times$ $150,000 = $2235

Add the city tax to the county tax, and that's your total property assessment for the year. Listed below are 21 of Florida's largest counties and their millage rates, followed by various city millage rates within these counties.

When you add county and city millage rates, it appears that Miami Beach, Miami, Gainesville, and Jacksonville are the most heavily-taxed areas in the state, respectively.

Municipality/Millage Rate

Alachua County: 19.1320		Broward County: 14.9142	
Gainesville	5.7310	Coral Springs	3.4092
		Deerfield Beach	5.4291
		Ft. Lauderdale	4.4326
		Hallandale	4.3064
Brevard County: 14.5795		Pembroke Pines	3.1014
Cocoa	4.3600	Plantation	1.9900
Cocoa Beach	3.6030	Sunrise	4.0000
Melbourne	3.3720	Tamarac	3.1890
Titusville	3.8640		

Municipality/Millage Rate (cont'd.)

Collier County: 12.8887

Naples	1.2229

Dade County: 16.8865

Coral Gables	5.2470
Hialeah	7.6000
Miami	9.5995
Miami Beach	9.9660
Homestead	8.4816
N. Miami	6.5420

Duval County: 20.1992

Jacksonville	0.5072
Jacksonville Beach	3.2313

Hillsborough County: 17.0325

Plant City	4.5471
Tampa	5.6890

Indian River County: 12.8399

Vero Beach	2.5000

Lee County: 13,7320

Ft. Myers	4.0000

Leon County: 15.7280

Tallahassee	2.9000

Manatee County: 15.0898

Bradenton	2.5255

Marlon County: 12.1300

Ocala	5.0800

Orange County: 12.2439

Orlando	5.0666
Winter Park	3.7200

Osceola County: 13.9636

Kissimmee	4.2953
St. Cloud	4.1790

Palm Beach County: 14.2584

Boca Raton	3.1224
Boynton Beach	8.1498
Delray Beach	5.3306
Jupiter	3.0000
Lake Worth	6.4191
Palm Beach	4.4483
W. Palm Beach	8.1401

Pasco County: 17.4860

Port Richey	3.0000
Zephyrhills	6.2000

Pinellas County: 14.8675

Clearwater	5.1000
Largo	3.2200
St. Petersburg	8.0517
Tarpon Springs	5.6406

Polk County: 13.4070

Lakeland	2.7000
Winter Haven	4.9000

Sarasota County: 12.5603

Long Boat Key	1.9288
Sarasota	4.0630

Seminole County: 12.6542

Altamonte Springs	3.1460
Sanford	5.8459

Volusia County: 14.9285

Daytona Beach	4.9830
Ormond Beach	2.0950

SECTION

IV

The Big Move

CHAPTER 21

Moving 101:
KEEPING YOUR POSSESSIONS AND YOUR SANITY WHEN YOU MOVE TO FLORIDA

Remember your school days when your teachers told you to put your thinking caps on? Guess what? If you're planning to hire a moving company to haul your most prized possessions to Florida, the first thing to do is put that old thinking cap back on. Only this time you'll need to put your "movers" cap on top of your thinking cap because if you hope to get there unscathed by the experience, you're going to have to THINK LIKE A MOVER.

You're going to have to learn how interstate movers arrive at their estimates (let alone their destinations). You'll need to understand the special services they offer and how they think when it comes to handling damage claims. Most important, you're going to have to learn their language—"Movespeak," so to speak. Because when you can talk in their terms, you'll be able to move mountains (not that moving your entire home won't be enough of a hassle).

So you say you don't want to bother with all of this? You don't need to take a course in moving? If 40 million Americans can change addresses every year, how hard can it be? Trust me when I tell you that an interstate move can be very tricky. Not to mention incredibly expensive if you don't know what you're doing. If you're still convinced that you can handle this on your own, remember that confidence is the feeling you have right before you understand the problem!

What does this chapter cover? Basically everything you'll need to know about making an interstate move. Things to look for when selecting a moving company. Understanding moving costs. Liability coverage and how to make it through the claim process. Packing. Storage. How to transport your cars to Florida. Even the most recent performance records of some of the country's oldest and largest long-distance movers.

Before we get started, please make a note to send away for a very important free booklet from the Interstate Commerce Commission, the government agency that oversees long distance carriers. It's called "When You Move: Your Rights and Responsibilities." Write to:

Interstate Commerce Commission
12th & Constitution Ave.
Washington, D.C. 20423

Basic Transportation Costs

The first thing people want to know when they make the decision to move is "what's it gonna cost?" Unfortunately there's no simple answer. It's like deciding you want to buy a car and asking a dealer about price. Do you want it stripped or with options? Do you want a luxury sedan or a fuel-efficient compact car? The questions go on and on until a number is arrived at. So it goes with moving. That's why the best way to get a fix on moving costs is to understand the myriad of possible charges that can be factored into your estimate.

When starting to calculate the actual cost of moving the contents of your home to Florida, the first thing the moving company will do is establish the approximate mileage between your new and old homes. This is determined by mapping out the shortest distance between points A and points B on *highways that are useable for truck travel.* With respect to costs, obviously the farther you move the more money it will run, but exactly how much depends on the mover who's providing the estimate. Rates will vary by mover (some discount by as much as 45%) and by season (June through September is prime time and generally more costly).

The next factor in determining moving costs is the total weight of your contents. Are you moving 500 lbs. (usually the minimum) or 5,000 lbs.? That's a tough one for the average person to figure out. The best way to determine weight is to have several movers come to your home and give you their best estimates. Or as I like to call them, their "SWAGS," for "Sophisticated Wild Ass Guesses."

In all fairness, these guys are pretty good at assessing contents. They can size up a kitchen, for example, by looking at the number of major appliances being shipped, the volume of dishes and glassware, the size of the table and the number of chairs, etc. They also know that if they see a home library on par with your local branch, a grand piano, and a wide screen TV, they're dealing with thousands more pounds than the average shipment. They'll calculate their prices accordingly, based on every 100 lbs. moved. For example, on the facing page is a breakout of the average price per 100 lbs. moved in 1987, taking both distance and weight into consideration. As you can see, when the distance increases, the rate per 100 lbs. increases. That is offset by the increase in weight, which actually reduces the price per 100 lbs. Since you won't have any control over the distance between your old and new homes, the best way to keep costs down is by having the biggest garage sale of your life so you ship a minimum of household goods.

Distance	Total Weight	Price per 100 lbs.
300 mi.	2000-4000 lbs.	$31.35
300 mi.	4000-8000 lbs.	$24.60
300 mi.	8000-12,000 lbs.	$21.30
600 mi.	2000-4000 lbs.	$41.00

Source: Household Goods Carrier Bureau

Even with a reduced load, however, weight and distance only help establish the *basic* cost of transportation. Basic transportation is defined as: 1) having use of the mover's truck; 2) taking the household goods out of your house and loading them on to the truck; 3) driving to your new home, and 4) dismantling the goods upon arrival and reassembling everything inside the new home.

Now comes the part where you discover that moving is like eating in an expensive restaurant where everything is "a la carte." Your entree will cost "X," but if you want a plate and silverware, be prepared to ante up.

Additional Transportation Charges (ATCs)

If your move originates and/or terminates in a high density area, there will very likely be additional transportation charges, or ATCs. This means if you're making that ever-popular move from New York to Florida, you're likely to be charged more.

Here's why. Let's say you're going from Brooklyn to Boca. The first stop is your old home. The moving company automatically assumes that the driver will have to contend with snarled traffic jams, construction delays, inaccessible entrances and other hassles associated with being in the New York area. To compensate the driver for lost time, you might pay as much as an additional $2.40 per 100 lbs. Incidentally, this applies not only to the five boroughs of New York, but Long Island (Nassau and Suffolk), Dutchess, Orange, Putnam, Rockland, Ulster, and Westchester counties as well as Fairfield County, CT. Some movers charge an additional .50 per 100 lb. charge (give or take a few cents) to go from New York to Florida as a way to compensate for an almost certain empty van on the return trip. This is due to the fact that there are a great many more people moving south than north.

These two ATCs will fluctuate by long distance carrier, and if you are able to hire one that discounts, you may not be charged extra at all. Or, if your estimate comes in even higher than I've indicated, it could be attributed to the fact that a 4% to 5% rate increase was approved by the Interstate Commerce Commission and put into effect in fourth quarter, 1989. Remember that rates are very much affected by the time of year you move. If you reserve a carrier in the height of the season (between June and September), the mover is likely to be so inundated with shipments, he'll be less inclined to negotiate a price.

Accessorial Costs

Besides basic transportation and additional transportation charges, long distance moving companies also have what they call assessorial or additional service charges. Examples of these include moving in and/or out of an apartment building, packing services, guaranteed pick-up and delivery, expedited service, exclusive use of a vehicle, and liability protection.

APARTMENT BUILDINGS

Let's start with apartment building charges, since so many people do move either in and/or out of one when going from a major metropolitan area to Florida. When movers have to deal with apartment houses, they feel entitled to additional compensation because they are forced to contend with elevators, extra stairs, and long carries, also known as excessive distances. This is when your apartment is far away from the nearest stairs or elevators and/or everything has to be hauled to a loading dock or to the van—which unfortunately had to be parked down the block. The theory is that all of this "shlepping" back and forth is time-consuming and adds extra wear and tear on the men. To remunerate them for the fact that they can't just park in the driveway of your private home, they might charge you anywhere from .65 to $1.05 per 100 lbs. for every 50 ft. they have to go after the first 75 ft.

Next, it's time to look at your "flights" situation. Yes, that's right. Unless you live on the ground floor, you could find that you'll have to pay for every floor the movers have to climb. In the New York area, you might pay as much as $1.05 per 100 lbs. for every flight above the ground floor. If the men must use an elevator, you could be charged as much as $1.45 per 100 lbs. for every floor. That's because access to New York area elevators is considered more restrictive, more crowded, slower, etc.

Should you be moving into an apartment building in Florida, the additional costs for stairs and elevators are less than New York rates. For every flight of stairs after the first floor, you could pay around .65 per 100 lbs. per flight. Elevator rides cost $1.20 per 100 lbs. per flight. "Woe is you" if you fell in love with a penthouse apartment!

Again, if you are leaving and/or moving into an apartment building, there's hardly anything you can do about it, so you might as well shop the competition and see which mover gives you the fairest shake.

Packing Services

When talking to movers about their packing services, remember that there are three aspects to consider. First is the packing materials you can purchase—dishpacks, wardrobes and other sturdy cartons. Whatever you can say about movers, they certainly have better boxes to offer than the local liquor store and supermarket. For your fragile and valuable items, they are definitely worth the money.

Next comes labor services. If you want the movers to pack your belongings at your old residence, they'll quote you a price. Likewise, if you want them to unpack your cartons at your new home, that's another charge. By the way, unpacking consists of unwrapping items and placing them on a table. It doesn't mean that the movers will actually set up your shelves and arrange your bookcases. Still, if you want to get settled as quickly as possible, having the movers unpack is a big time saver. Packing services seem to intrigue families who are moving. The prospect of not having to fold a single glass into an old newspaper or get newsprint all over your hands when you unpack is a wonderful fantasy! If you are uncertain as to whether packing services are worth your consideration, here are some things you should know.

If you pack yourself, you could have a difficult time getting reimbursed in the event there are damages. That is because the mover can say in no uncertain terms you did a poor packing job and that is the cause for the breakage. This does not mean you will have no recourse; you most certainly will, and we'll get into what to do in case you do have claims later on. On the other hand, if the mover did the packing in the mover's packing cartons and there is damage, they can't very well blame you. That means you can count on a reimbursement commensurate with the terms of your contract. The bottom line is that packing services are probably well worth their cost both in terms of convenience and claims. Remember also that reliable movers are known for their expert packing capabilities. They do it every day, so they should be good at it!

In terms of anticipating the costs of packing, it's virtually impossible without a mover's estimate. That's because it does not only depend on how much needs to be packed, how fragile the items are, etc., but also depends on your particular county's labor rates. Only when the moving company comes in to give you an estimate can you get a specific answer. The mover will refer to his tariff (list of prices, including a county-by-county breakdown of labor rates) and calculate a price based on that plus your particular shipment.

Storage Costs

If the thought of paying for every flight of stairs or elevator ride hasn't convinced you to have the biggest garage sale of your life, then maybe understanding storage costs will.

Unfortunately, storage can be a necessary evil under more circumstances than you can imagine. Often people will be forced to give up possession of their home to new owners before their Florida home is ready for occupancy or, an apartment lease may expire before the Florida apartment is available.

In other instances, you may be delayed in getting to Florida and will be unable to meet the van when they arrive. When this happens, the mover is within his rights to put your entire shipment in storage. It happens more often than you think, even with the most advance planning. That's why you should build storage costs, even for a few days, into your moving budget. Right off the bat you should know that like the price of everything else, storage costs less in Florida, to the tune of about 50%.

To calculate storage costs in either location, understand that there are three different charges involved. The first is warehouse handling. This covers the cost of having the mover drop your goods at the storage house's loading dock, move it from the dock to your personal containers and bring the items back to the dock when they're ready to be shipped to your new home.

In New York, warehouse handling costs an average of $3.90 for every 100 lbs. In Brevard County, for example, it costs around $2.50 per 100 lbs. The next cost is for storage itself. In New York, the first day could run you $1.85 per 100 lbs., with each additional day costing around .15 per 100 lbs. In Brevard County, you'll pay about $1.65 per 100 lbs. for the first day and .08 per 100 lbs. for each additional day. The final charge is for pick up and delivery to-and-from storage. In New York the price hovers around $15.00 per 100 lbs., but in Brevard County you can pay around $6.65 per 100 lbs.

Let's take a look at a real live comparison. We'll use a 4000 lb. shipment that gets stored for 30 days in both locations.

	New York	Florida*
WAREHOUSING	$ 156	$100
STORAGE	248	158
PU & DELIVERY	600	266
TOTAL COST	$1004.00	$424.00

*Brevard County

It's obviously expensive, but if you have to store your shipment and you have a choice as to where, do it in Florida.

Other Services To Consider

Most major long distance movers offer a variety of services that are worthy of consideration if they simplify the process for you at a cost you can afford. Here is a brief description of those services.

SPACE RESERVATIONS

If you want to be assured that your shipment is going to be picked up on a certain date, you can request that space be reserved for you on that date. It's just like making a dinner reservation. The big difference is that sometimes movers will charge extra for this privilege, particularly if it's between June and September.

EXPEDITED SERVICE

If you absolutely, positively have to be at your new home by a certain date and that means the moving company will have to speed up the amount of time it normally takes to make the trip, this is called ordering an expedited service. It is an expensive option because it forces the mover to put a special crew on and possibly give you exclusive use of a van in order to make your deadline. Unless there is an important reason for this or your employer is footing the bill, it's better to work within their system.

EXCLUSIVE USE OF A VEHICLE

There are some people do not want their shipment co-mingled with other shipments for fear of delays, screw-ups and other problems associated with sharing space. If this is a problem for you, you can request that your shipment be the only one on the van.

GUARANTEED SERVICE ON OR BETWEEN AGREED DATES

If you can't handle the fact that you won't know precisely what day your mover is going to show up on either end, then you can arrange for guaranteed service which provides that your shipment be picked up, transported and delivered on agreed-upon dates. Then if the mover fails to provide service on the days specified, you'll be entitled to compensation, the amount of which has been established up front, but which probably won't cover all the expenses you incur due to their failure to show up when promised. Some movers do not charge extra for guaranteed delivery.

Liability Protection

In addition to the services we've discussed, there is another important cost factor to consider when planning a move and that is liability coverage. By law, every interstate moving company must assume some liability against damage or loss when agreeing to move your household goods. Unfortunately, as with many types of insurance protection, liability insurance is just as much to help the company protect itself from you as it is the other way around. In other words, the whole idea behind liability insurance is that it limits the liability of the mover if they lose or damage your shipment. Still, it's the only game in town and you definitely want whatever coverage is available to you. Common sense tells you that 99% of the contents in your home were never built to be moved cross country. That's why the moving industry calculates that 25% of all moves report losses or damages. With a one-in-four chance of needing to make a claim, liability coverage is critical. It's what will stand between you and your sanity as you watch the moving van pull off for points south with everything you've ever acquired on board.

As the shipper, you have the right to choose from four different types of liability coverage that are available.

RELEASED VALUE PROTECTION

The first type of liability coverage offers protection, if you'll pardon the

223

expression. In this case, you agree to release your goods to the moving company without making a declaration of their value. Then if there is loss or damage, the mover is only obligated to pay you up to .60 per lb. per article. In other words, the dollar value of the items damaged is irrelevant. The only consideration when calculating reimbursement is weight. It plays like this:

The mover is testing his juggling skills with your favorite reading lamp and discovers he needs more practice. Lots more practice. Unfortunately, there rests the shattered lamp on your driveway. It doesn't matter if the lamp was a priceless heirloom or a free gift from your savings and loan. If it weighed 7 lbs., all you'd get is $4.20 (try not to spend it in all one in place). That would be the mover's maximum liability for the item. The only positive thing to say about this coverage is that the moving company doesn't charge you extra for it. It's part of their cost of doing business. However, if you do agree to this minimal protection, you must indicate your acceptance with your signature on the Bill of Lading (your contract). Otherwise the mover will automatically cover you for the second type of liability, thereby voiding this .60 per pound agreement.

MINIMUM DECLARATION

The second type of coverage available provides for up to $1.25 per pound times the weight of your total shipment. For example, if your goods weigh a total of 4300 lbs., (the average weight of an interstate move), the mover would be liable for losses or damage up to $5375. The reason this kind of coverage is called "minimum declaration" is because it does not allow you to declare a value of less than $1.25 per pound. You have to agree to the minimum $1.25 valuation.

The other big difference between this protection and the "released value" coverage mentioned earlier is that the actual reimbursement you receive is based on the depreciated value of the item that was lost or damaged. The weight does not matter, nor does the original purchase price. What does matter is the amount specified in the mover's list of "released values," which is really a depreciation schedule for thousands of household items. Now if the mover drops your favorite reading lamp and it breaks beyond repair, the moving company will compensate you based on the age of the item. If your lamp was three years old and originally cost $145, the current depreciation might be $75. Thus, you'd get $75. *And of course all of this is contingent on proving the mover's negligence.*

The cost of this "added protection" averages $5 for every $1000 in liability. Thus for our example of 4300 lbs. shipment, which had $5375 of declared value (4300 lbs. × $1.25 per lb.), the liability insurance would cost approximately $27.

LUMP SUM DECLARATION

The third type of liability protection available from the moving company is if you determine that your shipment is valued at more than $1.25 per lb. This way you can declare a specific dollar value, or a "lump sum declaration." The caveat here is that you must declare that the value of your goods exceed $1.25 per lb. times the weight of your shipment.

In other words, you can declare that your 4300 lb. shipment is actually worth $10,000 instead of $5375. By doing so, the mover will charge you the same $5 per $1000 of declared value; it will just cost more. For example, if you determine that your shipment is worth $10,000, you will then pay $50 for this liability protection.

Similar to claims made with the minimum liability coverage, reimbursements are based on the depreciated value of the item(s) lost or damaged. *When trying to determine how much to declare, consider the fact that today's household contents are actually worth an average $3.25 per pound.*

FULL VALUE PROTECTION

Full value protection or replacement cost coverage is exactly what it sounds like. It offers you full replacement value if, due to the mover's negligence, items are damaged or lost and cannot be totally restored. Similar to a homeowners' policy, however, there are deductibles which are taken into consideration, and of course the higher the deductible the lower the premium. The cost of replacement coverage can run around $8.50 per $1000 of valuation. This is the absolute maximum protection you can buy and although the cost may seem pricey, it is highly recommended.

Be aware that when you do buy liability protection from your mover, by law they must provide you with a copy of your policy, or some formal receipt at the time of the purchase. If they don't provide the necessary documentation, they will be held fully liable for any claim that is a result of their negligence.

Adding It All Up

OK, now that you have a feel for all the charges and services, there's still that burning question. How much is this going to set me back?

According to the Household Goods Carriers Bureau, a national trade association for long distance movers, the typical C.O.D. move weighs 4,314 lbs., goes 1167 miles, and costs the shipper a total of $2022. Of this amount, $1587 goes for basic transportation between point A and point B, or $51.15 per 100 lbs. The balance of $435 is for those ATCs or Additional Transportation Charges and accessorial services, such as packing and liability coverage.

When you are getting your estimates, it helps to understand that although each moving company will inevitably give you a different cost quotation, you can pretty much count on the percentage of costs being broken out as such:

Basic Transportation	81% of your cost
Packing Services	9%
Liability Coverage	4%
Accessorial Services	4%
Additional Transportation Services	2%

18 Great Ways To Keep Your Moving Costs Down

Unless you are one of those lucky souls whose company is paying the moving tab, at this point you are probably desperate for ideas on how to bring the costs down. As we discussed earlier, the real expense is in what you move, not where you move.

The key to saving money is to take a good hard look at every room in your house and categorize as many items in that room with one of the following designations:

- SELL IT
- DONATE IT
- TOSS IT
- GIVE IT TO FRIENDS OR FAMILY

Here are some thought starters on items that should be considered for one of these piles:

1. *FURNITURE*...if it's old and you're tired of it, if it's not going to match your new decor...if it won't fit in the new room sizes...it can be cheaper to replace than to move it and reupholster.

2. *TOOLS*...if you're moving from a house to an apartment you probably won't need most of them...and you probably won't have a place to store them either...will you really need the lawn mower anymore?

3. *BOOKS*...just hang on to your most treasured favorites...inquire about the cost of mailing them or shipping UPS vs. moving them.

4. *PLANTS*...In order to move your house plants to Florida, you must get a certificate of inspection issued by a Dept. of Agriculture agent from your home state. Contact the county office for inspection certificates. Under Florida law, your plants are subject to inspection upon arrival. Citrus plants are strictly prohibited.

5. *CLOTHES*...No need for your winter wardrobe anymore...leave it behind with friends and family for winter visits. Anything you know you won't wear again should never see the inside of the van.

6. *RECORDS*...100 record albums weigh around 50 lbs...purge your collection if you never listen to them anymore.

7. *TOYS AND HOBBY EQUIPMENT*...You know what the kids have outgrown. If they want it so badly, let them keep it at their place, or if they're still young and at home introduce them to the concept of charity.

8. *MISCELLANEOUS (JUNK)*...Every home has its own special assortment... you know where it's hiding. Is it worth several hundred dollars to have it follow you?

9. *RUGS*...Unless they're valuable or are desperately needed in your new home...leave them behind.

10. *ARTWORK*...Take only what you absolutely love, is an investment, or has such sentimental value it won't feel like home without it...otherwise say goodbye.

11. *MUSICAL INSTRUMENTS*...If the musicians in your home are no longer active, it's time to part company with their instruments. Pianos and organs are extremely expensive to move across country, require special handling and need tuning after a move.

12. *CHANDELIERS, CEILING FANS, AND LIGHT FIXTURES...These require special handling and cost you before they ever get on the van...it could be cheaper to buy new ones.*

13. *APPLIANCES*...If any one of your major appliances are on the brink of retiring, or have been known to break down in just stationary positions, don't take them...measure your new place first to make sure the refrigerator's not too tall, the washer and dryer will fit in the laundry area, etc. Any major appliances you move (TV antennas, air conditioners, washer and dryers) will need special disconnections and installations in addition to the cost of moving them.

14. *FIREPLACE EQUIPMENT*...It's unlikely your Florida home will have a fireplace...give the people who bought your place a "housewarming" present.

15. *FLAGPOLES, BASKETBALL BACKBOARDS, SLEDS, AND OTHER BULKY STUFF FROM THE GARAGE*...By now you've got the hang of this exercise...you know what to do with these things.

And for no extra charge, here are three other ways you can save some big bucks when you move:

1. *Try to Avoid Moving between June 1 and September 30*...That's when 60% of all moves take place and it's chaos everywhere. To handle the rush, movers operate on a 24-hour schedule. That means slower service and higher prices. If you do have to move then, at least try to avoid the first and last days of the month. That's when leases expire and when many people insist upon leaving. If you can postpone your move so that it takes place during the other ten months

of the year, you'll get a much better price and probably better service as well.

2. *Keep Your Receipts*...you can deduct allowable moving expenses from your income tax if you itemize deductions and complete Form 3903.

3. *Check Your Current Homeowners Policy*...Does it cover your belongings while you move? If it does, there may be no need to buy additional liability coverage from the mover; or perhaps you can add a rider to your policy which protects you during the move. That could be cheaper than the full value protection the mover is offering.

The time to do all this contemplating of what goes and what stays is before you start to get your moving estimates. Don't waste your time or the mover's until you know what will be an accurate reflection of the move itself.

Getting And Understanding The Estimates

When you start to solicit estimates, the first thing to know is that you can request one of two types—binding or non-binding. Some movers still charge for a binding estimate, but that's negotiable.

The most common price quotation is a non-binding estimate. 60% of all estimates fall into this category. By definition, this kind of estimate allows the mover to give you his best educated guess on the cost of your move, including additional transportation charges and special services. However, it does not bind the mover, commit him, or in any way guarantee that that's what you're going to actually end up paying.

In looking at the performance records of the biggest long distance movers, it appears that in at least 20% of the C.O.D. moves, people were ultimately charged a higher price then they were originally quoted. It makes sense that if a mover is not "bound" to a price, he'll be more inclined to appear competitive in order to get the job. In other words, there will be a greater tendency towards lowballing. On the positive side, at least what you do end up paying is an accurate reflection of your shipment because the final cost depends on the actual weight, not an estimated weight (which is often higher). Finally, a non-binding estimate gives you the greatest leeway when it comes to packing. In other words, if you're getting rid of furniture, books and other weighty possessions up until moving day, you'll end up paying for a lighter load than originally estimated.

With a binding estimate, the mover comes to your home, makes an assessment of the job and commits to a final price right then and there. This is great if you don't like surprises, but it could actually slow you up if at the last minute you make changes in what you plan to move. For example, if you didn't tell the mover to include the cost of shipping your piano because you were certain you could sell it, you'll need to get another estimate if that plan fails. If you don't request another estimate, the mover will not be obligated to take the piano because according to the contract you signed, he's not going to be paid to take it. In addition, he might not have room for it

228

if your shipment is co-mingled with others because he planned on your goods taking up only so much space. That's a last minute hassle you don't need. It's why binding estimates are fine for people who are very confident they know exactly what they're taking. Also, keep in mind that binding estimates are based on estimated weight so it's possible that you'll be overpaying. You see, if a mover is going to have to live or die by his price quote, he's going to build enough profit into it to cover himself for certain contingencies.

Regardless of which kind of an estimate you request, both must be put in writing in the Order for Service and the Bill of Lading (contract). Whatever you decide, you shouldn't get an argument from the mover. If a mover balks at giving you a binding estimate or pressures you to reconsider, you should reconsider...the moving company that is.

Finally, when it comes to making fair comparisons, I highly recommend that you get at least 3 different estimates. That should be sufficient enough to give you a sense of price and service. If there is a United Van Lines agent in your area, you should consider having them provide one of the estimates. As part of their service, they have created the "Bette Malone Relocation Service." I don't know who Bette is, but she sure has put together some of the most useful materials, worksheets, and reminders I've seen. The booklets give you step-by-step advice on every aspect of an interstate move. They also have a special booklet for people who are moving upon retirement. In addition, you can call their toll-free number for help with personal questions, needs, etc. This service is free of charge to customers. While I've never personally moved with United, I know that they have an excellent reputation, and in fact, were recently listed as one of the top 100 service companies in the country. It seems like a good place to start.

In addition, you may want to call Terminal Van Lines based in Clearwater. They specialize in Florida moves, but unlike the rest of the industry, they handle the entire transaction by mail. You fill out a form and tell them exactly what you're shipping and they'll get back to you with a firm price. They claim to offer deep discounts and at least from their literature, it looks like they have a very impressive operation. They've been around since 1919! It's probably worth your time to call 1-800-237-2887 and ask to speak to a relocation specialist.

Making A Final Decision About Which Mover To Hire

Given the vast number of personal circumstances that could impact your move, coupled with the options and services you can take advantage of, you absolutely positively must shop for the best deal. Prices and discounts will vary greatly. There are even some long distance movers who give special price breaks to seniors and veterans. However, and this is a big however, you get what you pay for. The cheapest quote may not be the best quote. Movers that lowball their estimates have to save money somewhere and you can be sure that somewhere is in their overall service. "Buying" a mover is like buying any other major purchase. Bargain hard but make your final decision based on price as well as other important criteria, such as these:

- *Personal Recommendations...*Do you actually know someone who used the mover and was pleased with the service? Or did you just get names from the Yellow Pages and are keeping your fingers crossed?

- *Overall Treatment...*How were your questions and concerns addressed when you spoke with representatives of the moving company on the phone and in person? Did you get a sense of genuine interest or were you intimidated, pressured or ignored?

- *Overall Appearances...*An industry spokesman highly recommended that you make an on-site inspection of the mover's offices and warehouse. Why? First to make sure they are where they say they are. There are known cases of movers who have a storefront address but are located in a place where you couldn't find them if you need to. Secondly, when you stop by, you can observe if the office is professionally run, if the warehouse is clean and organized, etc.

- *Better Business Bureau Reports...*It never hurts to check with your local office of the BBB to see if anyone has filed a report on the mover. If it confirms your worst suspicions, keep shopping.

INDEPENDENTS vs. THE LARGE NATIONAL CARRIERS

People like to buy brand names. It gives them confidence when they know there's a big company behind the product. When it comes to selecting a mover, the same theory applies. It's easy to understand why there's a certain comfort level in choosing a Bekins or United Van Lines over Joe's Fast Moving Company. If there are problems with an agent affiliated with a nationally-known company, at least there's another layer of people who can intervene—namely the home office. In addition, the agents who have signed agreements to become affiliated with the nationally-known moving firms have to do more than just keep up appearances. In order to keep their contracts they have to comply with a whole host of rules and regulations. In essence they have a lot at stake so they're not intentionally going to screw up. On the down side, they may not have the flexibility to be as price sensitive as you like because they have to split their profits more ways than the unaffiliated movers.

As for the strictly independent movers, some have excellent reputations and provide better-than-average service. In addition, they might be able to offer you very personal, flexible services at more affordable prices. The trade-off is if you do have problems or claims, you can count on having to spend a lot of money in long distance bills as you try to resolve the problem from your new home. Should you decide to work with a local independent mover, the on-site inspection of their facilities becomes even more important. In addition, you'll want proof that the firm is authorized by the Interstate Commerce Commission and other Interstate authorities to move goods out of state. Otherwise you could find that your insurance coverage is null and void.

Keep in mind that neither the size of the moving company nor claims that it is "bonded," "certified," or "insured" are any indication of reliability. However, if you see that the mover has a CMC (Certified Moving Consultant) designation, you know that at least they completed a program that required on-the-job training and passing a tough exam.

None of this guarantees that if you do your research, everything will go perfectly. What is the moving industry other than men and their machines? They do make mistakes, but if you do your homework and find a mover you have confidence in, you'll rest a lot better. If all of this seems like an awful lot of work, just remember that every tangible possession you hold dear will be put on a truck by complete strangers you'll never see again. If there are serious problems in transit or at your final destination, the only thread you'll be able to hang on to is the caliber of the company behind the name on the truck.

The ICC's Performance Reports

The Interstate Commerce Commission requires that every long distance carrier who transports more than 100 C.O.D. shipments a year report their performance to the ICC. You can request that your mover show you a copy of their performance report (provided they are large enough to have one), if that will make you feel any better. Just to give you an idea of what you would find, here are the results of the 1987 performance reports of the ten-largest long distance movers in the country by rank in various categories.

Ranking by Number of Shipments Per Year

MOVER	RANK	MOVER	RANK
Allied Van Lines	1	Atlas Van Lines	6
United Van Lines	2	Global Van Lines	7
North American	3	Wheaton Van Lines	8
Mayflower Transit	4	American Red Ball	9
Bekins Van Lines	5	National Van Lines	10

NOTE: Each of the 5 largest movers do over 50,000 commercial shipments a year. The majority are corporate transfers. If these carriers did not run professional operations, companies would not hire them to move hundreds of executives every year. Again, numbers do not guarantee quality, but they do indicate a trust and confidence on the part of volume users.

The following chart indicates that although Atlas and Wheaton give the least number of binding estimates, they are accurate in their non-binding estimates more than 95% of the time.

Estimates

MOVER	% of Est. That Were Binding	% of Accurate Non-Binding Est.
Bekins	65%	87.2%
Mayflower	63%	74.6%
Allied	55%	77.0%
American Red Ball	50%	88.3%
National Van Lines	48%	73.2%
North American	46%	53.0%
Global	45%	91.0%
United	40%	64.1%
Atlas	35%	95.5%
Wheaton	21%	97.4%

The on-time records indicated in the next chart are excellent, no doubt because time is money to everyone, but especially to long distance movers. The faster they go, the more moves they can make.

Pick Ups And Deliveries

MOVER	% On-Time Pick Ups	% On-Time Deliveries
North American	96%	92%
Allied	97%	96%
Bekins	99%	96%
United	98%	97%
Mayflower	98%	95%
Atlas	99%	96%
Wheaton	97%	99%
Global	91%	99%
American Red Ball	88%	98%
National	73%	97%

Claims

MOVER	% Of Shipments Not Resulting In Claims of $100 Or More	No. Of Days Between Claim & Settlement
North American	97%	11
Allied Van Lines	96%	13
Bekins	93%	15
United	97%	15
Mayflower	98%	11
Atlas	93%	14
Wheaton	95%	13
Global	96%	13
American Red Ball	95%	15

In looking at this chart, it appears that the biggest movers have relatively few claims due to damage or loss that amount to more than $100. And when they do, the claims are generally settled in two weeks or less from the time the claim is received.

Getting Your Cars To Florida

When most people start to think about moving, at some point the light bulb goes on and they say to themselves, "How are we going to get the car(s) down there?" That doesn't exactly fall under the domain of the mover who's packing up your house. Some end up driving the cars down themselves, happy to have space for special belongings they don't want the movers to haul. Others sell their cars up north and buy new ones in Florida. For those who want to hang on to their cars but don't want to drive themselves, there are two options.

The first is to drive the car to Lorton, VA (12 miles south of Washington, DC) and to load yourself and the car(s) onto Amtrak's Auto Train. 16½ hours later you'll be in sunny Sanford, FL (25 miles north of Orlando). Here's how this works. You pay an average of $69 per adult and $50 per child (ages 2-11) to board the train. Then you pay $108 per car boarded. Rates will vary by month and reservations need to be made a couple of months in advance since space is limited. Trains leave daily at 4:30 PM. Amtrak doesn't put you in sleeper cars, just regular coach seats. But at least you won't have to sleep in the car. For reservations or more information, call their toll-free number at 1-800-872-7245.

If this still turns out to be too much driving for you on either end, there's yet another option: having an auto transport company drive your car to your desti-

233

nation. One such company, Auto Driveaway, has been doing this since 1952, apparently with tremendous success. They move more than 50,000 cars a year, plus other vehicles. Based in Chicago and licensed by the ICC, they have 90 offices covering all 50 states. They even have offices in Canada and Europe. 35% of their business is transporting individual cars (vs. fleets) and they take pride in offering an important service to people who don't have the time or the stamina to undertake a long distance drive.

Here's how this works. You call and tell them you want your car to go from Long Island to Deerfield Beach on such and such a date. They match your request with a licensed driver who is 21 or older and who has called in requesting to drive a car from the New York area to a location in Florida that is close to your final destination. Then they start to do some serious checking. Through a computer search, they look into the person's driving record in all 50 states. They check references at the point of origin *and* destination. If the driver passes muster, he is photographed and fingerprinted. The driver must then post a cash deposit which he will get back if the car is undamaged and arrives on schedule. Incidentally, he is given a set number of days in which he has to complete the trip, based on the number of miles to be traveled. He is expected to drive 400 miles a day. As the car owner, you have responsibilities, too. You have to guarantee that the car is mechanically able to make the trip, that the tires are fine, the oil is checked, etc. In other words, if you were driving to Florida, would the car's condition be acceptable to you?

If you are interested in their standard or "casual" service, you pay based on the two states the car is traveling between. As an example, if the car is going from New York state to Florida state, the cost is $225 plus the first tank of fuel. This is provided you have a late model car (no more than 5 years old). Reservations should be made 2-3 weeks in advance, although this company has been known to help people who called on very short notice. Should you need your car driven to Florida immediately, Auto Driveaway has a professional expedited service. In this case, a paid employee of the company will drive your car to your destination. The cost is then based on total mileage. For example, a trip from New York City to Ft. Lauderdale (1267 miles) would cost $705 plus the first tank of gas. A trip from Chicago to Ft . Lauderdale (1304 miles) would cost $735 plus gas. Sure it's more expensive, but isn't it great that the service is available?

If you are interested in getting more information, check your white pages for Auto Driveaway. They have 11 offices in Florida and one in every major metropolitan area in the country. If you can't seem to make contact, call their toll free number at 1-800-346-2277.

NOTE: *Speaking of cars... If you have a leased vehicle, please check with your leasing company and find out if you can turn in your car in Florida at the end of the lease.*

Countdown To Moving Day

Moving to a new state requires orchestration beyond anything you've probably ever done before. That's why if you can do everything in your power *before* the move, you can avert crises which can be both grievous and expensive.

Why not take this checklist of things to do starting 8 weeks before the move and tape it to the fridge? It'll help you make sure the most important steps don't fall through the cracks. Then when the move goes smooth as butter, you can thank the American Movers Conference for coming up with this great trouble saver!

At Eight Weeks

- Call in several long distance carriers to give you a moving estimate. *Never take an estimate over the phone.* You want a mover to show up in person to assess your contents. Make a decision whether you want a binding or non-binding estimate.

- If you are moving with children, or are concerned about transporting pets and plants, write to the American Movers Conference for two excellent booklets: *Moving and Children* and *Moving with Pets and Plants.* They are free of charge. The address is 2200 Mill Road, Alexandria, VA 22314. Send your requests along with business size, stamped, self-addressed envelopes.

At Six Weeks

- Make a final decision on the mover and review costs, moving dates, insurance, packing, etc. Then request the "Order for Service." This document, signed by you and the mover, confirms everything in writing.

At Four Weeks

- If you are doing your own packing, start packing.
- If the mover is doing the packing, set a date for one or two days before the loading. *DO NOT give them permission to pack on moving day—it will be much too hectic.*
- Start the tossing, donating, selling, and giving-away process.
- If necessary, arrange for storage of rugs, carpeting and drapes. Have them dry cleaned and prepared first.
- Arrange for any repairs or work needed in your new home.
- If you are planning to bring your car(s) to Florida, make arrangements for transporting them if you don't plan to drive yourself.

At Three Weeks

- Arrange to have appliances, utilities, and telephones disconnected in the old house. Arrange for utility and phone hook-ups in the new house.

- Make travel arrangements and hotel reservations for your trip.
- Apartment dwellers—reserve elevator space for pickup and/or delivery day.
- Obtain medical, dental, and veterinarian records.
- Organize your car license, registration and insurance records.

- Get advice from your bank on special courier services specializing in transporting valuables such as jewelry, coin and stamp collections, furs, or the contents of your safe deposit box.

At Two Weeks

- Obtain, fill out and mail change of address cards. Send them to newspapers, magazines, utilities, creditors, social security office, insurance companies, post office, banks, friends and family, etc.
- Make special arrangements for transporting pets and plants.
- Take care of final banking and investment transactions. Make certain you will have enough cash on hand or a certified check to hand the mover on delivery day.
- Close out charge accounts from the local department stores.

At One Week

- Arrange for a baby-sitter on moving day if necessary.
- Transfer prescriptions to a new pharmacy.
- Stop delivery services (newspapers, dry cleaning, water softener services, trash collector, milk, etc.).
- Finish packing all but the essentials you'll need to live on.

One Or Two Days Before Loading

- Have mover pack any goods you agreed to.
- Defrost and dry the refrigerator and freezer if you are taking them with you. Beware that there are some restrictions on freezers. Discuss this with your mover.
- Pick up the cash and travelers checks you'll need for the trip and the mover.
- If traveling by car, check your tires, gas, battery, oil, wipers, etc.

Moving Day

- Be on hand when movers arrive to answer questions and give directions.
- Discuss the delivery arrangements with the mover.

- Have beds stripped and ready to be packed.
- Read the Bill of Lading (your contract) before you sign it. Keep it on your possession until your shipment is delivered, all charges are paid and all claims, if any, are settled.
- Inform the mover where you or your representative can be located at your destination.
- While you are in transit, keep in touch with the mover's agent at your destination.

More Moving Day Activities: Taking Inventory

Before the mover does any packing or loading, the first thing he does is prepare the inventory—a description of everything he's going to ship for you and the condition of each and every one of these items. You'll get a copy of this inventory and you should keep it with you.

Briefly, here's how the process works. The mover walks through the house or apartment and places a number sticker on each carton and piece of furniture. All the stickers will be the same color and lot number, but will have their own identifying number. At the same time, each piece will be carefully inspected and will be marked according to its condition (bent, chipped, rusted, scratched, soiled, cracked, etc.). It will also be indicated precisely where the condition appears on the item (lower left corner, side, tip, etc.). The mover will then designate certain letters of the alphabet and numbers to describe such conditions. That way, when he looks at the inventory at delivery he will know that Item Number #37, a dining room table, is CH-Sc-W, 10, 9, 8, 7, 4, 3, 2. Or, it's chipped scratched, and badly worn on the top, right, side, rear, front corner and bottom. You want to be there for this evaluation because that will be your only chance to argue the point if you disagree with the mover's assessment.

Smaller cartons will be labeled either "CP" (carrier packed) or the dreaded "PBO" (packed by owner). Since they will already be taped shut, the cartons will not be opened for inspection.

Getting Your Bill Of Lading

On moving day, you'll also get your copy of the Bill of Lading you've heard so much about. This is your contract for transporting your goods, and is, in effect, the receipt for your belongings. It will contain all the same information as your original Order for Service, but it must have one more important piece of information: the agreed liability coverage you have for this shipment. Don't sign it unless the numbers are correct.

The Day Of Reckoning...Weighing In

Remember when we said that if you had agreed to a non-binding estimate, your final bill would be determined by distance as well as the total weight of your shipment. On moving day, the mover will weigh the van on a certified scale before loading your shipment. That's the "tare" weight. Then after your shipment is loaded, the van will be weighed again. That's the "gross" weight. The difference between the two numbers is the "net" weight, and that's what your charges will be based on.

Should you so desire, you have the right to observe the official weighing. That means you should be prepared to go to the scales with the mover immediately before and after the shipment has been loaded. If that is not feasible, you can arrange for a reweigh before your goods are unloaded in Florida. Some movers do this automatically, particularly if the billed weight is appreciably higher than the estimated weight.

The important thing about weighing is that you be informed of the figure before delivery so that you will know precisely what the move is going to cost. You should arrange with the van driver to notify you of the actual charges at a certain phone number or address. Finally, if you received a binding estimate, your cost is firm before the move and the van will not be weighed.

Taking Delivery

Generally your belongings are combined on the van with other families' shipments who are moving in the same direction. This is one of the ways movers keep your costs down. However, that means that the move itself cannot be on an exact schedule. There can be delays and hang-ups at any point along the way, which is why you won't get a guaranteed delivery date (unless you request, and probably pay for one). The actual date of delivery can be on any one of several consecutive days agreed to in the contract (Bill of Lading). Legally, just so you know, they *cannot* deliver your goods any *earlier* than promised.

The mover is obligated to contact you by phone, telegram or in person if the delivery will be delayed beyond the agreed dates. That's why it is so important to make sure that the mover has a way to contact you at your destination. If you don't have family in Florida who can receive this kind of urgent call, see if you can arrange with the landlord, a new neighbor, the real estate agent or even your new employer to get this message. Or even better, get in touch with the mover's agent at the destination to make sure they have your new phone number if phones have been installed.

It is very important that you be at your new home when the mover does arrive. Unless otherwise agreed, unloading only takes place between certain hours on certain days. The common practice is between 8 AM and 5 PM, Monday through Friday. If you are not around, the mover will wait for no more than two hours. If you then miss the unloading time, your goods will be placed in storage at considerable cost to you. Movers can justify this because they cannot afford to be late delivering the next family's shipment. When they are ready to be redelivered, you'll pay for that second return trip as well. Ouch! Just be home!

C.O.D. ...You Must Have Payment On Delivery

When the van is starting to unload, this is no time to discover that the mover won't take your personal check or credit card. Individual shipments are called C.O.D. shipments because that's exactly what they are: cash on delivery, unless accepting your credit is something the mover agreed to in advance. Some movers will accept certified checks, money orders, travelers checks or cashier's checks. Be sure to work out your form of payment before you leave.

If your original estimate was non-binding, there's a good chance that the final cost will be higher. *By law, you are only obligated to pay the estimate plus 10% of the remaining balance at the time of delivery.* It helps to know that even if the mover who gave you the original estimate was off by a lot, you'll still only have to pay the estimated charge plus 10% at delivery. Upon request, you can have 15 to 30 days from that point to pay off the unpaid balance.

Did You Say Charge It?

For the first time, some of the larger movers will allow you to pay for your move with credit. Atlas Van Lines, Bekins, Global Van Lines, Mayflower, North American and United Van Lines either accept major credit cards or will allow you to establish credit with them. Not all agents participate, so you'll have to shop around. In fact, because this benefit is quite new, you can probably count on being told by a representative that the mover only takes cash. Ask that they double-check. They just might come back and say that you can pay with Visa or American Express. Obviously your credit has to be good, and you have to have a line open equal or greater than the amount you'll be charging.

Unloading...It's So Good To Be Home

Before unloading gets into full swing, get your copy of the inventory sheets. Check off the items as they're pulled off the van and do a preliminary check of their condition. If you see obvious damage, or something is definitely missing, show it to the mover and have it marked on your copy and the mover's copy of the inventory. Make sure all the reported losses and damages are listed before signing your name.

I can't stress enough the importance of this process. I know it will be an exciting, hectic time, and there will probably be lots of other more fun things to do. So decide in advance which adult is going to get this job. Someone has to do it. If you immediately report problems on your inventory or delivery receipt it will be a major factor in your favor when it comes to collecting on a claim.

What you are really doing is called "taking exceptions" and you may end up taking a little heat from the mover for it. In other words, the mover wants a clean receipt. He doesn't want you to indicate any losses or damages on the inventory because if claims are eventually paid to you, he'll be "charged back" for those claims. It's money that will come right out of his pocket. That's why he'll probably assure you not to worry about the damages. Instead, he'll tell you you'll have 90 days to make a claim, and by law he'll be right. But the longer you wait to make a claim, the harder it could be to settle, no matter who's at fault. So take the heat and take all the exceptions on anything you might end up submitting a claim for.

239

Filing Claims Against The Mover

If you can believe it, most moves are relatively disaster-free. The vast majority of claims involve losses or damages of $100 or less. This in spite of the 1001 details that could go astray at any time. Nonetheless, when claims are submitted by the shipper it can be a seemingly painful process. Movers will generally argue that items were improperly packed (and in lots of cases they are absolutely right), forcing you to prove negligence on the part of the mover. It's tricky. But then there could be items such as a leather couch, which was clearly marked in good condition on the inventory. If at the unloading it has grease marks or rips, you shouldn't have a problem with your claim.

Again, the actual reimbursement on a claim is totally dependent on the type of liability insurance you agreed to buy before the move. If you do have a claim, don't panic. There a number of things you can do to protect yourself. Here is a checklist of suggestions.

10-Step Checklist For Handling Claims

1. You don't have to unpack and inspect all of the cartons before signing the inventory sheet, but you should indicate any obvious damage to the carton's exteriors.

2. Concealed damage discovered at a later time can still be reported and claims submitted. Since you're going to have to provide some proof of the mover's negligence, leave the damaged items in the carton until the mover's claims adjustor comes to inspect the problem.

3. Claims for loss and damage can be filed within nine months of delivery, but if you wait that long you're cutting your own throat because the mover will have every reason to point a finger at you as the culprit.

4. When you do submit a claim, the mover must acknowledge it within 30 days, and within 120 days must deny the claim or offer you a settlement.

5. Get your claim forms from either the mover's home office or the destination agent. You may be required to submit them with the original billing and your Bill of Lading, so make sure you hang on to them.

6. When you do submit your claim, it must be in writing. However, you may want to find out if your mover has a toll-free number you can call to get instructions on filing claims.

7. Don't be afraid to be overly detailed in your claim report. Claim settlements are often delayed because the mover needs more information.

8. List lost and damaged items separately, along with estimates for repairs or replacement. You may be asked to justify a replacement cost. If you no longer have a receipt for the purchase, check mail-order catalogs or store ads for similar values.

9. If you incurred any hotel, living, or other expenses caused by the mover's delays, document them on the claim forms as well.

10. Finally, it's important to understand that the actual dollar amount you will receive from the mover for losses and damages is initially determined by the representative who pays you a visit when you've got a claim. In anticipation of getting the kind of adjuster who assumes your furniture was shabby to begin with, remember that your contract with the mover, or the Bill of Lading, specifies that if you are unhappy with a settlement made by the mover you can tell them you want to take the case to arbitration. This is at no additional cost to you. This way you'll at least have your case reviewed by an objective third party if it should ever come to that.

Arbitration

The American Movers Conference, a trade association representing over 1,000 moving companies, has developed a voluntary program for their members to help settle large claims. It's called the AMC Household Goods Dispute Settlement Program and it has been approved by the Interstate Commerce Commission (ICC). Most of the major long distance carriers have agreed to participate. When selecting a mover, you should find out if they are members of the AMC and if they have signed up for this arbitration program. If they are affiliated with this program, then either the mover or the shipper can request arbitration if a claim cannot be settled any other way. However, both parties must agree to the arbitration process. This is at no cost to the customer.

If you and the mover do agree to go this route, then the American Arbitration Association (AAA) an independent, non-governmental organization, appoints an arbitrator from its national panel. The arbitrators render a decision that is legally binding. Interestingly, according to the ICC's Performance Reports, it appears that the arbitration process is virtually never used by consumers who have claims of $100 or greater. I would like to think that this reflects the integrity of the moving companies. It makes sense that they would want to resolve their claims in order to avoid legal involvement. This is confirmed by the ICC's Performance Reports which showed that the average claim of $100 or more was settled within 14 days from receipt of the claim. That's pretty impressive.

Moving Costs And Tax Deductions

For those of you who itemize deductions on your federal tax return, you should determine if this move is tax deductible. If so, just complete IRS Form 3903 to claim an interstate move on your tax return. There are other provisions to be eligible to take this deduction:

1. You must be a full time employee who is employed for 39 weeks in the 12 months after the move (not necessarily for the same company).

2. Or you are a self-employed individual who works full time for at least 78 weeks during the two years following the move.

3. Students and homemakers entering the job market may be eligible, with certain exceptions. Check with your tax preparer.

Here is what you can deduct:

- The mover's bill;
- Transportation, food and lodging expenses en route (keep all your parking and tolls receipts), in addition to mileage charges at 9 cents a mile;
- Up to $1500 of your expenses in finding, purchasing, or waiting to move into a new residence;
- Up to $3000 of the costs of buying and selling a residence (such as an appraisal, escrow fees and commissions);
- Any security deposit lost as a result of breaking a lease.

Wrapping It All Up

Remember when we talked about putting your thinking caps on when you were planning your move? Now you can see how important it is to be knowledgeable about the process. Moving is one of the most highly emotional times in a person's life. It is a time of endings and beginnings, of intense feelings and infinite details. It's not necessarily a time in which you can think clearly. In fact you can count on it. That's why you should be kind to yourself and your family by organizing a smooth, uneventful and perfectly boring move. You'll have enough excitement without it.

SECTION
V

So This Is Florida: You're Going To Love It!

Florida Destinations

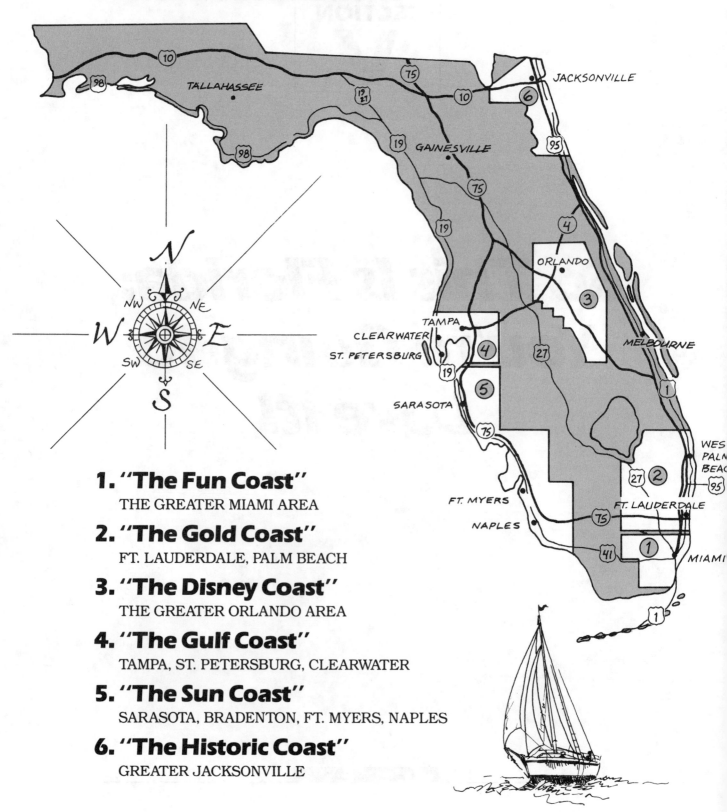

1. **"The Fun Coast"**
   THE GREATER MIAMI AREA

2. **"The Gold Coast"**
   FT. LAUDERDALE, PALM BEACH

3. **"The Disney Coast"**
   THE GREATER ORLANDO AREA

4. **"The Gulf Coast"**
   TAMPA, ST. PETERSBURG, CLEARWATER

5. **"The Sun Coast"**
   SARASOTA, BRADENTON, FT. MYERS, NAPLES

6. **"The Historic Coast"**
   GREATER JACKSONVILLE

CHAPTER 22

Destination Florida:

INTRODUCING THE CITIES AND COUNTIES OF THE SUNSHINE STATE

There are more than 400 cities, municipalities, towns and planned communities spread over Florida's 67 counties. Many of their names are as familiar as your own. Miami. Boca. St. Pete. Others may be unrecognizable to you, such as Longwood, Orange Park and Zephyrhills.

The purpose of this section is to shed light on the areas you know as a vacationer, but not necessarily as a prospective resident. Hopefully you'll also read about the areas you know nothing about. It's possible that therein lies the best place to move. No attempt will be made, however, to sway you to any one location. Your ultimate decision will be very personal, based on tastes, needs, and budget.

Housing prices, property taxes, wages, municipal services, education, job and business opportunities and even climate will vary from one region to the next. Even adjacent communities will not necessarily offer the same attributes. That is why you must make a decision based on your own careful study of several different locations.

So often, friends or family urge others to settle where they have. Unfortunately, their criteria for selecting a community doesn't always match the needs of the newcomer. Besides, isn't it human nature to cover it up when we've made a bad judgement call? It's like the guy who buys a new car and raves about it *ad nauseam*. Later you discover the truth; he hates the performance, it's always in the shop, etc. It's the same with home towns. People always *LOVE* the place, even if they hate it. Thus, if your only means of judging an area is one person's experience, there's more homework to be done.

FLORIDA REGIONS AND CITIES

To first acquaint you with the various cities and regions across the state, there is an alphabetical breakout of almost 100 different locations, along with their respective counties. They range from large metropolitan areas to the suburbs, small towns, planned communities, and "microwave municipalities" that have sprung up instantly as a result of urban sprawl.

Next to each city is the estimated population. Although these figures are only approximate, they are based on the most current available data and provide an indication of size.

To give you a sense of locale, each listing is also identified by a Region nickname and number. The nicknames, though fictitious, try to describe the area's key characteristics. And please...don't interpret their sequence. They are not ranked from best to worst or any other criteria. Regions are simply listed by their geographic location, moving from south to north.

Next you'll find a breakdown of the regions with listings of local and county Chamber of Commerce offices. I encourage you to contact as many you think necessary. The COCs are there to provide current information about their counties and communities. Generally, their staffs are very helpful to prospective newcomers. Services are normally free of charge.

One other note. Hundreds of beautiful communities have gone unmentioned, and residents will probably be happy about that. Everyone seems to feel the same way. "Close the doors after we move in." In other words, keep our town a secret. But that is not the reason for the omissions. Unfortunately, space constrains describing every locale, fabulous as it might be.

This section can serve as a valuable starting point, but it is, by no means, the definitive source.

Florida Regions

Region		Nickname	Counties
1	South	"Fun Coast"	Dade Monroe
2	Southeast	"Gold Coast"	Broward Palm Beach
3	Southeast Central	"Treasure Coast"	Martin St. Lucie Indian River
4	East Central	"Space Coast"	Brevard Seminole Volusia
5	Central	"Disney Coast"	Orange Osceola Polk
6	South Central	"Cattle Coast"	De Soto Highland Okeechobe
7	West Central	"Quiet Coast"	Hernando Pasco
8	Tampa Bay	"Gulf Coast"	Hillsborough Pinellas
9	Southwest	"Sun Coast"	Charlotte Collier Lee Manatee Sarasota
10	North Central	"Books & Breeders Coast"	Alachua Marion
11	Northeast	"Historic Coast"	Clay Duval St. Johns
12	Northwest	"Florida Panhandle"	Bay Escambia Leon Okaloosa

The Cities and Counties of Florida

City	Population	County	Region
Altamonte Springs	29,500	Seminole	4
Arcadia	6,100	DeSoto	6
Boca Raton	125,000	Palm Beach	2
Boynton Beach	48,000	Palm Beach	2
Bradenton	37,500	Manatee	9
Brandon	85,000	Hillsborough	8
Brooksville	7,100	Hernando	7
Cape Canaveral	7,000	Brevard	4
Cape Coral	55,000	Lee	9
Casselberry	18,000	Seminole	4
Clearwater	100,000	Pinellas	8
Cocoa/CocoaBeach	18,000	Brevard	4
Coconut Grove	30,000	Dade	1
Coconut Creek	20,266	Broward	2
Coral Gables	50,000	Dade	1
Coral Springs	70,773	Broward	2
Davie	35,654	Broward	2
Daytona Beach	60,000	Volusia	4
Deerfield Beach	43,994	Broward	2
Deland	16,500	Volusia	4
Delray Beach	46,600	Palm Beach	2
Dunedin	36,000	Pinellas	8
Ft. Lauderdale	151,048	Broward	2
Ft. Myers	40,000	Lee	9
Ft. Pierce	39,000	St. Lucie	3
Ft. Walton Beach	36,000	Okaloosa	12
Gainesville	85,000	Alachua	10
Greenacres City	23,000	Palm Beach	2
Haines City	12,500	Polk	5
Hallandale	37,919	Broward	2
Hialeah	180,000	Dade	1
Hollywood	124,448	Broward	2
Homestead	27,000	Dade	1

The Cities and Counties of Florida (Continued)

City	Population	County	Region
Jacksonville	610,000	Duval	11
Jupiter	22,100	Palm Beach	2
Kendall	280,000	Dade	1
Key West	26,000	Monroe	1
Kissimmee	25,000	Osceola	5
Lake Worth	27,000	Palm Beach	2
Lakeland	175,000	Polk	5
Largo	67,000	Pinellas	8
Lauderhill	42,747	Broward	2
*Longboat Key	5,900	Sarasota	9
Longwood	13,000	Seminole	4
Margate	40,117	Broward	2
Melbourne	58,200	Brevard	4
Miami	342,315	Dade	1
Miami Beach	98,000	Dade	1
Miramar	37,200	Broward	2
Naples	18,975	Collier	9
New Port Richey	13,100	Pasco	7
Oakland Park	24,620	Broward	2
Ocala	43,000	Marion	10
Okeechobee	4,500	Okeechobee	6
Orange Park	9,600	Clay	11
Orlando	150,000	Orange	5
Ormond Beach	29,000	Volusia	4
Palm Bay	42,500	Brevard	4
Palm Beach	11,000	Palm Beach	2
Palm Beach Gardens	20,300	Palm Beach	2
Panama City	35,000	Bay	12
Pembroke Pines	49,740	Broward	2
Pensacola	61,000	Escambia	12
Pinellas Park	39,871	Pinellas	8
Plant City	18,000	Hillsborough	8

The Cities and Counties of Florida (Continued)

City	Population	County	Region
Plantation	56,689	Broward	2
Pompano Beach	68,759	Broward	2
Port Charlotte	69,000	Charlotte	9
Port Orange	30,000	Volusia	4
Port Richey	2,600	Pasco	7
*Port St. Lucie	31,050	Martin	3
St. Augustine	11,891	St. Johns	11
St. Cloud	10,200	Osceola	5
St. Petersburg	244,000	Pinellas	8
Sanford	28,500	Seminole	4
Sanibel	4,200	Lee	9
Sarasota	51,000	Sarasota	9
Sebring	9,970	Highlands	6
Spring Hill	47,000	W. Hernando	7
Stuart	11,000	Martin	3
Sunrise	52,719	Broward	2
Tallahassee	120,000	Leon	12
Tamarac	34,403	Broward	2
Tampa	280,000	Hillsborough	8
Tarpon Springs	18,150	Pinellas	8
Temple Terrace	12,000	Hillsborough	8
Titusville	40,000	Brevard	4
Venice	19,000	Sarasota	9
Vero Beach	17,500	Indian River	3
West Palm Beach	68,000	Palm Beach	2
Winter Garden	7,500	Orange	5
Winter Haven	24,000	Polk	5
Winter Park	23,000	Orange	5
Winter Springs	18,000	Seminole	4
Zephyrhills	6,500	Pasco	7

*Longboat Key is also part of Manatee County. Port St. Lucie is also part of St. Lucie County.

Sources: Bureau of Economic and Business Research, University of Florida, The Florida Department of Commerce, Division of Economic Development, The Florida Chamber of Commerce

Florida Counties, Cities and Chambers of Commerce

The Chamber of Commerce offices report that the majority of requests for newcomer information come in via telephone. Even though people are generally given both addresses and phone numbers, in today's fast-paced world it appears that no one corresponds by mail anymore. Therefore we've provided phone numbers only. For the purists who still enjoy writing, the Florida Chamber of Commerce will provide a complete listing of offices across the state. Write to:

Florida Chamber of Commerce
136 S. Bronough St.
P.O. Box 11309
Tallahassee, FL 32302
Or call (why not?) 904-222-2831.

Region 1: South Florida
Dade and Monroe Counties
"The Fun Coast"

DADE COUNTY

Miami	305-350-7700
South Miami	305-661-1621
Miami Beach	305-672-1270
Coral Gables	305-446-1657
Homestead	305-247-2330
Hialeah	305-887-1515

MONROE COUNTY

Key West	305-294-2587

Region 2: Southeast Florida
Broward and Palm Beach Counties
"The Gold Coast"

BROWARD COUNTY

Coral Springs	305-752-4242
Davie	305-581-0790
Deerfield Beach	305-427-1050
Ft. Lauderdale	305-462-6000
Hallandale	305-454-0541
Hollywood	305-920-3330
Miramar	305-989-6200
Pembroke Pines	305-962-3302

Plantation	305-587-1410
Pompano Beach	305-941-2940
Sunrise	305-741-3300
Tamarac	305-722-1520

PALM BEACH COUNTY

Boca Raton	407-395-4433
Boynton Beach	407-732-9501
Delray Beach	407-243-7000
Jupiter	407-746-7111
Lake Worth	407-582-4401
Palm Beach	407-655-3282
West Palm Beach	407-833-3711

Region 3: Southeast Central Florida
Indian River, Martin and St. Lucie Counties
"The Treasure Coast"

INDIAN RIVER COUNTY

Vero Beach	407-567-3491

MARTIN COUNTY

Port St. Lucie	407-335-4422
Stuart/Martin County	407-287-1088

ST. LUCIE COUNTY

Ft. Pierce	407-461-2700

Region 4: East Central Florida
Brevard, Seminole and Volusia Counties
"The Space Coast"

BREVARD COUNTY

Cocoa/Cocoa Beach	407-636-4262
Melbourne (S. Brevard)	407-724-5400
Titusville	407-267-3036

SEMINOLE COUNTY

Altamonte Springs	407-834-4404
Longwood/Winter Springs	407-831-4991
Sanford	407-322-2212
Seminole	407-392-3245

VOLUSIA COUNTY
Daytona/Beach	904-255-0981
Ormond Beach	904-677-3454
Pt. Orange	904-761-1601

Region 5: Central Florida
Orange, Osceola and Polk Counties
"The Disney Coast"

ORANGE COUNTY
Orlando	407-425-1234
Winter Park	407-644-8281

OSCEOLA COUNTY
Kissimmee	407-847-3174
St. Cloud	407-892-3671

POLK COUNTY
Winter Haven	813-293-2138
Lakeland	813-688-8551

Region 6: South Central Florida
DeSoto, Highland and Okeechobee Counties
"The Cattle Coast"

DESOTO COUNTY
Arcadia	813-494-4033

HIGHLAND COUNTY
Sebring	813-385-8448

OKEECHOBEE COUNTY
Okeechobee	813-763-6464

Region 7: West Central Florida
Pasco and Hernando Counties
"The Quiet Coast"

HERNANDO COUNTY
Brooksville	904-796-2420
Spring Hill	904-683-3700

PASCO COUNTY
New Port Richey	813-842-7651
Zephyrhills	813-782-1913

Region 8: Tampa Bay
Hillsborough and Pinella Counties
"The Gulf Coast"

HILLSBOROUGH COUNTY
Brandon   813-689-1221
Plant City   813-754-3707
Tampa   813-228-7777

PINELLAS COUNTY
Clearwater   813-461-0011
St. Petersburg   813-821-4069
Tarpon Springs   813-937-6109

Region 9: The Southwest
Charlotte, Collier, Lee, Manatee
and Sarasota Counties
"The Sun Coast"

CHARLOTTE COUNTY
Port Charlotte   813-627-2222

COLLIER COUNTY
Naples   813-262-6141

LEE COUNTY
Ft. Myers   813-334-1133

MANATEE COUNTY
Bradenton   813-748-3411

SARASOTA COUNTY
Sarasota   813-955-8187
Venice   813-488-2236

Region 10: North Central Florida
Alachua and Marion Counties
"The Books & Breeder's Coast"

ALACHUA COUNTY
Gainesville   904-372-4305

MARION COUNTY
Ocala   904-629-8051

Region 11: The Northeast
Clay, Duval and St. Johns Counties
"The Historic Coast"

CLAY COUNTY
    Orange Park   904-264-2651

DUVAL COUNTY
    Jacksonville   904-353-0300

ST. JOHNS COUNTY
    St. Augustine   904-829-5681

Region 12: Northwest Florida
Bay, Escambia, Leon, and Okaloosa Counties
"The Florida Panhandle"

BAY COUNTY
    Panama City   904-785-5206

ESCAMBIA COUNTY
    Pensacola   904-438-4081

LEON COUNTY
    Tallahassee   904-224-8116

OKALOOSA COUNTY
    Ft. Walton Beach   904-244-8191

FLORIDA NEWSPAPERS

There is no better way to become knowledgeable about a community than by reading the major newspaper serving the area. Everything you could possibly want to know about the area is found there: real estate, employment and business opportunities, local issues, entertainment and culture, recreational activities, building and development and much more. For $7 or $8 a month, you could order the Sunday edition of a Florida newspaper, have it mailed to your home and begin to get a feel for an area without leaving your armchair. Order several newspapers and compare different areas. It's the best investment you could make.

Here is a roster of the major local papers.

Florida's Daily Newspapers

Ft. Lauderdale News/
Sun-Sentinel
101 N. New River Dr.
Ft. Lauderdale, FL 33301-2293
(305) 252-1511

Ft. Myers News Press
2442 Anderson Ave.
Ft. Myers, FL 33901
(813) 335-0200

Gainesville Sun
P.O. Drawer A
Gainesville, FL 32602
(904) 378-1411

Florida Times Union
1 Riverside Ave.
Jacksonville, FL 32202
(904) 359-4111

Miami Herald
One Herald Plaza
Miami, FL 33132
(305) 350-2111

Naples Daily News
1075 Central Ave.
Naples, FL 33940
(813) 262-3161

Owendyando Sentinel
633 N. Orange Ave.
Owendyando, FL 32801
(407) 420-5000

St. Petersburg Times
P.O. Box 1121
St. Petersburg, FL 33731-1121
(813) 893-8111

Sarasota Herald-Tribune
P.O. Box 1719
Sarasota, FL 34230
(813) 953-7755

Tallahassee Democrat
P.O. Box 990
Tallahassee, FL 32302
(904) 599-2100

Tampa Tribune
P.O. Box 191
Tampa, FL 33601
(813) 272-7711

CHAPTER 23

"The Fun Coast"

THE GREATER MIAMI AREA

In 1964, Jackie Gleason glorified Miami and its beaches as the "Sun and Fun" capital of the world. Some 25 years later, the "Great One" has still got it right. You feel the heat and the beat as soon as you arrive. Although this "City of the Future" is also very much a part of Florida's "Gold Coast," the 120-mile stretch along the Atlantic Ocean, Miami is different. Unlike Ft. Lauderdale, Boca Raton, and Palm Beach, Miami is truly an international metropolis.

No longer the sleepy southern resort haven, the Miami area has been transformed into one of the most glittering, exhilarating, multi-national Meccas of the 20th century. Today's Miami and surrounding Dade County offer a myriad of cultural, recreational, and educational facilities. Brickell Ave., in the heart of Miami's business district, has evolved into one of the foremost trade capitals in the free world. Add to that the irrepressible Latin influence, with its vast financial and cultural offerings, and this place is paradise in the fast lane.

Could we possibly be speaking of the same Miami that is also known as "God's waiting room?" Yes! And while we can't deny that a good part of the Miami area is inhabited by retirees, you're bound to see as many "33s" and "45s" as you do "78s"! Actually, the "social security" crowd down here looks so damn good, only the IRS knows for sure . . . The funny thing is that many of you are so familiar with places like Biscayne Blvd., Collins Ave. and the Tamiami Trail, it probably seems odd to be asking questions about South Florida living. But with Dade County's 1.7 million residents residing in one of 27 incorporated municipalities, even the most devoted tourists would be hard put to describe all those neighborhoods.

"The Fun Coast"

THE GREATER MIAMI AREA

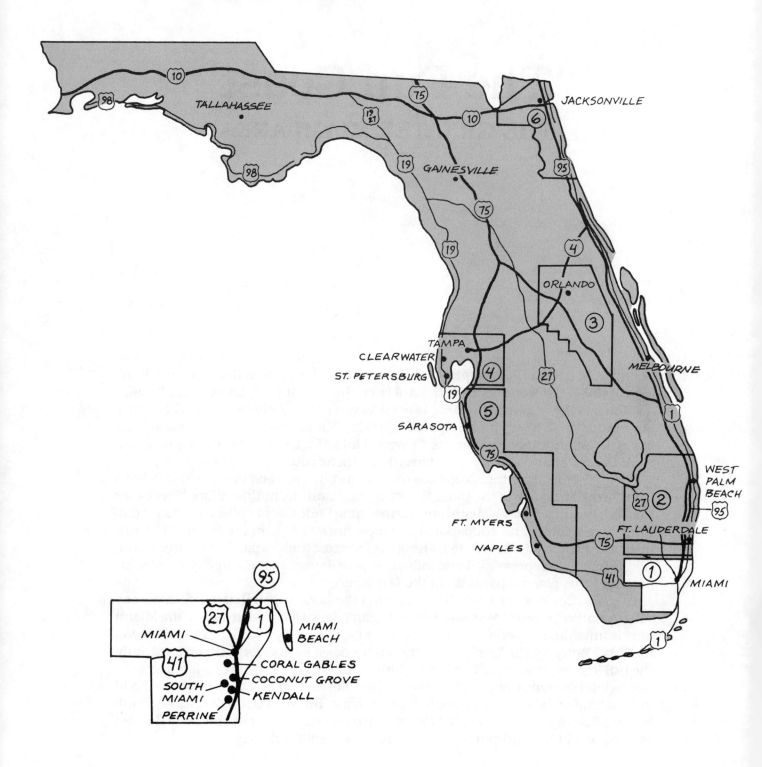

Here is a brief tour of some of the communities in and around Miami.

COCONUT GROVE

If you plan to work in Downtown Miami and would give anything to live within 10 to 15 minutes of the office, take a look at quaint-but-sophisticated Coconut Grove. This little pocket of South Miami is only 3 sq. miles wide, but offers something for everyone.

Aside from the easy commute, there's no shortage of recreational and cultural activities, including the famous Coconut Grove Arts Festival each February and the annual Renaissance and Shakespeare Festivals at the Vizcaya museum.

The Grove attracts both the creative (it's an artists' and writers' colony) and the executive types, as well as the wealthy. Housing options range from ultra-fancy condominiums to beautiful old homes that are architectural monuments.

Some say that along with Coral Gables and South Miami, Coconut Grove real estate is the "hottest" around. Young professionals are especially attracted to the area because of the fine public schools (believed to be the best in South Florida) and the quiet, lush neighborhoods that are strictly residential. For $100,000 you can buy a small 3BR/2BA home and end up next to a million dollar home on the water. That's what Miami is about. The little house next to the large estate.

Unfortunately, the Grove is also known for being a high-crime area. But those who want the urban paradise of the cinemas, a potpourri of elegant restaurants, a sophisticated shopping experience, the bohemians, and the chic, take the good with the bad.

SOUTH MIAMI

This small, quiet bedroom community is tucked between Coral Gables and Kendall and has evolved into an ideal first home for transferred executive and their families. Although some of the most desirable and elegant neighborhoods in all of Dade county are found here, there are plenty of modestly-priced houses and lots and nearby parks and recreation centers. Property taxes are lower than the Gables for what some consider to be better values.

Whatever type of home you choose, each is perfectly situated. You're either 20 minutes from the ocean, 20 minutes from Downtown or 20 minutes from Miami International Airport. Getting around the city is easy now that there's a South Miami Metrorail station in the heart of the business district. This rapid transit system provides easy access to Greater Miami. Shopping is fun with the *Bakery Centre*'s mixed-use complex of boutiques, galleries and restaurants.

KENDALL

In nearby Kendall, you'll find one of South Florida's largest malls, Dadeland, and a landscaper's dream center, "The Falls." It's also a New Yorker's dream. It's got a Bloomingdales! Pity the poor folks who moved down 10 years ago and had to go through withdrawal.

With more than 275,000 residents, Kendall is a very popular suburb south of US 1. There's a wide variety of housing choices including modern townhouse condos in the $70,000 range and 3/BR homes for about $140,000. Here the lots are small, but the area is ideal for young families who care just as much about parks, tennis courts, swimming pools, daycare and good security.

There are also many beautiful, affluent neighborhoods such as Snapper Creek, Hammock Lakes, and Pine Acres. These upscale developments offer luxurious single-family homes built around lakes and canals.

PERRINE-CUTLER RIDGE

If you've got rich blood, or even rich relations, you can consider one of the most exclusive areas of South Dade. Located south of Kendall, between S.W. 168th St. to the north, S.W. 137th on the west, Biscayne Bay on the east and S.W. 216th on the south, you can easily pay $1 million for an estate on Old Cutler Road. Even if you can't afford to buy, there's no extra charge for drooling at Cutler Oaks, Hammock Oaks and Kenwood Lakes. The average 4/BR home goes for $500-$600,000. This unincorporated area of Dade county has the highest density of county parks and also offers a public golf course. For those in the money, private clubs abound.

CORAL GABLES

Perhaps you know Coral Gables as the home of the University of Miami, but did you know that it was also the first planned community in the country? What's more, it is home to over 100 multinational corporations, giving it a worldwide reputation for financial and business savvy. In fact, Coral Gables was cited by the Harvard Business Review as one of three global cities in the world (Paris and Honolulu are the other two).

Despite the fact that EXXON, Dow Chemical, Delta Airlines, Rockwell International, Lockheed, DuPont and other corporate giants share the landscape, strict zoning regulations keep business in the business district and homes in the residential areas. Never the twain shall meet. A vision of George Merrick, a prominent land developer in the 1920s, he sent his builders to Italy and Spain to study housing design before a single lot was sold. His dream was to build a modern city with Mediterranean charm. Today, the 50,000 residents of "The City Beautiful" enjoy a very special lifestyle. Nestled along Biscayne Bay, they can choose from sprawling 4- and 5-bedroom homes or more affordable two-bedroom condos.

North Gables is elegant and vast. South Gables is for the young and the restless (not to mention the dual-income professionals with two kids and a housekeeper). 3/BR homes range in price from $180,000 to $250,000.

MIAMI BEACH

The recent infusion of multi-millions to restore the glamour and beauty of Miami Beach has paid off handsomely. It no longer has to rest on its laurels. Instead, as a result of the "sandlift," this most famous stretch of beach rests on a new wooden walkway. Once again the early morning joggers and late night strollers can enjoy the breathtaking views of Biscayne Bay and the Atlantic Ocean.

Miami Beach is on the rebound and is predicted to be one of the up and coming "hot" markets. Right now you can buy an older home and renovate. If you can hold on for at least another seven years, you'll probably own some very prime real estate.

Miami's South Beach, the historic Art Deco district, is by far the trendiest neighborhood. Within this 80 square block radius, you'll find lots of singles and young married professionals enjoying the glitter and pastels of the 1920s along with modern luxury apartment buildings, such as South Pointe Towers at the tip of South Beach. The newly-built Miami Beach Convention Center, one of the ten largest in the country, is another sign that this former resort haven means business. Big business.

"The Gold Coast"
FT. LAUDERDALE, PALM BEACH

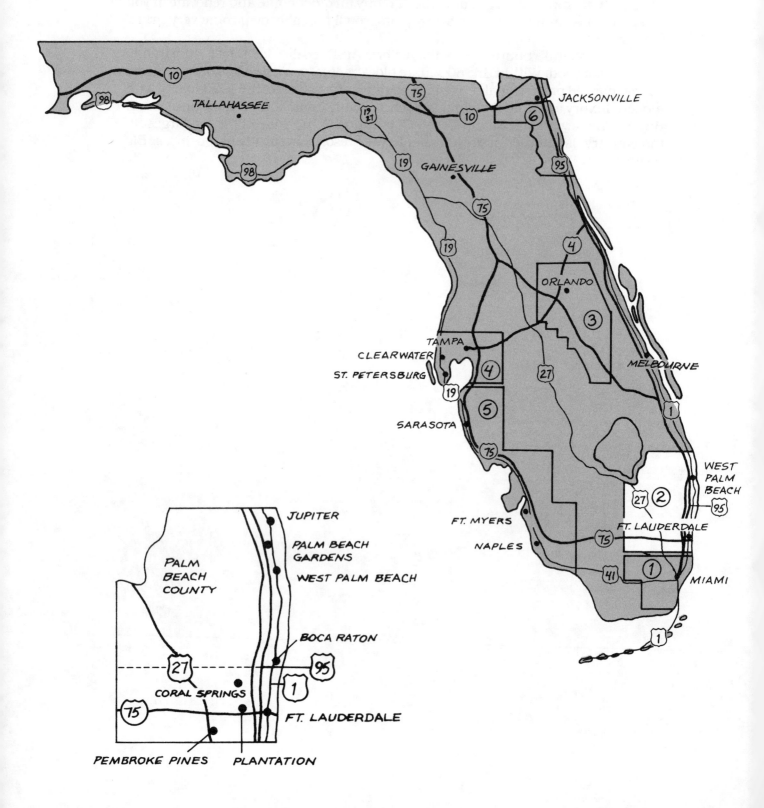

CHAPTER 24

"The Gold Coast"

FT. LAUDERDALE AND THE
PALM BEACH AREA

There is so much personal wealth on the "Gold Coast" of Florida, it is said that if everyone cashed a check on the same day, the banks would bounce.

While the area's greatest claim to fame is that it's an exclusive vacation haven for the jet set, Broward and Palm Beach Counties have also evolved into a prime locale for high-tech industries.

Although tourism is still a mainstay of the "Gold Coast" economy (it attracts two million visitors a year), it is also a bustling trade center. Major communications, computer, electronic and other scientific manufacturing concerns contribute greatly to the area's financial health, without polluting the environment.

On the residential front, Ft. Lauderdale and the Palm Beach area offer some of the finest neighborhoods and homes in the country. Between the glittering waterfront, the ever-present 75 degree climate, the cultural and recreational facilities, the sense of community feeling, and the incredible choice of housing, you can understand the appeal to its more than 1.75 million residents.

Let's first take a look at some of the offerings of Broward County, starting with its flagship city, Ft. Lauderdale.

FT. LAUDERDALE

Ft. Lauderdale is often called the "Venice of America." It has 165 miles of waterways, six miles of oceanfront, canals and beaches. If you're fond of boating, sailing, deep sea fishing or just plain dining with a view of the water, you'll love it here.

Located in the center of Broward County, this city is the largest of the county's 28 communities. It offers its 150,000 residents a full spectrum of modern architecture or old-fashioned Mediterranean charm. The median asking price for a single-family house is $110,000, almost always including a pool. As with any waterfront community, housing prices will vary depending on whether you have a view of the water, or a view of the homes that have a view of the water. Given that boating is synonymous with the Ft. Lauderdale lifestyle (more than 38,000 boats are docked here), housing prices along the canals move up or down with the depth of the water (the deeper the level, the bigger the boat that can be parked in the backyard).

The recent migration of employees who have come to work for the high-tech corporations have changed the makeup of the community. Older residents are moving farther north, young families are taking their places.

For the snowbirds, the oceanfront condominiums is where the action is. Prices start at just under $100,000. One neighborhood taking shape for young professionals is Bermuda Riviera. The public schools are very good, the area is lush and new housing abounds. Lots for custom-built homes sell for $150,000 to $250,000. If you can do without the waterfront view, you'll find plenty of attractive houses in the $175,000 range.

Two other communities that have become quite popular are Sea Ranch Lakes and Lauderdale-by-the-Sea. As their names indicate, both are off the intracoastal waterways and are naturally very prestigious addresses.

For all residents, recreational facilities abound. There are 23 parks, 500+ tennis courts and 65 golf courses in the area. The Hugh Taylor Birch State Park contains 180 acres of inland waterways, nature trails and more.

CORAL SPRINGS

Doesn't it seem that everyone is moving here, or at least considering it? If you have a young family, want an excellent school system, 16 soccer fields, an abundance of shopping, and beautiful homes at reasonable prices, you'll see why this is one of the most successful planned communities in the country. Tucked in the northwest corner of Broward County, this city epitomizes what young families are searching for in today's hectic world. How young is it? Statistics indicate that 37% of the population are 17 or younger with the median age being 30. And it's growing fast—at a rate of about 3500 new residents a year, adding to the current population of 70,000. Developed by Westinghouse Electric back in the 1960's, it has been transformed from farmland to suburban chic. Houses go from modest to magnificent, the school system achieves scores well above the national and county levels in tests, and the recreation facilities are some of the most well-run in the state. In 1988, $16 million in new projects were underway, including a new community center, a major local park and other municipal improvements. Also planned is a major Olympic-style aquatic and training complex open to the public.

The average home offers three bedrooms, two baths, and a pool in a price range of $120,000 to $160,000. The typical lot size is 80 × 110 and many of the streets are situated on winding, green cul-de-sacs.

From an employment perspective, prospects are good. Coral Springs is considered to be the economic and business hub of Northwest Broward, with more than 30 major financial institutions. Coral Square Mall and Sample Blvd. provide the shopping highlights in town, with endless strip centers providing all the convenience stores.

PEMBROKE PINES

In southwest Broward County is the totally-residential community of Pembroke Pines. Every type of housing is available, including a top-rated mobile home site at the western edge of the city.

Pembroke Lakes, a beautiful neighborhood developed 25 years ago, offers both lakefront and non-lakefront homes. Off the water you can buy an attractive 3/BR 2/BA with a pool for anywhere from $90,000 to $160,000.

For commuters, the Pines is situated an easy 25 miles from either Miami or Ft. Lauderdale, and is conveniently located between the Florida Turnpike and US Route 27.

Residents can enjoy the year 'round pleasure of the C.B. Smith Park, a 300-acre park offering every major sporting activity. Pembroke Lakes and Racquet Club, a city-owned facility, offers 18-hole golf courses, swimming and tennis.

PLANTATION

Situated 15 minutes west of Ft. Lauderdale is another fine planned community called Plantation, a strictly-zoned residential area that is ideally suited for active families. It's considered to be a modern, progressive, beautifully-kept city that offers prestige with value. Many homes here are selling for over $175,000, with the median price at around $100,000. This well-landscaped bedroom community offers a small town atmosphere and some lovely older homes on nice-sized pieces of property. Many of the 50,000 plus residents are commuters to Miami or other office parks in nearby Ft. Lauderdale.

Light industry and financial institutions currently utilize over 1 million square feet of new office space, and retail shopping focuses around the huge Broward Mall, a major tourist attraction as well as anchor for hundreds of surrounding shops and mini-malls. The community is also known for its exceptional recreational facilities, including 284 acres spread over 37 parks. Tennis, swimming, and indoor recreation centers offer 80 different programs for both young and old, making it a very special place to raise a family.

PALM BEACH COUNTY

Nothing compares with the natural beauty and luxurious surroundings of the Palm Beach area. It is the most closely situated city next to the Gulf Stream, providing a mild, comfortable climate all year, not to mention 47 miles of some of the most glorious beaches in the world. If there was such a thing as beauty contests for cities, Palm Beach would surely be an annual winner. While it is still known as the ultimate winter resort arena for high society (it's a favorite stop for HRH, Prince

Charles), it has also fast become a magnet for high technology industries. IBM, RCA, Burroughs, and United Technologies are just some of the multinational corporations that have made a name for themselves here. This strong influx of dollars to the economy has freed the area from being totally dependent on tourism and its 12 months of fabulous weather.

Stretching north of Broward County along the Atlantic coastline, Palm Beach is growing in population at a rate of 2,000 people a month. By the year 2000, the population will reach 1 million. But due to the large expanse of the area (2,578 sq. miles), it will have a far lower population density than Broward or Dade Counties.

In today's market, the Palm Beach area is indisputably Florida's premier residential locale. The average house costs $133,000, compared with Broward's $105,000 and Dade's $104,000 median asking prices. But Palm Beach is not known for its average homes. There are more magnificent estates per square mile here than anywhere in the southern U.S. Almost all of the homes are either oceanfront or Intracoastal. Add to that its proximity to the ultra-extravagant Worth Ave. shopping district, and you've got housing prices that could support third world countries. Even small houses here go for about half-a-million. No wonder Palm Beach County is considered the high end of the spectrum in the Gold Coast, with large upscale developments dotting the landscape, excellent public schools, superb municipal services and a quality of life that is unparalleled.

BOCA RATON

When you buy in Boca, you pay for a lifestyle and they throw in the house. Boca residents are the first to tell you that their address makes a statement about how they want to live. They want a country club existence and all the amenities year 'round. They want luxurious, modern surroundings; money is no object. People pay more to live in Boca than just about anywhere else in the state. The line-up of mansions that cover North and South Ocean Boulevard tell the story.

Most of the housing in Greater Boca centers around prestigious club developments, such as Fairfield, Boca Pointe and the famed Polo Club, where everyone expects to find Chris Evert on the tennis courts; often she is.

In the West Boca Market, there is a new Arvida development called Broken Sound where young families are snapping up gorgeous homes for anywhere from $200,000 to $1 million. On the waterfront in Boca Bay Colony and Walker's Cay, a contemporary 3/BR starts at $400,000 and only the buyer knows how high is up. If it's an older neighborhood you aspire to, you can look to Old Floresta, one of the Boca originals. Slightly inland, it has the same feel as Coral Gables, with quiet, lush streets and old Spanish homes. Most of the houses are 3/BR's on large lots, starting at $400,000. Right next door is New Floresta, where you can find copies of the homes in Old Floresta, only larger. Prices start at $260,000.

WEST PALM BEACH

I take their word for it when I'm told there are 50,000 palm trees in West Palm. That's almost one tree for each of the 68,000 residents. This is the largest city in Palm Beach County and a thriving commercial town. Although it's sometimes viewed as the black sheep of the Palm Beach families because of its fluctuating real estate values, it is definitely a city on the rebound.

"The Downtown/Uptown Project"—a major overhaul of the residential and business districts—is revitalizing the whole area. Lots of older homes, ranging in price from $120,000 to one million dollars, are undergoing renovation; in five years, it's predicted that most of West Palm will be a great place in which to have invested.

If you're interested in fabulous lakefront condos, take a look at Trump Plaza, the Trianon and the Waterview. Units start at $150,000 and go up to a half a million.

The El Cid district, 5 minutes from downtown West Palm, is like a checkerboard. One house can be a handyman's special for a $120,000 while next door can be a fabulous renovated home for twice that.

PALM BEACH GARDENS

Located just west of North Palm Beach, Palm Beach Gardens has become known as the home of the PGA National. It was conceived to be a country club community for avid golfers, and it has certainly lived up to its expectations. Four championship golf courses have been built on the PGA National Golf Club complex.

This totally-planned luxury community spans over 2300 acres, offering a multitude of individual villages and residences while protecting the natural beauty of the terrain. The area is set in the midst of perfectly manicured lawns, lakes, woodlands and fairways. It's a golfer's dream (and a golf widow's nightmare). Parks and recreation such as Lake Catherine Park and Plant Drive Park offer every major sporting interest for residents, including a 240-acre wilderness reserve and wildlife sanctuary.

Townhouses start at $100,000, but it doesn't take too long to arrive at custom building for $1 million. The new Ryder Cup development is creating even more elegant housing options.

JUPITER

At the northern tip of Palm Beach County is a large residential community most renowned for its favorite son, Burt Reynolds. Thanks to his successful Burt Reynolds Jupiter Theatre, this city is not just an asterisk, but a hot spot on the map. It's situated just where the sub-tropics begin in the U.S. Jupiter Inlet joins the three branches of the Loxachatchee River with the Intracoastal Waterways. New homes, townhouse condos and apartments have sprung up since the early 1980's, offering residents a magnificent place on the water at favorable prices.

Across the River-of-Turtles, Jupiter faces lovely Tequesta. Here residents find a small-town living environment with lots of sophistication. In just the past few years, this sleepy little town on the marina has spawned beautiful, affordable oceanfront condos.

"The Disney Coast"
THE GREATER ORLANDO AREA

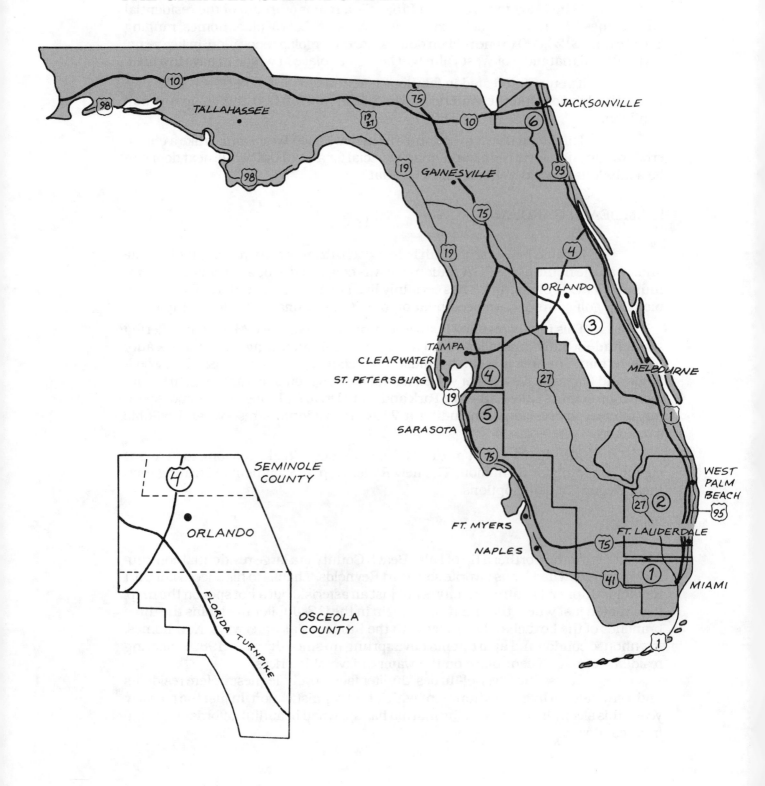

CHAPTER 25

"The Disney Coast"
THE GREATER ORLANDO AREA

How seriously can you take a region whose biggest claim to fame is a mouse that roared? Pretty damn seriously. Thanks to the Disney Dynasty and the more than 20 million visitors its parks and attractions bring in every year, there's more going on in the Orlando area on a single day than in Kansas during an entire year. Sorry, Dorothy.

But it's not just that the tourists are descending. They're staying. Moving in by the droves. That's why this lake-filled region in central Florida, with close to a million residents, is growing at a speed usually associated with Space Mountain. According to *Inc.* magazine, it's now the third fastest-growing city in the country. Yet while Orlando and surrounding Osceola and Seminole counties are experiencing this rapid development, builders are quick to mention that they're working hard to maintain the region's natural beauty and bounty. The sentiment is that you can still experience southern country living . . . if you don't mind the cranes. Since 1984, more than $360 million dollars has been spent on redeveloping downtown Orlando. Among Florida's key cities, the biggest plans for government office space are showing up in the heart of this city. Last year a new 218,000 sq. ft. state office tower—a $23 million dollar project—broke ground. The country is about to spend $150 million on a new court house and the $100 million home for the new basketball franchise, the Orlando Magic, should be completed by year's end.

What's interesting is how many detractors thought that a Florida locale without a "REAL" coast line would be as popular as a skunk at a picnic. They guessed wrong, grossly underestimating people's desire for a beautifully wooded region that offered jobs, low-cost housing, a desirable quality of life . . . and no hurricanes. One of the first things you notice when you arrive is how well kept is the "City Beautiful." They take clean living seriously, which must be why you can't buy chewing gum at the airport. Whether you're coming or going, you are not going to mess up their home!

One of the other things you may notice is that although citrus is still the second-largest industry in central Florida, there are a lot less oranges in Orange County these days. Hotels, motels, restaurants, shopping centers, and tourist attractions are sitting on top of what used to be miles and miles of groves.

As far as making a living is concerned, the under 5% unemployment rate tells you that if you're out of work in Orlando, it's by choice. Tourist attractions, the burgeoning $12 million retail sector and over 800 manufacturing concerns provide an endless stream of part- and full-time job opportunities. In spite of Florida's famous reputation for low incomes, people can make a decent living here. The average household income is $33,000, which is not bad when you consider that living costs and taxes are very moderate.

On the corporate side, Orlando is one of the fastest-growing high-technology centers in the U.S., with more than 300 firms employing 50,000 people. This includes Westinghouse, Martin-Marietta, Harris Corp., and AT&T Technologies, to name a few. Entrepreneurs in the high-tech service sector are also thriving.

Culture is as near as the Loch Haven Art Center and several other performing arts centers. The beaches are a short 45-minute drive to the Daytonas. You can shop till you drop, or you can spend the entire year outdoors (there are 200 lakes and 3000 acres of parks). As one former New Yorker now turned real estate agent said, "You don't come here to play bridge."

Housing is beautiful, spacious, versatile and inexpensive, relative to the east coast. You can pick from Mediterranean, Victorian, and contemporary styles in price ranges that still raise eyebrows. The median asking price is $78,000 (meaning half sold for more, half for less). The average selling price is just under $105,000. And it can buy you one of the nicest 3- or 4-BR homes you've ever seen. It's understandable that *Newsweek* magazine recently ranked the Orlando area the 7th best place to live and work in America!

However, according to local experts, growth is not without its problems. Those who have moved north of town to Altamonte Springs and Longwood for the newer homes and larger pieces of property will be the first to tell you about the commuter's nightmare to downtown. Interstate 4, the major north and south thoroughfare, is a virtual parking lot during rush hour. City and state authorities are to be commended for their long-term planning solution. The first circular highway in Florida, the Eastern and Western Beltway, is currently under construction. Although this is a 10-year project, every stretch of expressway that allows drivers to circumvent the clogged arteries will bring welcome relief. In the meantime, if you're planning to live and work in the area, try to choose a location that goes against traffic!

Here is a brief overview of some of the surrounding cities and communities you should explore.

ORLANDO

If you are intent on rolling out of bed and being at the office shortly thereafter, your best bet is to look in either Winter Park or in the southwest quadrant of town. Winter Park is a beautiful, old established community where one home is lovelier than the next. People pay another $20,000 or $30,000 to be in this area because the school district has an excellent reputation, the gourmet restaurants and prestigious boutiques make the right statement, and because property values remain high. Many residents are so convinced of the locale's desirability that in order to get a new home, they buy an old one, tear it down and start over.

South of Kirkman Rd. is the exclusive Windermere section. Homes on Lake Butler and Chase Rd. are already in the $150,000 to $250,000 range, but surrounding areas are quite reasonable and on the verge of exploding. Arnold Palmer's Isleworth and Bay Hill are two luxurious golf club communities rising in popularity. Finally, MetraWest is a brand-new multi-use development in this area, complete with commercial and residential properties, a golf course and loads of amenities.

SEMINOLE COUNTY

Suburban sprawl best describes lovely Seminole County, a fast-growing area 10 to 15 minutes north of Mickey's house. But as close as Walt Disney World is in distance, is as far away as it is on the minds of those who live here. The residents of Longwood, Altamonte Springs and Lake Mary live, work and play in the area; the tourist attractions are a million miles away.

Longwood is Seminole County's oldest city and is considered the choice bedroom community for young families. Planned communities and country club-like developments offering custom built houses and townhomes have sprung up so fast, anything older than 15 years is a veritable antique.

Sweetwater Oaks is a successful new home development worth looking at. For a beautiful condominium village, try The Springs. Units start at $140,000. Keep in mind that central Florida's condo market is not anywhere near as vast as it is on the east and west coasts.

Lake Mary, a small but attractive suburb north of Longwood, has captured the hearts and pocketbooks of one of the biggest developers in Florida. This is where the famed Jeno Paulucci's Heathrow community is situated. This "private world-class community" is *the* place for big spenders, with custom built houses ranging in price from $300,000 to $2 million. Even the AAA is so convinced of its unique aura that it is constructing its new national headquarters here. As desirable as this area may be, given the high-volume traffic patterns, it's best to look this far north only if you plan to work or have a business in the immediate area.

Due south of Longwood is Winter Springs, a quiet but pleasant community that is building a reputation for great-looking but affordable homes. The Tuscawilla subdivision and Deer Run community are worth looking at.

OSCEOLA COUNTY

Kissimmee and St. Cloud in adjacent Osceola County are enjoying the spillover of Orlando's boom. Although still considered a major resort area, or the best place to park your camper when you come to town, newcomers who want to live in rural surroundings think these are very decent, hospitable communities.

Whichever areas you explore, Arlene Carozza, a Merrill Lynch broker in Winter Park, encourages you to keep two things in mind. "Don't view your first home purchase in Orlando as your last one. People come down here to buy like it's their final resting place, even if they're 35." The problem occurs when they discover they want something very different in a house style or location and decide to sell. If they've purchased a brand-new home, that can take forever and there are no guarantees on profits. For the best values and resale possibilities, it's probably best to start out with a modern house that's youngish but not brand-new. Secondly, Ms. Carozza recommends that you not gravitate to homes on large pieces of property. "Everyone wants these big lots until the summer's rainy season hits. Like clockwork, it comes down every day at 4:15. With that kind of precipitation, you're bound to be mowing the lawn every 5 days. All of a sudden having a big backyard is a drag."

CHAPTER 26

"The Gulf Coast"

TAMPA, ST. PETERSBURG AND CLEARWATER

If living on the Gulf of Mexico isn't enough of an incentive to consider relocating to the Tampa Bay area, perhaps you've never seen the spectacular sunsets. Or maybe you're not aware of the progressive business climate here. For good measure, let's throw in the Tampa Bay Buccaneers and an outstanding assortment of parks and recreation centers, the diverse cultural arena, the powdery beaches, and some of the most exciting housing choices in the state. No wonder John Naisbitt calls Tampa a "Megatrend" city.

If you think Tampa doesn't sound like a great place to live, you'll find yourself outvoted. The "Gulf Coast" is growing at twice the rate of anywhere else in Florida and for that matter, at six times the rate of the rest of the country.

Tampa, St. Petersburg, Clearwater, and their surrounding communities are growing at this dizzying pace because everything you could ever want is here. We are told that the quality of life, the easy economic existence, and the opportunity for an active, productive lifestyle are unparalleled.

Let's first explore the Hillsborough County side of the blue, blue Tampa Bay.

TAMPA

Hillsborough County is a sprawling land mass, covering 1,062 square miles. With a current population of 800,000, this "hot-to-trot" area is bracing itself for an even-bigger population surge by the year 2000. By then, this bustling Gulf Coast county should have more than one million residents.

"The Gulf Coast"

TAMPA, ST. PETERSBURG, CLEARWATER

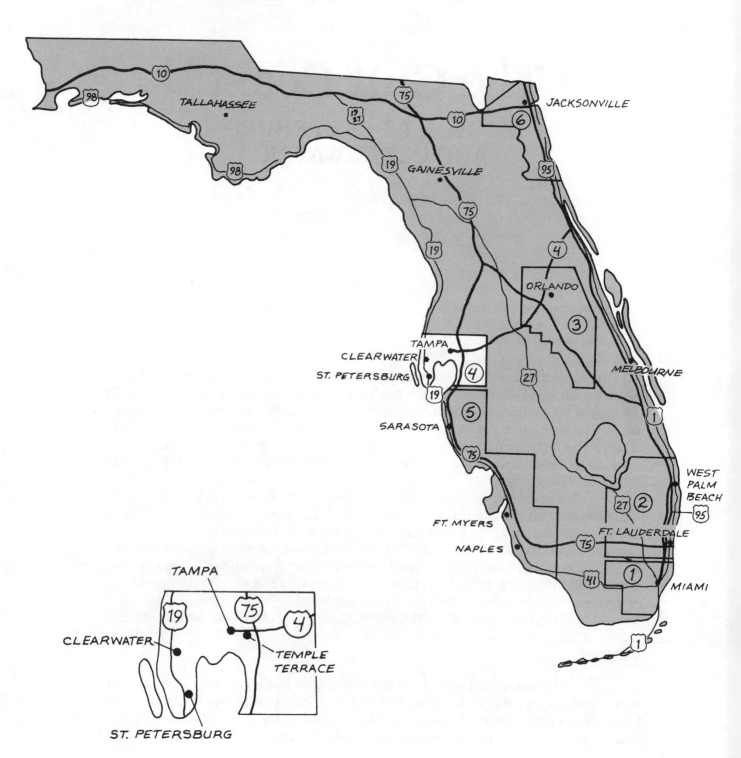

What's interesting is that it's not the retirees who are putting down stakes; they tend to head further north into Pinellas County; instead it's young families, the business professionals, and even the singles. The median age here is only 32; not only are they young, they're better-educated than their native counterparts. Their skills and expertise have contributed to the sheer vitality of the profitable business environment.

Newcomers are being drawn to the area by the ever-increasing number of light industry, high tech and service-related businesses. In fact, some of the largest U.S. corporations have set up regional headquarters here. Honeywell, Anheuser Busch, Citicorp Services, Xerox, Johnson and Johnson, and Metropolitan Life are just some of the firms adding to the low unemployment levels, the burgeoning economy…and to the impressive skyline.

Serving as a cultural magnet is the brand-new Tampa Bay Performing Arts Center, which faces the Hillsborough riverfront in downtown Tampa. This three-theatre complex brings in local and national talent for dance, drama, and music. Practically next door, a convention center is scheduled for completion at the end of 1989. When opened, it will be one of the largest in the country.

TAMPA NEIGHBORHOODS

Choosing a neighborhood is one of the greatest challenges of moving into this area. There is such a wide variety to pick from—modest and modern, old and stately, ritzy, preppy and everything in-between. Much of the appeal is that wherever you settle, you feel part of a small community, in spite of Tampa's continuous growth.

Attractive, contemporary single-family homes begin at $60,000, and as with the rest of Florida, you can fall in love with the custom homes. Prices start as low as the $70s, average in the $140s, and choices are breathtaking in the $200,000 range.

In northern Tampa numerous developments have sprung up, including Avila, Carrollwood, and Cheval. Homes in these exclusive areas appeal to the young and successful…or about-to-be successful. There are some lovely homes in the $60,000 and $70,000 range, and some spectacular waterfront properties for $200,000 and up. In the northeast quadrant, the new 5900-acre planned community of Tampa Palms was recently named "Florida's Best Environmentally Planned Community" by the Florida Association of Realtors. Buying into any of these contemporary residential villages entitles you to use of all the amenities you could possibly want: pools and clubhouses, an 18-hole golf course, schools, shopping and recreation facilities…even canoeing at River Park. Condos start at $85,000. Single-family homes range from $160,000 to $675,000. The typical home has 3500 to 4000 sq. feet of living space. That's a lot of living!

The waterfront district is on the south side of town. For those who have the resources and inclination to renovate the mansions and bungalows, the elegant Hyde Park and Bayshore Blvd. sections offer some unique and special finds. It's a great place to live when you work downtown—you're only minutes away. High-rise condos range from $100,000 to $200,000, although you can still pick up some units for $50,000 to $90,000. You can count on private homes selling in the $325,000 range.

Davis Island is hot as a pistol. In this private and quaint enclave at the tip of Hyde Park, you'll find older, sprawling homes. The average selling price is $150,000, with some of the larger houses going for twice that. To preserve the beauty and tranquility, no new houses are being built.

TEMPLE TERRACE

This very pleasant and progressive incorporated city is located in the northeast section of Tampa. The strictly-residential community is small (with 11,000 plus residents) and is actually a bedroom community for the University of South Florida. It's also known for the Temple Terrace Golf and County Club, one of the oldest courses in the state. According to John Barfield at Tam-Bay Realty, the average single-story Spanish-style home, including a 4/BR 2/BA arrangement with a pool, goes for $150,000. The typical lot size is 100 x 100.

BRANDON

Located 15 minutes east of Tampa via the Crosstown Expressway, Brandon is the largest unincorporated area in Tampa Bay. With an estimated population of close to 100,000, this is one of the most rapidly-developing communities around. It offers extensive choices of beautifully-appointed planned developments. Similar to other newly-built neighborhoods, you can spend $60,000, $160,000 or $260,000. Although many people moved here with the intent of commuting to business in Tampa, an increasing number are finding career and entrepreneurial opportunities in the retail and service sectors right in their own backyards. New industrial and office parks are cropping up like weeds.

St. Petersburg And Clearwater

Across the beautiful Tampa Bay is Pinellas County, home of St. Petersburg and Clearwater. Although it is Florida's second-smallest county in land area (309 sq. miles), it has the third-largest population (815,000). When you look at a map, you'll discover that Pinellas County is actually a 30-mile long peninsula, surrounded by the Gulf of Mexico to the west and south and Tampa Bay on the east.

Interestingly, this fast-growing region is another part of the state that was always known as a retirement community. It used to be said that if you thought the people in Sarasota were old, you should see their parents in St. Pete, but surprisingly, the median age here is 45. With a large migration of young career families, St. Pete and Clearwater are rapidly evolving into a business force to be reckoned with. City leaders are hard at work to encourage and promote municipal, industrial and public cooperation to create a prosperous but environmentally-sound atmosphere.

Aside from tourism, major industries include citrus, food production, electronics manufacturing, the optical and pharmaceutical fields, and the service trade.

For the sports buffs and weekend recreation seekers, Pinellas County is heaven. There are several PGA championship golf courses such as the famous Innisbrooke Resort and Golf Club. World-class tennis is at its best at Bardmoor Country Club. Baseball fans can rejoice between February and April when Spring Training comes alive. The St. Louis Cardinals train at Lang Field in St. Petersburg, the Philadelphia Phillies at Jack Murphy Stadium in Clearwater and the Toronto Bluejays at Grant Field in suburban Dunedin.

ST. PETERSBURG

Is there anything bad to say about a place that's nicknamed "The Sunshine City?" After breaking a world's record for 700 consecutive sunny days, the city was thusly named. It wasn't a fluke, either. The area averages 361 sunny days virtually every year. What's great about St. Pete is that you can live, work, and play in the same town, making for a very high quality of life. It's all here. The jobs. The housing. The beauty. The recreation.

The northeast part of town offers luxury condominiums, older homes and waterfront properties. On the south side are the older and more moderate private homes. Most were built in the 1940s and 1950s. The median housing price in St. Petersburg is just under $65,000. Tierra Verde and the Skyway section offer gorgeous waterfront properties starting at $200,000.

CLEARWATER

This year-round beach resort community is also an up-and-coming business community as well. The appeal to weary workers from the east is that there's virtually no traffic and congestion in what is considered a small but cosmopolitan environment. There's lots of new housing going up between $80,000 and $100,000, some of it in heavily wooded neighborhoods. Villas of Lake Arbor has constructed a beautiful townhome development, complete with a dock area. 2 and 3/BR condos start at $70,000.

Another area to explore in Pinellas County is Tarpon Springs, a gorgeous community 15 minutes outside of Clearwater. Here you'll find a mix of charming old estates and brand-new developments.

Finally, the coastal community of Largo, is a very fast-growing area on the peninsula. This incorporated city of 67,000 calls itself the "City of Progress," but in no way do they have the corner on that market. They are, however, at the highest elevation above sea level in Pinellas County. At least they can claim to offer the best views. Actually, the whole Tampa Bay area is a natural wonderland. And with the abundance of commercial activity, it's no doubt a business wonderland as well. It may be a region of contrasts, with young and old pursuing their own productive lifestyles, but it's all one big happy family under that continuous bright sun.

"The Sun Coast"

SARASOTA, BRADENTON, FT. MYERS, NAPLES

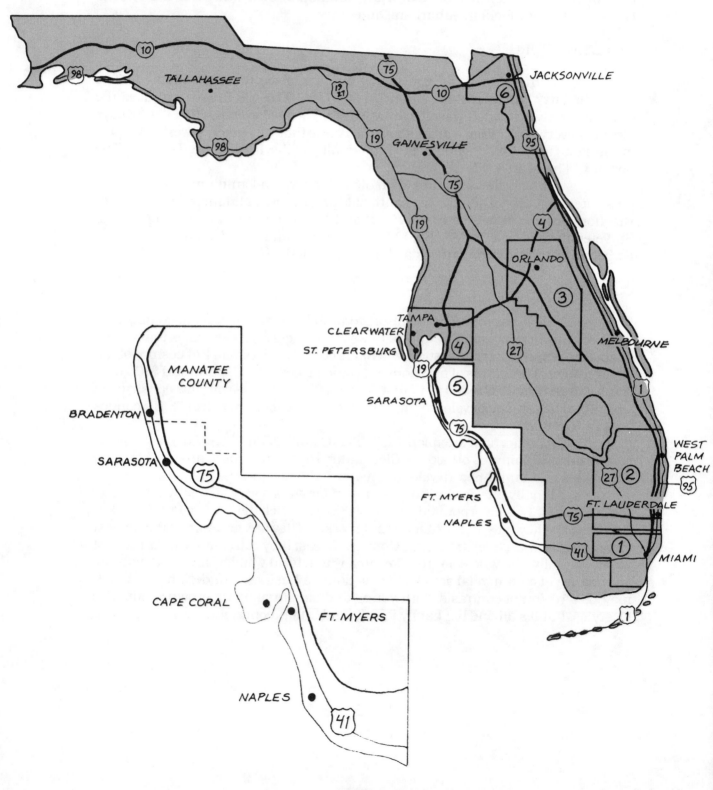

CHAPTER 27

"The Sun Coast"

SARASOTA, BRADENTON, FT. MYERS AND NAPLES

The southwest coast of Florida is one of the most picturesque and serene in the state. It has an abundance of culture and natural beauty; the architecture, homes and shopping are very elegant, and it's in a class by itself when it comes to hassle-free lifestyles. It's also one of Florida's best kept secrets, and residents are anxious to keep it that way.

Actually, the 110-mile stretch of paradise off the Gulf of Mexico could have many names: "The Seashell Coast;" "The Platinum Coast (there's a *lot* of money down here);" or "The Culture Coast"—all would describe the attributes of this Sarasota, Ft. Myers and Naples locale.

Those lucky souls who have discovered the region that is off the beaten path are less-than-anxious to get the word out. They would like nothing more than to keep their paradise safe, small and uncontested. As one Naples resident pleaded, "Please continue sending everyone to the east coast. Forget we're even here."

But ready or not, more and more people are exploring this sunny side of the state. Traditionally, the area was a retreat for the midwesterners. Bob Mayer of Century 21 in Sarasota said, "The whole state of Ohio is down here." But times are a-changing. New Yorkers, who are famous for only looking at Miami and Boca, have discovered there's a west coast and are coming in droves. "They can't believe we've been here all the time."

Let's start off with Sarasota, the heart of the coast in terms of size, population, events and activities and versatile housing choices.

Sarasota

If you've never seen the sights of Sarasota, never browsed around fashionable St. Armand's Circle or eaten in one of the fine restaurants on Siesta Key, you're in for a big treat. Sarasota has it all and more.

For those whose biggest fear about Florida is that there is no culture, you should see what tiny Sarasota brings to the party. In the early 1900s circus master John Ringling settled here and dreamt of turning the town into a cultural magnet; he succeeded. Today there are more museum exhibits, art offerings, theatrical events, symphonies, and operas than anywhere else in the state.

Sarasota's 50,000 residents take a great deal of pride in their Van Wezel Performing Arts Hall, Asolo State Theatre, The Ringling Museum of the Arts, The Florida Studio Theatre, The Florida Symphonic Band and the Sarasota Opera. If you are a patron of the arts, this is the place to be, but don't get the impression that Sarasotans sit around all day and listen to La Boheme. The ideal subtropical climate and ample private and public sporting facilities make this place an outdoor person's paradise.

Golfers especially have some wonderful developments to choose from. Gary Player, the South African pro, is building a new residential golf club community, which promises to be a deluxe complex of homes and condominiums. Everyone is talking about Prestancia at the south end of town. This elegant golf club community offers a mix of single-family houses and condos. Starting prices are around $180,000, but you can spend a million dollars if you prefer. The Oaks, an Arvida development, is another spectacular community where single-family homes start at $200,000. Close by, east of Bee Ridge Rd., is the exclusive Bent Tree Country Club development, another upscale golfer's paradise. Donald Regan recently retired here. Inland are Pelican Cove and The Meadows, large and elegant self-contained communities offering top notch services, amenities, facilities and a vast assortment of luxury homes and condos. Close to downtown is the older but elegant Harbor Acres.

Realtors spoke of the action happening on the Sarasota/Manatee county line. Sections of new and reasonably-priced homes are available starting from $80,000; also in this part of town is Palm Aire, a country club complex offering houses, condos and two fine golf courses.

Off the shores of Sarasota are two of Florida's most famous keys, Long Boat Key and Siesta Key. Here you'll find some of the most spectacular waterfront homes and condominiums, world-class dining and shopping, and the most beautiful white sandy beaches you've ever set foot upon.

Manatee County/Bradenton

Sandwiched between Sarasota to the south and Tampa Bay to the north is mighty Manatee County, which is taking off like wildfire. Everything is bright and new here: Homes. Shopping centers. Schools.

The city of Bradenton and surrounding Anna Maria Island and Palmetto are taking the spillover from Sarasota and Pinellas Counties due to the lower-priced waterfront properties, beautiful beaches, good school systems and even its own sewage and water systems. This is a rarity, and anyone who is aware of the seriousness of the water shortage problem across the state should make a note that Manatee County has a 15-year supply on hand.

According to Jay Getz of Golden Gate Relocation in Bradenton, many people who work in St. Petersburg are choosing to live in Manatee County instead of Pinellas because the rebuilt Sunshine Skyway Bridge actually makes commuting to work faster and more convenient. Also, housing prices are very reasonable and the sizes of the lots may be larger.

Among the areas to look at, Ellenton Parrish to the north and east of town has new homes priced at $80,000 to $125,000, and growth over the next five years is expected to be sizeable; in Northwest Bradenton, the Azalia Park section is a lovely community with big brand-new homes selling between $150,000 and $250,000. West of I-75 is a new golf course community called Tera; homes and condos are reasonably priced between $85,000 and $150,000 . . . but the place that has everyone's tails wagging is the River Wilderness, a "hot" new development with 2 championship golf courses. This exclusive complex on the north side of the river is selling homes at $200,000 and up (that doesn't include the $5000 membership fee). It's pricey, but perfect.

Ft. Myers

Thomas Edison had more than one bright idea when he settled in Ft. Myers back in 1855. You've never seen coconut palms quite like those found in this scenic "City of Palms." With one of the most versatile shorelines in Florida, this burgeoning young community is making a name for itself. Situated off Pine Island Sound, the Caloosahatchee River and the Gulf of Mexico, the 40,000 residents enjoy year 'round natural beauty and quality planned developments.

Most of the growth and development is centered around the south side of town, which is most convenient to the shopping and business districts. San Carlos Park is one of the most popular communities, offering beautiful newly-built homes starting in the $60,000 range. Just about everything here is under $100,000, which is why it's attracting young families.

Also south is The Landings, a beautifully-appointed golf and tennis development right on the river. Here you'll find a large selection of houses, condos and villas in the $120,000- $180,000 range. Waterfront properties in this area start at $130,000 and up. The Town and River complex is known as a quality buy. For even more luxurious surroundings, look to The Forest, Eagle Ridge, and The Fiddlesticks, which has one of the top 30 golf courses in the state. Houses, villas, and condos start at $200,000 with many styles coming in at $300,000. River access, which feeds into the gulf, makes this an ideal location for boaters.

CAPE CORAL

Just across the river is lovely Cape Coral. Looking at a map, you wouldn't realize that this gulf-front community is the second largest city in land size in the state, covering 103 sq. miles. That gives its 60,000 residents plenty of room to spread out. Although there are frequent complaints of excessive traffic and congestion crossing the single span bridge during the height of the season, people are quick to point out that you just take the good with the bad. Expansion bridges are in the works.

Connie Mack was one of the original developers in this quiet retirement area. More and more young families are moving in to take advantage of the affordable housing and water-oriented recreation. The school and health care systems are some of the finest in the southwest.

Naples

This former tiny and remote fishing village is now one of the most charming and graceful communities in the state. For a city of only 18,000, this joint is jumping! Like so many regions of Florida that were once viewed as retirement havens, you can't keep the young people away. They've diversified the economy and expanded industry to the point where the half-dozen business and industrial parks are surging. Naples is now home to art galleries, culture, nightlife entertainment and delightful boutiques along their version of 5th Ave.

All of Naples sugar-sand (quartz) beaches are open to the public and provide year-round water activities. There is some spectacular oceanfront property, and relative to the east coast, you don't have to spend close to a million to get it. A half-million buys something palatial. But honestly, anywhere you go here is a winner. Most of the action is east of Route 41. Kings Lake and Lely are two beautiful gulf communities that offer condos, villas and homes in the $100,000 to $200,000 range. Old Naples, Moorings and Park Shore are other elegant neighborhoods attracting newcomers.

North of Naples is the Westinghouse community of Pelican Bay, an environmentally-protected area that offers some of the most breathtaking views in town.

CHAPTER 28

"The Historic Coast"

GREATER JACKSONVILLE

Covering 840 sq. miles of land, Jacksonville is actually the largest city in the country. And it's growing so fast, its 600,000 residents are concerned that it will lose its small-town feel. But not to worry. This "Big Bold New City of the South" is ready for just about anything, because this region, rich in history, has seen it all. Jacksonville and nearby St. Augustine are often called the "First Coast" due to their early discovery in 1513 by Spain's Ponce de Leon. The desirable river cities endured hundreds of years of territorial battles between Great Britain, Spain, France and even the Timucua Indians.

Today's Jacksonville offers a unique blend of lifestyles, from cosmopolitan to country. The cultural, social and housing options are vast, and recreation is everywhere. With almost 75 sq. miles of rivers, creeks and lakes in the city limits, water sports are always nearby. Community beaches dot the shoreline for 50 miles to the north and south. The city takes great pride in its beautifully planned neighborhoods, its system of well maintained parks and green belt areas, and its non-stop cultural calendar, renowned galleries and museums. But the big appeal is the cost of living. It's one of the lowest in the country, certainly lower than its large counterparts across the state. In addition it has a strong and diverse economy, which is supported in part by being a banking and insurance capital of the entire Southeast.

The city's hospitals have an outstanding medical reputation which so impressed the famed Mayo Clinic that they opened a satellite center there recently.

Housing choices are exciting and versatile. What's your pleasure? A recreational environment? A country place? A riverfront home? A restored home

283

"The Historic Coast"
GREATER JACKSONVILLE

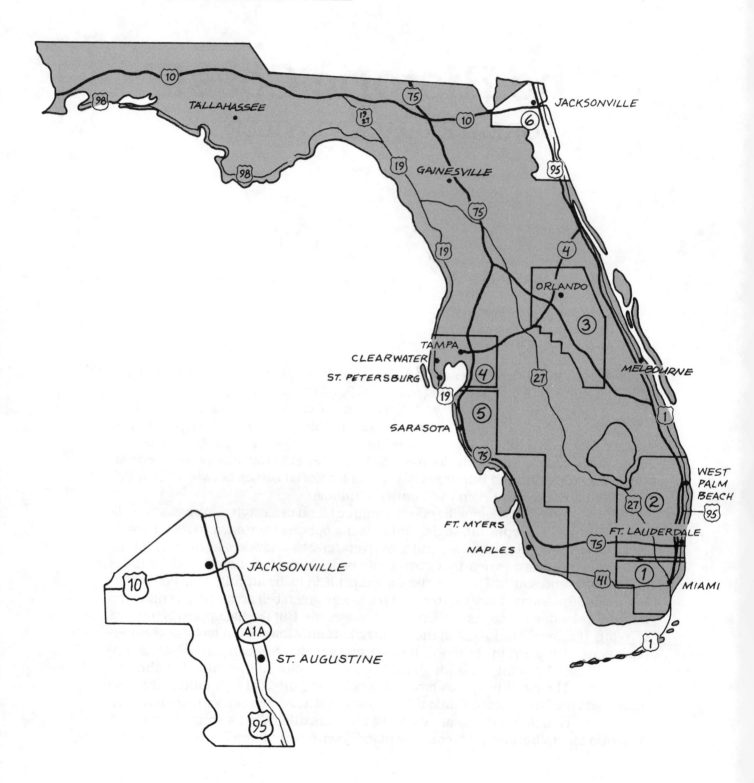

in one of the rich, historical sections? It's all here. Asking prices are modest-to-reasonable for both single-family homes and condos. The average 3/BR 2/BA home with 2000 sq. feet of living space costs between $50,000 and $100,000. Larger custom-built homes start at around $150,000.

In spite of its size and its resources, Jacksonville is not exactly top-of-mind when people start to consider areas of Florida for a relocation, yet in all the interviews we conducted, the "happy" factor was overwhelmingly high here. We have heard nothing but positive comments from newcomers—about the incredible friendliness, the strong community feeling, the varied weather and change of seasons, the employment and business opportunities, the affordable lifestyles, and the high quality of life.

No wonder so many people fought to claim this land as their own.

SECTION VI

What Every New Resident Should Know

CHAPTER 29

Florida Laws:

WILLS, TRUSTS, AND EVERYTHING IN BETWEEN

Whenever the subject of Wills, probate or other matters arise that have to do with protecting one's own interests, I'm reminded of this story. A friend of the deceased went to the cemetery to pay his respects. Unfortunately, after hours of searching he was unable to locate the gravesite. He called the widow to explain his dilemma.

"You told me your husband was buried in the Good Samaritan Cemetery. Why can't I find his plot?"

"It's simple," she responded. "Look for the one that says Ruth Stern."

"But that's you," he said with surprise.

"Certainly," she said. "Before he died, I made sure everything was in my name."

It's amazing how sharp are the instincts when it comes to protecting what's rightfully ours, and this is a good thing. Yet oftentimes we make important decisions, not really knowing from a legal perspective if they will work to our advantage or not. Fortunately Florida laws, including those pertaining to wills, trusts, estate taxes and other important family matters, generally favor its residents. Certainly when it comes to the two sure things in this world, "death and taxes", it's better to be in Florida than just about anywhere else. Nevertheless, you should probably anticipate making some changes in your estate plan once you have a basic overview of Florida's legal and tax structure. Many laws will have an immediate and direct effect on your personal and financial affairs.

By reviewing the questions and answers that are relevant to your circumstances, you'll have a good understanding of what to anticipate before you meet with your new legal and accounting professionals. In the meantime, please note that the following information is both current and accurate to the best of our knowledge. However, it is intended for instructional purposes only. *Before you take any legal action with respect to your estate, seek the advice and counsel of a knowledgeable attorney.*

LEGAL RESIDENCY

Q. What do I need to do in order to establish that I'm a resident of Florida and how long does it take?

A. Florida has no fixed waiting period for establishing residency. However, in order to show your intent to make Florida your legal residence, you must first establish a home or permanent dwelling place. Proving your intent can be accomplished by filing a sworn statement with the Clerk of the Circuit Court for the county in which you reside. There is a $6 filing fee for recording this "Affidavit of Domicile." If you forward a copy of this Affidavit to your former state's tax collection agency, that will provide further proof that you have severed your ties with that state and now consider yourself a permanent, legal resident of Florida.

Proof of legal residency is an issue the state of Florida does not take lightly. There are numerous tax benefits offered to permanent, legal residents, and thus, the state agencies who monitor taxes and revenues go after those who try to claim resident status on their tax returns. In particular, New York state has enacted strict legislation to prohibit New York business owners, who are "snowbirds," from claiming legal residence in Florida as a way to avoid heavy taxation. There are other laws on the books in both states pertaining to tax evasion. In fact, recently the two states agreed to cross-check tax information. Thus, if you plan to maintain homes in both states for a while, you should check with your attorney before you do anything that might be questioned later on.

Q. What are the residency requirements for voting?

A. Eligibility for voting requires that you be 18 or older, a citizen of the United States, and a permanent resident of Florida and the county where you intend to vote. You have up until 30 days prior to an election to register with the Supevisor of Elections in your county. Since there is no waiting period for residency, there is also no waiting period for voter registration.

Q. Does Florida have minimum residency requirements for anything?

A. Yes. In order to get a divorce, at least one of the parties to the marriage must have lived in Florida for six months or longer before the filing of the petition for the dissolution of the marriage. Also, anyone wishing to run for public office in Florida must generally satisfy certain residency requirements, depending on the office and the city in which the election is held.

FLORIDA TAXES

Q. What is the current sales tax in Florida?

A. As of February, 1988, the retail sales tax is 6%. However, medical, pharmaceutical and most food purchases are exempt. The exception to this is meals purchased at restaurants.

Q. Is it true that Florida has no personal income tax?

A. Yes it's true, thanks to the express prohibition against personal income taxes contained in Florida's Constitution. Moreover, it seems unlikely that this ban on personal income taxes will ever be lifted since this would require a Constitutional Amendment which the majority of people in Florida would have to approve.

Q. Are there any other taxes that Florida does not levy?

A. Florida is the only state in the Southeast which has no annual franchise tax, although it does have an intangible tax (discussed later on). Moreover, although Florida has an estate tax, it does not cost the state anything. Here's why. The IRS allows a credit (reduction) against federal estate taxes for state death taxes. The amount of this credit is based on a specific formula. Florida accepts this state death tax credit, less inheritance taxes paid to other states (if any), as the amount owed to Florida for estate taxes payable by a deceased Florida resident. This means that a portion of the total estate taxes are paid to Florida instead of to the IRS. In essence, the IRS and Florida are sharing the total tax dollars that otherwise, but for the state death tax credit, would go solely to the IRS.

Q. Is there a property tax imposed by the state?

A. Although Florida residents pay real estate taxes, they are not levied by the state. Instead, property taxes fall under the jurisdiction of the city, county and/or special districts. However, it's the state that requires that all real property be assessed at its full, fair market value. The tax collector in the county where you are moving can tell you what that assessment will be. But here's an interesting twist: although the state requires that all homeowners be notified of any increases in the assessed value of their property during the previous year, they do not have much time to take action. Specifically, the tax rolls must be completed by July 1 of each year (although extensions may be applied for and are frequently granted), and a notice of the proposed property taxes must be given to each homeowner. Homeowners have only 25 days following the mailing of this notice in which to file a petition objecting to the proposed increase. Consequently, you better move fast if you disagree with a hiked assessment!

Q. What exactly is Florida's Homestead Tax Exemption and how can I take advantage of it?

A. The Homestead Tax Exemption is a tax break that entitles permanent residents to exclude the first $25,000 of their home's assessed value in determining their real property tax. In order to qualify, you must be a permanent, legal resident of Florida. Secondly, you must both purchase and occupy a home in Florida by January 1 of the year in which you are applying for the tax exemption. To receive the homestead exemption, you must file an application with your county's Property Appraiser's office by March 1 of the year in which the exemption is to apply. In addition, there is a $500 homestead exemption available to widowed, blind or disabled residents, as well as a complete exemption for certain disabled veterans. The Property Appraiser's office can inform you of your eligibility.

Q. What exactly are the Tangible and Intangible Tax Laws?

A. In some respects, they are Florida's answer to the income tax dilemma. Since the state does not impose an income tax on individuals (it is prohibited by Florida's Constitution), the state has to collect revenue somehow. One way is from the Tangible Personal Property Tax, which is imposed on all personal property used in a commercial enterprise. This includes such things as business supplies, fixtures and furnishings, etc. The amount of this tax is based on the owner's declared value by April 1 or a 25% penalty can be imposed. The Intangible Personal Property tax, which applies in lieu of a franchise tax, is imposed on certain types of intangible assets owned by a Florida resident such as stocks, bonds (except bonds issued by the state or by the federal government), mutual funds, accounts and notes receivable, mortgages secured by non-Florida properties and other taxable securities. Cash and interests in limited partnerships are exempt from the intangible tax.

Each January, residents receive an intangible tax return form which must be completed and returned by June 30 of that year. The intangible tax rate is very low: a maximum of $1 for every $1000 of assessed value. That means a portfolio would have to be valued at over a million dollars before the tax bill reached $1000. There is a $20,000 exemption for individuals and a $40,000 exemption for married persons (even if all the securities are in one person's name). Due to this generous allowance, many taxpayers owe a nominal amount of tax, or nothing at all. You can see why some residents feel the intangible tax is a nuisance, but it's still on the books.

Please note that there is a separate one time, intangible tax of $2 for every $1000 of assessed value of all notes, bonds, and other obligations for the payment of money which is secured by a mortgage on real property located in Florida (this nonrecurring intangible tax is payable when the mortgage is recorded).

Q. Is there a Florida corporate income tax, and if so, how is it assessed?

A. The state's corporate income tax structure is based on federal taxable income, with certain adjustments, and is imposed on every corporation (foreign or domestic), organization, association, and financial institution that does business or generates income within the state. The rate of this tax is 5.5%, and is applied to that portion of the corporation's Federal taxable income, less a $5000 exemption, which is allocated to Florida based on certain income appointment rules.

Q. Are there other taxes or fees charged for doing business in Florida?
    A. Yes. Counties and incorporated municipalities are authorized to levy taxes and/or fees for businesses operating in their jurisdiction. These fees are for "Occupational Licenses" needed to conduct business. Since the charges for these licenses vary considerably, contact the city clerk or county tax assessor for more details.

WILLS AND TESTAMENTS

Q. Is my old Will going to be considered legal and valid in Florida?
    A. That depends. The Will you drew up in another state will be valid when you move to Florida, in so far as distributive provisions are concerned, provided that the execution of your Will meets all of the execution requirements under Florida law, such as having two witnesses, etc.

Q. Are there any advantages to drawing up a new Will?
    A. Most definitely. There are three good reasons to execute a new Will once you've established residency in Florida.

   1. A Last Will and Testament should always indicate your current legal address so that it is clear under which state's laws the Will is to be executed.

   2. The witnesses to your current Will presumably live in your old state, which could make it difficult to locate them if the Will is probated. Further, unless the Will is a self-proving Will (discussed shortly), Florida law requires that a Will be proved by having the witnesses, resident or not, affirm that they saw the decedent sign the Will. That may mean bringing an out-of-state witness to Florida, most likely at the expense of the Estate. Alternatively, a Will may be admitted to probate in Florida upon the oath of any attending witness taken before a commissioner appointed by the court. This alternative approval may apply if a witness is not physically capable of making the trip to Florida, for example. Thus, the estate may be facing additional expenses, as well as additional time, in order to prove the Will. It therefore pays to create a new Will, which contains a proving clause. This would avoid having to locate witnesses after the decedent's death.

   3. Another reason why it's important to prepare a new Will is that it's possible that the person or trust company named as Personal

Representative (or Executor) in your current Will may not be qualified to act as such in Florida. Florida law requires that the personal Representative either be (i) another legal resident who is 18 or older, or (ii) a non-resident who is either a spouse of the decedent, a legally adopted child or adoptive parent of the decedent, a blood relative of the decedent, or the spouse of a person otherwise qualified to serve. Any trust company incorporated in Florida or any state banking corporation that is qualified to exercise fiduciary powers in Florida is also qualified to act as a personal representative. If your executor does not qualify, the court is required to appoint someone who does.

Q. If I have an attorney draw up a new Will for me, should it be "Self-Proved"?
A. Yes. Given the obstacles described above, having a "self-proved" Will in Florida is very important! A "self-proved" Will is one that has been properly notarized, and contains certain language making a court appearance (or other affirmation) by the witness unnecessary. In other words, the court allows the Will in probate on the strength of the notarization and the self-proving language alone.

ESTATES

Q. What rights does a surviving spouse have to the estate of the deceased spouse?
A. If the deceased spouse was domiciled in Florida at the time of his death, the surviving spouse is given the opportunity to file for an elective share of the decedent's net probate estate if the surviving spouse is unhappy with what had been willed to that spouse. This elective share amounts to 30% of the fair market value of the assets of the probate estate (excluding non-Florida real estate), computed after deducting (i) all claims against the estate and (ii) all mortgages, liens or security interests on the probate assets. It is important to note that non-probate assets such as life insurance contracts, jointly-held assets with right of survivorship and assets held in trust are not subject to the elective share.

Q. What happens to real estate owned in a state other than Florida at a resident's death?
A. If you die in Florida and have property in Illinois, for example, then there will be two probates—one in each state. In Florida, this procedure is called an ancillary administration. Some states will not release personal property to Florida without a probate administration, even if the main one is underway in Florida. Check with your hometown attorney to determine your former state's rulings on property left by a deceased Florida resident.

Q. What happens to the estate when a Florida resident dies without a valid Will (i.e., dies intestate)?

294

A. Under Florida law, an intestate decedent's estate is distributed as follows:

1. If there are no surviving lineal descendants of the decedent (children, grandchildren, etc.) the decedent's surviving spouse receives the entire estate.
2. If there are surviving lineal descendants of the decedent, the decedent's surviving spouse receives the first $20,000 of the estate, plus 50% of the remaining estate. The decedent's lineal descendants (i.e., children, grandchildren, etc.) receive the balance of the estate.
3. If any of the surviving lineal descendants of the decedent are not lineal descendants of the surviving spouse, the surviving spouse receives 50% of the entire estate and the balance of the estate is divided equally among the decedent's lineal descendants.
4. If there is no surviving spouse, the entire estate is divided equally among the decedent's lineal descendants.
5. When there is neither a spouse nor a lineal descendent, the estate goes to the descendent's parents equally, or if none are surviving, decedent's brothers and sisters or their descendants.
6. If no person exists in these categories, the estate is divided equally between the decedent's maternal and paternal grandparents and their lineal descendants.
7. If no person exists in these categories, the estate passes to the heirs of the last deceased spouse of the decedent.
8. Finally, if no person qualifies, the estate becomes the property of the State of Florida.

PROBATE

Q. What is probate?

A. Probate is the legal proceeding for validating and administering the last Will and Testament of the deceased, passing title to assets and protecting beneficiaries and creditors of the deceased.

Q. Why is probate such a dreaded procedure?

A. When most people think of probate, the first two things that come to mind are exorbitant costs and spending a lot of time with lawyers. However, if you select a qualified personal representative to settle the estate, who in turn selects a reputable attorney, the fees paid to the lawyer should be a modest amount for the work that is performed. Court fees are determined by a Florida statute and are considered to be reasonable.

Q. How can you anticipate the cost of Executor's fees?

A. It used to be that the state dictated the fees for an executor handling the probate proceedings. Now the Probate Court simply states that the fees must be "reasonable." To clarify what is reasonable, Florida has categorized estates by their size. Estates under $25,000 require "summary administration," which can typically be handled by an attorney in one court appearance. The next category is called "family administration," and this is for taxable estates that do not exceed $60,000 or consist of any real property. The intent here is to allow the family to settle the debts of the deceased, clarify the distribution of assets and to present the estate to the court for prompt disposition. If the estate is larger than $60,000 the standard probate proceedings must take place.

Keep in mind that the size of the estate may be less relevant than the complexity of the estate when trying to predict legal fees. In other words, a million dollar estate could be settled quickly if it consisted of two homes, a car, and cash. A $200,000 estate could take forever to settle if the deceased had three ex-spouses, 2 heirs (one of which can't be found), and a $50,000 lien against his property.

Q. Florida used to be known for dragging out probate proceedings. Is that still true?
A. Unless there is just cause, an estate that is not required to file a federal tax return gives the personal representative 12 months to submit the final accounting and petition for discharge. If a tax return is due, the representative has 12 months from that due date. The exception to this is the sizeable estates which may become involved in major tax disputes.

LIVING WILLS

Q. Does Florida allow "Living Wills"?
A. Yes. In 1984, the legislature passed a bill which allows competent adults to make declarations regarding the use of life-prolonging devices on themselves, should it ever be necessary. The law states that you can make the decision to withdraw or withhold these measures.

JOINT TENANCY

Q. What is joint tenancy with right of survivorship?
A. Joint tenancy with the right of survivorship, as the name suggests, means that two or more persons, including but not limited to spouses and/or family members are declared equal owners of the bank accounts, house, stocks and securities, etc. and that upon the death of one of the co-owners, the jointly-held assets automatically pass to the surviving co-owner or co-ownees. This form of ownership eliminates the need to go through the probate courts (and therefore avoids the delay) in order to pass title to the surviving co-owner or co-ownees. This also saves the expense of attorney's fees, court costs, and the fees paid to a personal representative.

Q. Is joint tenancy always advisable?

A. Not in every case. While it is an effective method for the prompt transfer of assets, problems are known to occur when one of the spouses is still alive, but mentally or physically incapacitated. Unless the able spouse has durable family power of attorney, he or she would have to petition the court to act as the guardian for the spouse so that they could act on the disabled spouse's behalf. This can be a very long and expensive process at a time when it is neither emotionally nor financially possible. There are also federal estate tax reasons why a joint tenancy may not always be the best solution.

Q. Is it still necessary to draw up a Will if the children are already listed as joint tenants with rights of survivorship for the entire estate?

A. Yes. In the tragic event that your children predecease you, a Will indicates the residual beneficiaries. Of course, if you die first, and this provision is in force, probate will be unnecessary, since the jointly held assets will pass to your children, as joint-owners, by operation of law.

Q. Should an adult child be listed as a joint tenant with right of survivorship on bank accounts and other assets?

A. If the adult child is the only lineal descendant, then there should be no problem. If there are other siblings however, and they are not listed as joint tenants, then at your death, the ownership and complete control of the jointly-owned assets passes by operation of law to the surviving joint owner (the adult child) who is free to do as he wishes with respect to these assets. This may start World War III, since the other siblings have no ownership or control of these assets. Therefore, you may wish to either include the other siblings as joint owners or have the assets held in a living trust for the benefit of all siblings.

LIVING TRUSTS

Q. What is a Living Trust?

A. When you set up a living trust, you enter into an agreement with a trustee to hold legal title to your property and estate. Subsequently, all or a portion of your assets are transferred to that person. In the agreement, it states how the income from the assets will be distributed, and who will be the beneficiaries. If you so choose, you can elect to have yourself as the sole beneficiary until your death. The trust agreement also spells out the distribution of your assets after your death and how long the trust is to last. It even dictates what assets the trustee can invest in, how the trust shall be managed, as well as the amount of compensation the trustee shall receive.

Q. Why should you set up a Living Trust?

A. At some stage in many people's lives, they reach a point where due to a spouse's illness or death, or their own illness, they are unable to care for themselves or their property. With a Living Trust, drawn up when the individual was of sound mind to make the best possible decisions for him- or herself, the person is assured that his estate will be protected.

Q. Are there any other reasons to set up a Living Trust?

A. Yes, the most important one is that assets in a trust avoid the probate procedure. Thus there is no delay in transferring the assets to the surviving spouse or other party. Nor is there the major expense of working with the probate court. In other words, if the trust provides for the distribution of the assets on your death, or provides for the trust to continue, there will be no probate of your assets (assuming you had no assets outside of the trust).

Q. What happens if the trustee violates the terms of the Living Trust?

A. The matter will be resolved in a civil court, not in probate court.

Q. Is it still necessary to have a Will even though the Living Trust exists?

A. Yes. A Living Trust only applies to those assets which are owned by the trust. In many instances, people limit the assets that they place in a trust to marketable securities, real estate, life insurance and other investments. For whatever reasons, they do not refer to family owned non-incorporated businesses, jewels, furs and collectibles, furniture, and cash and debts owed to the deceased. These are assets that if owned by the decedent in his name at death end up as part of the probate estate and therefore, have to be validated in probate court. A lawyer or financial planner well versed in trusts can show you how to avoid the probate trap all together by the inclusion of a "pourover clause" in a Will.

Q. Who should be appointed the trustee in a Living Trust?

A. Legally, you have the right to appoint yourself as the trustee. In this case you would indicate in the trust at what point you would be willing to turn the trust over to a "successor trustee," such as a family member or close friend. Alternatively, you may appoint a corporate trustee, such as a bank or trust company, to serve as a trustee or as successor trustee. If appointed, the trust department of a bank or trust company would be responsible for overseeing the administration of the trust. One of the major advantages of having a bank or trust company serve as trustee is that the company's personnel are trained and experienced in this very complex area of trust administration. Another advantage is that the corporate trustee's existence is perpetual, and therefore, does not terminate upon the death of an individual. Too often a trustee is appointed who predeceases the trust's beneficiaries or who becomes too ill or incompetent to continue with his duties and responsibilities as trustee. When shopping for a corporate trustee, the amount of fees to be charged needs to be compared and analyzed in relation to the reputation of the corporate trustee.

Q. Once a Living Trust is established, is it always irrevocable?

    A. No, it can be designed to be amended, changed, or completely revoked at any time for any reason . . . provided the contingencies are clearly spelled out in the trust document. A Living Trust may, by the terms set forth in the agreement, be made irrevocable in which case the person creating the trust will not be allowed to amend or revoke the trust once it has been created.

Q. Is a Living Trust a matter of public record?

    A. No. Only the attorneys, the beneficiaries, the trustees, and the IRS need know about the trust.

Q. What kind of expenses are involved in setting up a Living Trust?

    A. Obviously there will be attorney's fees for preparing the trust document. In addition, there will be fees paid to the trustee at regular intervals. Typically, trustees receive commissions on the income of a trust, plus an upfront fee when the trust goes into effect. Moreover, upon the creation of an irrevocable trust, there may be gift taxes imposed.

Q. What does Florida law say about the power of attorney?

    A. Florida is one of the few states that allows a concept called "Durable Family Power of Attorney." Essentially, this is a power of attorney which may be granted only to a family member. Generally it provides that if a family member becomes incapacitated, senile or otherwise incompetent due to a serious illness or injury, the spouse or adult children can transact business for that person. This authorization must be in writing—while the person is capable of agreeing to the transfer of power. The power of attorney privilege cannot be bestowed if the person has never agreed to it and is now unable to carry on.

TESTAMENTARY TRUSTS

Q. What is a Testamentary Trust?

    A. Simply, it is a trust whose terms are set forth in your Will. After the death of the "testator" and the probate of the Will, the trust goes into effect.

Q. How does it compare with a Living Trust?

    A. A Living Trust is set up while you are alive and continues after your death. Assets owned by you at the time of your death may be transferred to this trust by way of pourover clause. A Testamentary Trust, the terms of which are included in your Will, does not go into effect until after your death.

Q. Why would anyone create a Testamentary Trust?

    A. Many people want to dictate precisely how their money will be spent upon their death, preventing a spendthrift child or a relative with poor judgment from improperly using the funds. Alternatively, you may want to provide for the support of a surviving spouse who is an invalid, so that he or she does not have to be responsible for managing and investing the remaining assets in your estate. A testamentary trust can accomplish these objectives.

It's Time To Review Your Plans

Moving to Florida would be the perfect time to have an attorney and certified financial planner, proficient in estate and tax planning, review your Will and Trusts. Since many of the laws have changed in the past few years, certainly you will want to do everything possible to protect your family as well as you can from a large tax burden and other problems associated with inattention to the details of an estate.

Editor's note: This chapter on Wills and Trusts was edited by Nick Jovanovich, a tax attorney with the law firm of English, McCaughan & O'Bryan in Ft. Lauderdale. Mr. Jovanovich heads up the firm's tax practice, consisting of all areas of federal and state taxation. This includes estate and gift tax planning and corporate law. Mr. Jovanovich received his law degree from Florida State University and his LL.M. degree in Taxation from the University of Florida. He is a member of the Florida and the Georgia State Bars and is admitted to practice in the United States Tax Court, as well as the United States Claims Court. He is a Florida Board Certified Tax Lawyer and is also a Certified Public Accountant in the State of Florida. He is a member of the American Association of Attorneys–Certified Public Accountants and is a member of the Greater Fort Lauderdale Tax Council and the Estate Planning Council of Broward County. Mr. Jovanovich has authored numerous tax-related articles and is a frequent speaker on tax-related subjects.

Mr. James Gallagher, an attorney in Baldwin, NY (Long Island) assisted with the editing. He is a member of the New York, Florida and Federal Bars and has been admitted to the Southeastern District to practice before the tax court. A graduate of the Florida State University College of Law, he was the former senior tax consultant at Price Waterhouse CPA's. He has also been associated with the Manhattan law firms of D'Amato & Lynch and Lowey, Dannenberg, Knapp, PC. In his private practice, he concentrates on tax law and real estate.

For further discussions with Mr. Jovanovich and Mr. Gallagher, you can contact them at the following addresses:

Mr. Nick Jovanovich, Esq.
English, McCaughan & O'Bryan
100 NE 3rd Ave., Suite 1100
Ft. Lauderdale, FL 33301
(305) 462-3301

Mr. James M. Gallagher, Esq.
Attorney-At-Law
2249 Derby Road
Baldwin, NY 11510
(516) 223-0993

CHAPTER 30

The Rules of the Road:
DRIVING IN FLORIDA

The laws pertaining to owning and driving a car in Florida are very clear-cut and not unlike those in most states. The speed limit is 55 mph, there's right turn on red, and you must have a valid driver's license and registration.

On the positive side, getting around can be a pleasure since the majority of roads are new and well maintained, the predominant mild weather conditions make for easy visibility and finally, large and ample street and highway signs reduce the incidence of accidents and getting lost.

So why do Florida drivers have the highest blood pressure levels than, perhaps, anywhere else in the country? It's due to the "Sunday Driver" phenomenon. For some Florida motorists, every day is Sunday. I refer, of course, to many of the seniors who have difficulty with just two minor driving skills. Starting and stopping. It is not my intent to be disrespectful, but it is true that one of the biggest adjustments newcomers have is trying to keep their cool when they find themselves behind another motorist who thinks that anything over 30 mph constitutes a drag race. What's the answer? According to my father-in-law, a former leadfoot from the midwest, you should avoid driving behind cars where all you see is a hat behind the wheel. If you see a hat *and* a cigar, pull over. You're not going anywhere for a while.

Here are some other important answers to questions regarding Florida's rules of the road.

Q. Do new residents need a Florida driver's license?
A. Yes, and they must apply within 30 days of accepting a job, entering

301

children in public school, registering to vote, or filing for the homestead exemption.

Q. *Do you have to take an exam even if you have a valid license from another state?*
A. Yes, you will be required to take both a written exam and a driving test. Your hearing and vision will also be tested.

Q. *What is the minimum age requirement for a license?*
A. 16. At age 15, a person can get a Restricted Operator's License, which is a learner's permit.

Q. *What is the cost of a Florida driver's license?*
A. A Florida license costs $15, and first-time applicants are charged an additional $4. If you have a clean driving record (no prior convictions for the past 3 years) your license will be good for 6 years, expiring at midnight on your birthday.

Q. *Where do I apply for my driver's license?*
A. At any Division of the Driver's License Office. Check the phone book for the nearest location. Every testing office has copies of the *Florida Driver's License Handbook*.

Q. *Does every car owner need a Florida Auto Tag?*
A. Yes. All residents who own and operate cars must apply for an official Florida license tag (license plate) at the county tax collector's office. This must be done within 10 days of accepting employment, operating a business or enrolling children in school. If you are a disabled veteran or are applying for personalized plates, you must do this through the Division of Motor Vehicles in Tallahassee. *Write to: Department of Highway Safety and Motor Vehicles, 2900 Apalachee Parkway, Neil Kirkman Building, Tallahassee, Fl 32301.*

Q. *What does it cost to license and register your car?*
A. License plates are issued for a 5 year period with the cost being assessed by the weight of the vehicle. Cars up to 2,499 lbs. pay $19.60; 2,500 to 3,900 lbs., $27.60; and cars 3,500 lbs. and up, $37.60. This is an annual registration fee. Once paid, you will receive a revalidation sticker in the mail to affix to the plate.

Q. *Does Florida allow vanity plates?*
A. Yes, for an extra $12 a year, you can apply for a personalized plate. In addition to personalization, you can also order a special Challenger plate for $25 or a Collegiate plate for $17.00. The collegiate plate allows you to select from one of nine state-supported universities. You can submit an application for these plates at any time. The vanity charges mentioned above are annual fees.

Q. Does your car have to be inspected?

A. Starting in 1990, the state will start to impose annual emission control inspections. In addition, certain counties do require their own inspections. Check with the city clerk's office to find out about local laws.

Q. What about auto insurance?

A. The 1988 Florida Legislature issued new statute's governing auto insurance. They have imposed a mandatory requirement that every owner of a 4-wheel vehicle carry insurance called PIP, for Personal Injury Protection. Motorcycles and 3-wheel vehicles are excluded. As Florida is a "no fault" insurance state, liability insurance is optional.

Q. Can you get a Florida Auto Tag without PIP insurance?

A. No. When you apply for the auto tag, you must provide proof of personal injury protection. You can purchase a policy from any insurance agency licensed in the state.

CHAPTER 31

Where The Care Is:

AN OVERVIEW OF
FLORIDA'S HEALTHCARE SYSTEM

A move to a new state automatically means finding new doctors and trying to secure the best available healthcare. This is of particular importance if you are moving to Florida with an elderly parent and/or children. This chapter provides an overview of Florida's health care system, and will also direct you to the local medical societies so that you can contact physicians when you move into town.

In 1989, there were 305 licensed hospitals in Florida. Almost a third of those were located in the 78-mile stretch from Miami to Palm Beach. I think it's safe to say that if your medical needs require frequent hospitalization, you'll certainly have ample choices on the east coast. Dade County alone has 44 in-patient medical facilities; Broward and Palm Beach Counties have 28 and 21 hospitals respectively. The second largest concentration of hospitals is in the Tampa Bay region. Pinellas County (St. Petersburg/Clearwater) is home to 23 hospitals; across the bay to Tampa, Hillsborough County has 16. Orange County (Orlando) just licensed two new hospitals this year, bringing their total to 9. Volusia County (Daytona Beach) has 8 hospitals.

While no county is without at least one hospital, there's no question about the great disparity of care across the state. With the exception of the Jacksonville area (which has 13 hospitals plus the famed Mayo Clinic), the farther north you go in the state, the farther away you are from abundant medical care. As in other states, the rural areas of Florida are hardest hit. Not only are there fewer hospitals to choose from, but many of them are financially unstable. To try and keep these facilities operational (profitable would be too much to ask), they are becoming affiliated with larger regional facilities; this strategy should prove to be advantageous to patients with regard to the quality of care, but it will invariably mean higher medical costs.

Interestingly, the true measure of available care is not the quantity of hospitals but the quantity of beds. In that department, Florida fares better than the national average. There are 4.3 beds for every 1000 people in the state, but only 2.9 beds are ever utilized at any given time. At least you know it's unlikely you'll ever be turned away, unless you don't have medical insurance. More than 50% of the hospitals in Florida are privately owned. That means the uninsured and the poor have immense difficulty getting treatment.

WHAT'S THE DIAGNOSIS?

Florida can boast of three prominent diagnostic clinics: The Cleveland Clinic in Ft. Lauderdale, The Mayo Clinic in Jacksonville, and The Watson Clinic in Lakeland (central Florida). These privately-owned centers have filled a much needed void. Their state-of-the art diagnostic capabilities offer patients the very latest medical technology, analysis and treatment.

THE CLEVELAND CLINIC

Opened in February, 1988, this renowned diagnostic center has developed a reputation for helping people who have tertiary medical problems (several complex medical conditions at the same time). Although this multi-specialty group practice is most widely recognized for its transplantations (heart and kidney), and the treatment of gastrointestinal conditions, they also provide diagnosis and treatment for more than 30 different specialties. For example, this clinic was responsible for the development and refinement of bypass surgery. When hospitalization is recommended, patients are admitted to nearby North Beach Community Hospital. Heart surgery is performed at Broward General. For more information:

The Cleveland Clinic
3000 W. Cypress Creek Rd.
Ft. Lauderdale, FL 33309
(305) 978-5000

THE MAYO CLINIC

Located in Jacksonville and affiliated with its own St. Lukes Hospital, this internationally acclaimed medical center specializes in the diagnosis and treatment of over 30 different medical conditions. Their staff of 75 physicians offers a full range of services, and is tied in to the Rochester, MN-based headquarters, which employs over 900 physicians. For more information:

The Mayo Clinic
4500 Pablo Rd.
Jacksonville, FL 32224
(904) 223-2000

THE WATSON CLINIC

This well respected center in Lakeland specializes in the diagnosis of 35 different medical conditions. However, they are best known for their work in cardiovascular and thoracic surgery, gynecologic oncology, ophthalmology, and endocrinology (the treatment of diabetes). In addition, they have their own kidney dialysis unit and offer the latest nephrology treatment. For more information:

The Watson Clinic
P.O. Box 95000
Lakeland, FL 33804
(813) 680-7000

TEACHING HOSPITALS

If you would feel comfortable being in close proximity to a large teaching hospital affiliated with a university's medical residency program, you'll want to make note of the six located throughout the state. These include:

W.A. Shands Hospital	Gainesville	(904) 372-0111
Jackson Memorial	Miami	(305) 325-7429
Mt. Sinai Medical Center	Miami Beach	(305) 674-2121
Tampa General	Tampa	(813) 253-0711
Orlando General	Orlando	(407) 277-8110
University Hospital	Jacksonville	(904) 350-6899

Medical Costs In Florida

How do medical costs compare on a county-by-county basis? Before you can weigh the difference between a doctor's visit in Miami vs. Gainesville, you should know that overall, you'll pay more in Florida for medical care than you will in many states in the U.S., even New York.

This is due to the fact that demand for medical services is extremely high, given that the state is home to a higher percentage of people 65 and over than anywhere else in the country. Since seniors typically require twice the amount of medical care than those who are under 65, their needs drive overall costs up.

Fortunately, the quality of Florida health care is considered better than average. Many of the facilities are new, offering the latest available equipment and treatment, but the old hospitals are good, too.

In Florida, the age of a hospital is not indicative of the quality because it has some of the toughest licensing requirements in the country. Both new and old have to meet stringent conditions in order to remain in operation.

On a county-by-county basis, you can expect to pay more on the east coast than in other parts of the state. Dade County is by far the most expensive place to receive medical care.

To give you a better feel for average charges by region, refer to the chart of the Health Care Cost Containment Board's annual survey of physicians' charges on the facing page. They have compared the costs of everything from a basic office visit to specific surgical procedures on a zip code-by-zip code basis.

Now although these figures are somewhat dated (1987 data), they were the latest available at the time of this printing. Even presuming that they've gone up in price, at least you can get a sense if the area you want to move to has high, low, or in-the-middle medical costs.

FLORIDA BELIEVES IN A PATIENT'S RIGHT TO KNOW

One thing the state can be commended for is being extremely conscious of the patient's right to be informed. As you've just learned from the last chart, Florida publishes cost comparisons for medical services and was the first state in the country to do so.

The HCCB (Health Care Cost Containment Board) in Tallahassee, the bureau which was established to monitor medical costs and control hospital budgets, publishes not only this information but numerous other patient's guides.

One of their useful pamphlets is called "Outpatient Surgery." It's a guide to more than 300 procedures that are considered safe enough to be performed without a stay in the hospital. And should you then decide to go ahead with the surgery, you can refer to their guide to facility fees. On a county-by-county basis, you can find out how much a hospital will charge for a certain outpatient procedure. In addition, the HCCB also compares the average charges and services of nursing homes across the state. If you know you will be placing a family member in a home, this free information can be requested. You just need to specify the county or counties you are considering.

To obtain any of these free booklets, call their toll-free consumer hotline once you are in Florida. That number is 1-800-342-0828. Outside Florida, the number is 904-488-1295. Or, you can write to:

State of Florida, Health Care Cost Containment Board
325 John Knox Rd., Suite L-101
Tallahassee, FL 32303

You might also want to note that should you ever have a problem resolving a hospital bill, the HCCB will intercede on your behalf. While they can't guarantee that the matter will be resolved in your favor, they will work with you until the discrepancy has been resolved.

1987 Average Physician Charges
By Zip Code (last 3 digits)

3-Digit Zip Codes...	322 Jacksonville	326 Gainesville	328 Orlando	331/332 Miami
Medical				
Office Medical Service	$ 29	$ 25	$ 29	$ 40
Hospital Medical Service	111	105	106	148
Emergency Room Service	104	76	71	99
Cardio. Stress Test	174	182	182	222
Surgical				
Chest X-Rays/2 views	$ 39	$ 37	$ 42	$ 46
Hernia Repair	813	762	725	1007
Total Hysterectomy	1625	1600	1595	2155
Cataract Removal	1561	1684	1707	1933

3-Digit Zip Codes...	333 Ft. Lauderdale	336 Tampa	337 St. Petersburg	342 Sarasota
Medical				
Office Medical Service	$ 33	$ 28	$ 26	$ 26
Hospital Medical Service	124	111	99	96
Emergency Room Service	94	82	78	67
Cardio. Stress Test	200	185	176	177
Surgical				
Chest X-Rays/2 views	$ 44	$ 34	$ 35	$ 37
Hernia Repair	849	780	638	707
Total Hysterectomy	1889	1943	1431	1350
Cataract Removal	1915	1811	1775	1435

THE BUCK STOPS WITH THE PATIENT

Florida has laws on the books to ensure that all hospital and nursing home patients will be kept informed of their condition as well as apprised of any recommended procedures or treatments. Patients have the right to refuse medical treatment and are encouraged to request a second opinion.

In addition, everyone who is admitted to a hospital or nursing home is given a list of his rights relating to the quality of care. The State of Florida's Department of Health and Rehabilitative Services encourages patients, friends, and family members to carefully read that list of rights.

There is no reason for someone to be dissatisfied with their care and treatment in a Florida hospital. Every facility has staff members whose most important function is to help patients receive the best possible care.

How To Find A Doctor In Florida

There are in excess of 42,000 licensed physicians in the state and more than 9,000 dentists. How hard could one be to find? Very hard when you're new in town and have neither the vaguest idea who these practitioners are, let alone where they are. That's why the medical associations throughout Florida are so helpful. They can direct newcomers to local doctors and dentists and refer you to those who specialize in a particular condition or problem. Obviously if you can obtain the name of a qualified physician through a referral from a friend or family member, that's great. Their positive experience with a doctor is much more reassuring than thumbing through the Yellow Pages looking for one who has an appealing name. But if you need a physician's referral, then by all means call the local medical association; and no, they are not on commission, as one elderly client insisted.

A listing of some of the non-profit societies that can be of assistance can be found on the page 312. Next to each location is the local area code. Refer to the Yellow Pages for additional listings.

Florida's Nursing Home Facilities

If your elderly parents are in Florida, and you expect to be placing them in a nursing home facility soon, this section will help you.

It is said that if you think the people are old in Sarasota, you should see their parents in St. Pete. Now I know why. There are 76 nursing homes in the area (Pinellas County). That's almost 15% of the 518 licensed nursing home facilities in the state. And if you add to that the number in nearby Hillsborough and Manatee Counties, there are well over 100 available nursing homes in the area.

What's so interesting about St. Pete is not the number of available homes in the area, but the number of seniors who live there and are *not* patients in homes. One of the reasons it's so easy for the elderly to manage is that there is an abundance of special Federal programs that help with the 3 M's of senior care: meals, mobility and medical. Many of the programs are free or low-cost. In fact, the whole community is so geared to the aged that it is used as a model for other communities across the country.

The chart on the facing page provides a breakdown of the number of nursing homes, by county.

HOW ARE THEY DOING?

What everyone wants to know is not how many nursing homes there are, but how good they are. According to Florida's Dept. of Health and Rehabilitative Services, every year the homes' services and care improve. In April, 1989 the Dept. released its annual survey of nursing facilities across the state. The survey is developed as a result of unannounced visits to all 518 licensed homes. The results?

43% of the nursing homes in Florida were considered superior (exceeding the minimum standards), 45% were standard (meeting the minimum standards) and 10% were conditional (did not meet the minimum standards).

Through this survey process, the Dept. has been successful in closing nursing homes that had no business being around. With the threat of sanctions and moratoriums, it has been able to keep the facilities that are only borderline-acceptable from deteriorating.

Florida *is* known for doing outstanding work in the area of rehabilitative nursing. It is not unusual for patients to improve so much that they can return home. In addition, many of the homes are quite nice. The facilities, amenities, and services make it a very pleasant living environment.

From the negative perspective, Florida has the same problems as any other state. Keeping a qualified, competent staff on board is the single biggest challenge. In addition, the shortage of nurses and aides is more acute in Florida because of the vast number of hospitals and homes that require these skills. Competition is fierce and loyalty is hard to come by.

Number of Nursing Homes by County

Brevard	11	Orange	21
Broward	27	Palm Beach	40
Dade	45	Pasco	14
Duval	22	Polk	16
Hillsborough	26	Sarasota	20
Lee	11	Volusia	24
Manatee	11		

How To Find The Right Nursing Home

As was mentioned earlier, the Health Care Cost Containment Board publishes a booklet comparing nursing home services and charges throughout the state. If you know that you will be placing a family member in a home, call or write for the free brochure. The address and phone are listed on page 308.

In addition, the Dept. of Health and Rehabilitative Services can provide you with a list of licensed nursing homes in any region of the state. The list will provide the name, address and phone number, the home's most recent rating, whether the home accepts Medicaid and/or Medicare patients, and the recreational activities that are available.

To obtain this information, you can call the Dept. in Tallahassee at (904) 487-3513. Write to:

State of Florida, Dept. of Health and Rehabilitative Services
Office of Licensing and Certification
2727 Mahan Drive
Tallahassee, FL 32308

You might also want to make a note that in late 1989, the state will be opening 11 regional offices of the Dept. of Health and Rehabilitative Services to be of further help to families who will be placing someone in a home. They will be available to refer you to homes, help with admitting problems, or with problems that occur once the patient is admitted. The planned offices will be in Pensacola, Gainesville, Jacksonville, Tallahassee, Tampa, St. Petersburg, Winter Park, Ft. Myers, West Palm Beach, Miami and one more location to be announced. Call directory assistance for the number or call the main office in Tallahassee if the listing is not yet available. Call (904) 487-3513.

Medical Societies In Florida

County	Area	Society	Phone
Broward	Ft. Lauderdale	Medical Association	(305) 525-1595
Broward	Ft. Lauderdale	Dental Association	(305) 772-5461
Dade	Miami	Physician Referral	(305) 324-8717
Dade	Miami	Dental Society	(305) 667-3647
Palm Beach	Palm Beach	Medical Society	(407) 433-3940
Palm Beach	Palm Beach	Dental Association	(407) 586-5332
Orange	Orlando	Medical Society	(407) 898-3338
Orange	Orlando	Dental Referrals	(407) 647-7660
Hillsborough	Tampa	Physician Referral	(813) 972-7234
Hillsborough	Tampa	Dental Referral	(813) 536-9427
Pinellas	Clearwater/St. Petersburg	Health Department: St. Pete	(813) 894-1184
Pinellas	Clearwater/St. Petersburg	Health Department: Clearwater	(813) 461-2727
Pinellas	Clearwater/St. Petersburg	Dental Association	(813) 323-2992
Duval	Jacksonville	Medical Society	(904) 355-6561
Duval	Jacksonville	Dental Society	(904) 359-6013
Volusia	Daytona Beach	Medical Society	(904) 255-3321
Volusia	Daytona Beach	Dental Referrals	(904) 255-9039
Brevard	Melbourne/Titusville	Medical Society	(407) 632-8481
Brevard	Melbourne/Titusville	Dental Society	(407) 773-2242
Sarasota	Sarasota	Home Health Services	(813) 365-0714

CHAPTER 32

Making The Grade:
AN OVERVIEW OF FLORIDA'S PUBLIC SCHOOLS

I f you have children of school age, no doubt one of your greatest concerns about moving to Florida is the quality of its education. For the past several years, the state has worked diligently to overcome its reputation for sub-standard public schools. From the looks of it, they're making progress. Student Assessment Scores have risen—not miraculously, but at least steadily. Almost 50% of Florida's high school students are now taking the SATs (Scholastic Aptitude Test), indicating a desire for higher education among half of the enrollees.

Given the tremendous population growth the state has experienced, it's a wonder that they've been able to manage the public schools at all. What school system do you know which could adjust to an addition of 50,000 new students each year? Not many. So their task is tough. But according to the annual Commissioner's report, they're seeing daylight.

Still, you probably want to know how you, a total stranger, will be able to assess the caliber of a particular school when you're considering a specific community in Florida? It's a good question. Unfortunately, the answer is subjective. *Your* passion may be someone else's poison. Some people want a large school district; others think the smaller the better.

To sort out the differences between school districts located in areas attracting the greatest number of transplants, this chapter provides an overview of the most recent statistical data gathered by the Florida Department of Education.

Just bear in mind that numbers never tell the whole story. For example, student assessment scores are only composite scores. Thus, they don't reflect the capabilities and achievements of individual students—only the averaging of all students from honors to non-English-speaking.

Although numbers won't answer all your questions by any means, they do provide some indication of the status of education in a given district, relative to averages in other districts. It's a good starting point.

As a next step, there's nothing like a personal tour to get a feel for what lies ahead. If your child is going to spend the next four to six years or even twelve years of his life in a particular school system, you owe it to him to interview the principal, the teachers—whoever you can persuade to talk to you about their particular program.

When visiting schools, take notice of the learning environment, available facilities, after school programs and extra curricular activities, the cleanliness of the school, and the overall feeling you get walking the halls. How would you feel as a student there, or better yet, what would your children have to say?

The other important step is to talk to prospective neighbors, realtors, clergy or other interested parties. What do they say about one school *vs.* another? What schools are their children attending? Their advice could be invaluable.

Finally, talk to your child's current teachers and get their opinion about the type of programs, schools or educational requirements they think would be of value to your son or daughter. As long as you're making a change, is there anything you could look for in a school system that would enhance their abilities, talents or interests?

Armed with all of this input plus the statistical information, you should have a good feel for what to look for as you examine some of Florida's public school districts. If you don't have confidence in one, there are 66 more to choose from.

Florida's Public Schools

School District#	6	13
Region:	South	South
County:	Broward	Dade
Serving:	Ft. Lauderdale Area	Miami Area
Phone:	305-765-6274	305-376-1429

Estimated Population by Age

0–14	186,079	349,376
15–24	139,541	251,018

Ethnic Background

White/Non-Hispanic	83.3%	35.85%
Black	12.2%	19.4 %
Hispanic	3.8%	43.7 %

Number of Schools

Elementary	98	177
Middle/Junior High	27	40
Senior High	21	33
Exceptional Student	8	3

Teacher's Salary Ranges

Bachelor's	$21,050–$32,180	$21,250–$32,411
Master's	$22,950–$34,000	$24,250–$35,411
Specialist	$24,704–$35,824	$26,250–$37,411

Ratios

Teachers:students	1:19	1:18
Teachers aides:students	1:7	1:15
Counselors:students	1:432	1:390

Student Achievement Assessment Tests	Math	Reading	Math	Reading
Grade 3	93	96	92	94
Grade 5	90	90	87	86
Grade 8	85	88	83	85

High School Graduates

Percent entering college	62%	67.8%

Source: Florida Department of Education, Division of Public Schools, May, 1988

Florida's Public Schools

School District#	50	29
Region:	South	West Central
County:	Palm Beach	Hillsborough
Serving:	West Palm Beach Area	Tampa Area
Phone:	305-684-5000	813-272-4000

Estimated Population by Age

	50	29
0–14	130,536	164,750
15–24	89,842	130,588

Ethnic Background

	50	29
White/Non-Hispanic	82.1%	76.3%
Black	12.2%	12.9%
Hispanic	4.9%	9.9%

Number of Schools

	50	29
Elementary	62	96
Middle/Junior High	17	26
Senior High	14	13
Exceptional Student	2	10

Teacher's Salary Ranges

	50	29
Bachelor's	$21,000–$32,177	$18,000–$28,378
Master's	$22,600–$33,777	$19,420–$24,797
Specialist	$23,800–$34,977	$20,129–$30,507

Ratios

	50	29
Teachers:students	1:15	1:16
Teachers aides:students	1:4	1:4
Counselors:students	1:624	1:399

Student Achievement Assessment Tests

	Math	Reading	Math	Reading
Grade 3	94	97	92	94
Grade 5	90	90	87	88
Grade 8	89	91	82	86

High School Graduates

	50	29
Percent entering college	53%	44.6%

Source: Florida Department of Education, Division of Public Schools, May, 1988

Florida's Public Schools

School District#	52	58
Region:	West Central	West Central
County:	Pinellas	Sarasoto
Serving:	Clearwater–St. Petersburg	Sarasota
Phone:	813-462-9270	813-953-5000

Estimated Population by Age

0–14	116,793	33,058
15–24	92,314	25,146

Ethnic Background

White/Non-Hispanic	90.2%	93.3%
Black	7.7%	4.8%
Hispanic	1.4%	1.4%

Number of Schools

Elementary	73	18
Middle/Junior High	19	5
Senior High	15	4
Exceptional Student	5	4

Teacher's Salary Ranges

Bachelor's	$19,100–$29,750	$20,000–$26,268
Master's	$20,500–$31,150	$21,500–$30,914
Specialist	$21,300–$31,950	$22,500–$33,394

Ratios

Teachers:students	1:15	1:17
Teachers aides:students	1:5	1:6
Counselors:students	1:34	1:408

Student Achievement Assessment Tests

	Math	Reading	Math	Reading
Grade 3	91	95	94	97
Grade 5	87	87	92	93
Grade 8	83	90	91	95

High School Graduates

Percent entering college	55.1%	60.1%

Source: Florida Department of Education, Division of Public Schools, May, 1988

Florida's Public Schools

School District#	5	48
Region:	East Central	East Central
County:	Brevard	Orange
Serving:	Melbourne, Titusville	Orange Area
Phone:	407-631-1911	407-422-3200

Estimated Population by Age

	5	48
0–14	66,951	124,025
15–24	53,976	104,760

Ethnic Background

	5	48
White/Non-Hispanic	88.9%	79.6%
Black	7.9%	15.1%
Hispanic	2.0%	4.2%

Number of Schools

	5	48
Elementary	41	71
Middle/Junior High	12	19
Senior High	10	10
Exceptional Student	4	10

Teacher's Salary Ranges

	5	48
Bachelor's	$19,000–$28,705	$18,000–$28,580
Master's	$20,785–$30,490	$19,885–$30,405
Specialist	$21,510–$31,215	$20,810–$31,330

Ratios

	5	48
Teachers:students	1:16	1:17
Teachers aides:students	1:9	1:4
Counselors:students	1:420	1:365

Student Achievement Assessment Tests

	Math	Reading	Math	Reading
Grade 3	96	98	91	95
Grade 5	93	95	86	88
Grade 8	90	94	86	90

High School Graduates

	5	48
Percent entering college	55%	58.1%

Source: Florida Department of Education, Division of Public Schools, May, 1988

318

Florida's Public Schools

School District#	1	16
Region:	Crown	Crown
County:	Alachua	Duval
Serving:	Gainesville	Jacksonville
Phone:	904-373-5192	904-390-2255

Estimated Population by Age

0–14	34,244	147,789
15–24	51,325	106,098

Ethnic Background

White/Non-Hispanic	76.1%	72.1%
Black	19.1%	24.7%
Hispanic	3.3%	1.8%

Number of Schools

Elementary	20	95
Middle/Junior High	5	21
Senior High	4	17
Exceptional Student	4	7

Teacher's Salary Ranges

Bachelor's	$17,200–$29,060	$18,000–$30,600
Master's	$19,000–$32,258	$19,100–$32,726
Specialist	$20,458–$34,582	$20,200–$23,742

Ratios

Teachers:students	1:17	1:18
Teachers aides:students	1:5	1:4
Counselors:students	1:405	1:412

Student Achievement Assessment Tests

	Math	Reading	Math	Reading
Grade 3	92	94	90	96
Grade 5	88	90	86	89
Grade 8	86	92	86	89

High School Graduates

Percent entering college	62.7%	50.2%

Source: Florida Department of Education, Division of Public Schools, May, 1988

Florida's Public Schools

School District#   **37**

   Region: Panhandle
   County: Leon
   Serving: Tallahasee
   Phone: 904-487-7250

Estimated Population by Age

0–14	35,794
15–24	44,276

Ethnic Background

White/Non-Hispanic	71.9%
Black	25.7%
Hispanic	1.5%

Number of Schools

Elementary	22
Middle/Junior High	6
Senior High	4
Exceptional Student	7

Teacher's Salary Ranges

Bachelor's	$16,000–$28,419
Master's	$17,213–$29,995
Specialist	$18,503–$31,286

Ratios

Teachers:students	1:17
Teachers aides:students	1:4
Counselors:students	1:363

Student Achievement Assessment Tests

	Math	Reading
Grade 3	91	95
Grade 5	88	91
Grade 8	80	86

High School Graduates

Percent entering college	41%

Source: Florida Department of Education, Division of Public Schools, May, 1988

SECTION VII

And In Conclusion...

CHAPTER 33

And Now A Word From The Real Experts:

THE PEOPLE WHO'VE RELOCATED TO FLORIDA

In preparing the manuscript for *Destination Florida*, my wife and I spoke to scores of families, young and old, who had permanently relocated to Florida at some point in the 1980s.

Although their reasons for leaving their homes up north differed, their hopes and goals about Florida were one and the same. They wanted to enjoy a hassle-free lifestyle. They wanted home to be a place that was clean, affordable, and easy to maintain. And they wanted access to recreational activities on a year 'round basis. That's Florida in a nutshell!

Did it all work out? For thousands of newcomers every year—absolutely! We spoke with retirees, pre-retirees and young families who told us they'd found paradise and would never leave. We also spoke to those who found trouble in paradise. In more cases than you can imagine, the move to Florida precipitated another move. Back north. Statistically, I'd heard that for every two families who move to Florida, one moves out within two years. It's probably close to the truth. In part it has to do with the transience of corporate employees. But in many instances, it's a result of some major league disappointment with Florida living.

What makes the difference between a successful relocation and one that borders on disaster? And how is it that some people adjust and swear by the place and others end up swearing at it? The answer seems to lie in a process you may have forgotten from your school days. It's called homework. Or research. Or just plain old hitting the pavement and making observations about an area—before making the move.

Overwhelmingly people told us that their greatest dissatisfaction had to do with where they chose to live. They had either picked a development, a community, an area of the state—or all three—that were not suited to their needs or tastes. Adding to the dilemma was that they were owners, not renters. And thus, their obligations and commitments posed serious problems when they wanted to leave.

If you haven't heard by now, selling a condominium or even a single family home can be very difficult in areas that are overbuilt or are on their way to being overbuilt. This includes the Orlando, Miami/Ft. Lauderdale and Tampa Bay markets specifically. The word on the street is you can get rid of cancer faster than you can get rid of a condo.

In retrospect, a lot of people admitted that had they done a better job of investigating, they might not have had the same regrets.

Also, we were amazed at the consensus about certain geographic locations. Those who had moved to the East Coast loved it, provided they had found a way to make a decent living. If they were retired when they moved down, they didn't start enjoying it until they got actively involved in something; anything.

Folks on the west coast were generally very enthusiastic about their move but begged me not to spread the word. They were very concerned about overcrowding and congestion and were fearful that a huge migration of newcomers would ruin their tranquil environment. A family friend in Naples said, "Don't you dare send anyone else down here. You just tell people that the east coast is wonderful." A newly retired couple in Cape Coral said they were aghast at the congestion and felt they should apologize to the natives for all the years they came down as vacationers and added to the crowds.

People we spoke to in Gainesville and Jacksonville were, by and large, very happy with their choice of relocation. In Jacksonville particularly, they found relief in the closest thing in Florida to a change of seasons. "I couldn't stand the oppressive heat all year long," one woman said. "At least here it cools down."

In Gainesville, the university offers residents culture, sports, and other activities. "Although it's not a big city, it offers many of the same features, without the high cost of living."

Tampa residents seemed to appreciate the diversity of the area in terms of housing, employment, recreation, culture, etc.

In Orlando however, there were mixed feelings. On the one hand there were complaints of rush hour traffic, overbuilding, and of a lack of community feeling due to the city's devotion to tourism. Others were happy with the low cost of living, the woodsy, lake-filled environment and the great housing values.

One of the most interesting conversations was with a woman whose family had moved 16 (yes 16) times—with five children! No we did not speak to her while she was recuperating at the Betty Ford Clinic (which is where you would have found me). To the contrary, she was calm and enthusiastic in spite of the fact that she had changed hometowns with greater frequency than some people change their oil! This past move was from Muncie, Indiana to Jacksonville. She told us that she had developed a theory about adjusting, and it's as good as any I've heard.

"You go through three important phases after a relocation. Phase One is the first three months. Here you are so busy setting up house, learning your way around, and getting your new life in order you don't have time to be homesick or lonely. Phase Two is from month three to month six, and that's when "Post Moving Blues" sets in. Maybe you haven't made friends yet, there's less to do in the way of organizing, and the excitement has worn off. Phase Three starts at six months and goes to your first anniversary. Hopefully that's when things take a turn for the better, when you become more active in the community, make friends, reach out for things to join and do." You get the sense that if you can make it through the first year, it's all going to work out.

Here are some other valuable comments straight from the horse's mouth. We asked people the following questions and here is what they told us:

1. With respect to the move itself, what advice can you offer?

"Get rid of all your old furniture. It's expensive to move and it will look stupid in your new place."
G.H., Boca Raton

"We moved everything down—the living room and dining room furniture, the boys' bedroom sets, our bedroom furniture. Then within six months, we chucked all of it. We wasted all that money moving it here."
M.R., Tampa

"I sold off everything and our move still cost $3800. I wish I'd shopped around for a mover more."
H.N., Cape Coral

"We used Fogarty to move and they were great. They were reasonable, on time, and they paid promptly on the living room couches that got water damaged."
A.B., Coral Springs

"We used North American and didn't have any complaints. They did what they promised. I think they lost two cartons, but they paid the claim right away."
M.E., Clearwater

"I've moved 16 times across country and I've always been happy with United, Atlas and North American."
C.B., Jacksonville

"I should have gotten a firm price commitment because when we had to pay the mover, it cost us an extra thousand bucks. That was one surprise we could have done without."
A.W., Coral Springs

"You can't check out a mover enough. Get everything in writing. Promises mean squat."
S.S., Long Boat Key

"Let the mover do your packing. It's one less headache and they have to take responsibility if they damage something."
S.H., Ft. Lauderdale

"I wish we'd let the movers pack. It was impossible keeping the kids out of trouble with all the boxes around. And the house was an absolute mess for two months."
M.A.H., Orlando

"If you're going to let the mover do your packing, insist that they schedule this before moving day. Most of the damage occurs when they pack on moving day while they're trying to do inventory and load the truck. "Also, avoid storage, if possible. No matter how careful they are, something usually gets lost."
C.B., Jacksonville

"I'll never move again unless my husband pays the movers to pack. Our backs are still killing us."
T.M., Deerfield Beach

"We moved here in July and it was bloody hot. I suppose it would have been an easier move in the fall, but the summer went fast and we eventually got used to the heat."
D.H., Sarasota

We moved from Chicago in January. It was hell leaving in the middle of a huge snowstorm. But we made it and when we woke up the next day and it was 70 degrees, we were glad we hadn't waited another day."
S.M., Tampa

"We moved in October, and it was perfect. The movers weren't that busy so we got a cheaper rate, the weather was perfect, not too hot, and the kids got such a kick out of swimming then that they took to Florida immediately."
C.Z., Winter Park

"We moved in June. Unfortunately so did the rest of the world. Our delivery was delayed because the movers had four other families before us. It was pretty hot, too."
D.E., Cape Coral

"We moved in June because we wanted the kids to go to day camp in Florida and meet kids before school started. It was hot, it cost us more money because the movers charge more in June, but we were glad we did it. The kids made friends and started school feeling confident."
R.S., Coral Springs

"If you have two cars to move, drive one and hire a professional driver to take the other. If there's two of you in one car at least you can take turns. It's too long a trip for one person."
H.H., Sarasota

"We sold one car before we left and bought a new one in Florida. That worked out great."
B.W., Gainesville

"We hired "Driveaway" to bring our car down. It was cheap, less than $200, the guy got there when promised, and he delivered the car cleaner than how we gave it to him."
A.B., Coral Springs

"We moved down before we sold our house. Everyone told us we shouldn't leave it vacant, but it worked out fine. As it turns out, it took much longer to sell than we expected. I'm glad we didn't wait."
D.H., Sarasota

"I was afraid to leave our house empty so we waited to move until it was sold. We moved right after it got sold and then flew back for the closing. It just took longer to sell than we expected."
R.P., Plantation

"The real estate agent found a family to rent our house because it wasn't selling. Our neighbors were hurt. They were afraid they'd trash the place and "there goes the neighborhood" kind of thing. But they were lovely people and it worked out great. They bought the house a year later."
L.M., Ft. Myers

2. *If you had to do it again, would you buy or rent when you first moved down?*

"We rented a 2-bedroom apartment when we first moved down and we stayed there for a year. Thank God. The area we were sure we should buy a condo in would have been a big mistake. We ended up buying on the other side of town, close to our temple and close to where our friends lived. We're very happy there."
M.N., Boca Raton

"Rent. Definitely. We bought a big house 10 miles outside of Orlando because we were so sure it was what we wanted. But we hated the community and when we tried to sell 20 months later, we didn't even get a bite. We moved to Connecticut anyway, and would you believe two years later the house finally sold to friends of friends?"

D.B., *Longwood*

"I wished we'd have rented at first. Our friends talked us into buying. They said if we rented, we'd have to move again when we bought. Guess what? "We moved again anyway because we weren't happy in our condo development. And what a problem selling we had. Oi. Don't ask."

S.A., *Sunrise*

"We never thought about renting, but when we came down to look around, we realized it doesn't have the same stigma it does up north. You can rent some beautiful houses for practically nothing, so it's not like you have to be in some dinky place on the wrong side of the tracks. We rented for almost a year and then had a house built—but not in Pinellas County where we were. It turned out we liked Hillsborough County better."

S.M., *Tampa*

"If we had rented instead of bought, we would have been able to do more homework. We didn't really check out the school districts, the cost of living in different areas or the resale market. We bought a 4-bedroom house right away because we fell in love with it. I mean you can't compare how gorgeous all these houses are to New York. We got our dream house for $175,000. The problem was we ended up in an area that didn't have enough kids. We should have bought in a community that had amenities like a clubhouse and a pool so they could meet other kids. It would have made their adjustment much easier, but we can't sell now. We're stuck. The resale market stinks.

G.A. *Casselberry*

"We bought in a condo development that turned out to be very poorly managed. But we didn't know any better. They all looked so nice. We figured they're probably all about the same. But that's not true. I also wish we'd bought closer to the water. I guess if we'd rented we'd be in a better position to buy something more to our liking."

A.R., *Hallandale*

"The maintenance fees for the condo we bought when we first came down were outrageous. Why? Because the development was not well run and it kept costing the owners for more and more repairs. We sold our unit at a loss and bought a house. Would you believe that was cheaper to maintain?"

S.Z., *Hialeah*

"Anyone who buys when they first move down here is looking for trouble. I don't care if you've been coming to Florida your whole life. Living here is very different. You may think you know what you want until you've got it. Then you find out a year later you need something different. It would save people a lot of money and aggravation if they rented first. What's so terrible?"

H.H., Sarasota

"When I was a freshman in college, the university did not permit you to live in an apartment. You had to live in a dorm. We thought that was the pits, but when we were sophomores we understood the logic. Dorm life helps you meet people, acclimate yourself to your new life, figure out what you want to do next—it gives you time to decide. I wish Florida had a similar law for newcomers. You know, you have to rent for a year before you can buy so you have time to get to know the place before you make a big commitment. If we'd have rented, we wouldn't be sitting with our house on the market so we could move to the west coast, which we now know is more to our liking."

E.G., Plantation

"We bought a house right away because I wanted my kids to have a backyard to run around in and to start in one school and stay there. I wouldn't have done it any differently, even though we didn't know anyone here or really know the area."

M.W., Orange Park

"If you work with a good relocation agent like Watson in Jacksonville, it shouldn't be a risk to buy. By the time they hook you up with a real estate agent, they know exactly what you're looking for and where to find it."

C.B., Jacksonville

3. *What advice can you offer newcomers to make the transition and adjustment period easier?*

"Don't expect to make friends overnight. And don't expect the welcome wagon or welcome parties like I did. I was so insulted. Not one person rang our bell when we moved into our development. I soon learned that people are so busy with their activities, they aren't sitting around waiting for new neighbors."

J.A., Pembroke Pines

"We weren't "joiners" in New York, but you have to be in Florida. Everybody belongs to something. A temple. A bridge club. A country club. If you don't join, it's hard to meet people."

Everyone!

"Come down with a good attitude. I didn't. I tried not to like Florida. I missed my children. I wasn't ready to move. But after a while, you realize it's a good life down here. A very good life. It's hard not to enjoy."
E.L., Hollywood

"I'm a very outgoing person so I just assumed we'd make friends quickly. We met people right away, but we didn't make good friends. It takes about a year until you feel comfortable with a good group of friends. Don't be afraid to stop seeing some people so you have time to get together with others who might be more compatible. We don't socialize with one single person we met when we moved in."
B.B., Tarpon Springs

"Sign your kids up for as much as possible. Get them enrolled in school and after-school activities. My daughter was like a magnet for us. She kept bringing home girls and then I'd meet their mothers and we'd go from there."
S.M., Tampa

"If somebody would have told me it takes a year to adjust to Florida I would have thought they were crazy. But it really does."
Everyone

"We spent the first six months pining for our friends and family up north. We didn't join anything, even though we got invited to practically every day. And we absolutely hated it here. We couldn't figure out why everyone was so crazy about Florida. Until we broke out of our shells and got active in organizations. Then it was a completely different world—busy and fun. Don't sit home waiting for people to come to you. You'll sit there forever."
F.R., W. Palm Beach

"My husband is a very private person. He doesn't like anyone to know our business. And believe me, when we first moved down, no one did. We stayed to ourselves and they didn't even know we existed. That's because new people are nothing special. They say 1000 people a day move to Florida. I believe it. That's why you have to pave your own way."
N.D., Cape Coral

"The first thing you should do is join a house of worship, even if you aren't religious. It's for social reasons. A temple or church is where the whole family can meet people. It's especially good for meeting other couples."
D.R., Sarasota

"Join a church. You don't have to be religious, but you'll probably want to meet people who have the same family ethics and values."
R.E., Gainesville

"If you work with a relocation service, that helps because they'll recommend areas that match your needs. We liked the homes in this one suburb, but moving there would have meant my husband had a long commute to his job. They saved the day by showing us better areas for us. That made our adjustment much easier."

M.W., Jacksonville

4. Are you happy with the area you chose?

"We bought in Longwood, outside of Orlando. We bought a great house, but we never felt like we'd moved into a real community. Or a hometown. Orlando is a very transient place and it caters to tourists. How many times can you go to Disney World? Or shop? That's all there is to do. You're not by the water, either."

D.B., Longwood

"We absolutely love Sarasota. It's paradise. It doesn't have the congestion of the east coast, and we have all the beauty. Plus there is so much to do. The theatre. Cultural activities. Tennis. The beaches. We couldn't have picked a better spot."

D.H., Sarasota

"Tampa is a very interesting city. It's still the south, so it has the slower pace. But it's also very cosmopolitan. Because of all the industry and corporations here, there's a big influence from the north. We have a lot of cultural events, great restaurants, attractions and all that. But there's also that neighborhood feeling, too. There are lot of different pockets of areas, each one a little different from the next. You can get the best of both worlds here. And it's very affordable."

S.M., Tampa

"We love Coral Springs. It's all young families, the schools are good, we're in the middle of all the action in Boca or Miami, when we want it. And when we don't, we've got our beautiful community to enjoy."

A.W., Coral Springs

"Clearwater has made us very happy. It's got culture. The water. Lots of activities. It's very pretty. The houses are lovely. We highly recommend it."

M.E., Clearwater

"Here's what we discovered. The east coast of Florida is for the country club set—the tennis and golf people who have to live in a place that offers both right on the premises. The West coast is for people who are much more independent and have a variety of interests to pursue. I mean you can play golf in Sarasota, but you can also enjoy a concert in the evening, too."

M.E., Clearwater

"Plantation is a great place. Everyone is so nice. Everything is so accessible. Nothing is a hassle. We bought a lovely condo in a very well-run development and we're very happy here."

R.P., Plantation

"We moved to Naples 12 years ago from Chicago. It was a quiet, charming community. We absolutely loved it. Now there are so many people here and it's so congested in season, we're saddened by what's come of our home. Don't send anyone else here, please. Tell them the East coast is wonderful. We don't have the culture and the activities they may want."

L.M., Naples

"If you're a working person in Naples, it can be hard. It's an expensive area to buy in and there's almost nothing to rent."

G.B., Naples

"We vacationed in Ft. Myers for many years, but always thought Cape Coral would be a better place to retire. We've been here for six months and know we made a mistake. You can't imagine how crowded it is. It takes forever to run just a few errands. My daughters are thinking of relocating here with their families and we're trying to encourage them to stay right in Elgin."

H.N., Cape Coral

"Jacksonville is a great part of Florida. The weather is mixed, offering a nice change of pace. The businesses are growing and diversified—they aren't dying. Your kids can get a good education here. The cost of living is very reasonable, and there's culture."

C.B., Jacksonville

"So far we love it!"

R.S., Gainesville

5. *What's the biggest surprise you've had about Florida living?*

"We're so busy. Sometimes too busy."

Everyone

"There's so much to see and do, we feel guilty if we're just lying around on a Sunday reading the paper."

L.L., Orlando

"The blue skies. I never realized how beautiful weather every day can make you feel good about life."

A.B., Coral Springs

"I miss the change of seasons a lot. I wish there was more variety of weather. My 2-year-old asked me what I was holding. I said "It's a sweater, honey." She just looked at me like what do you do with it?"
  J.M., Tampa

"At least on the east coast, it's very hard to find a doctor. You can wait for six weeks before getting an appointment."
  V.M., Boca Raton

"The wages are so low. You hear it, but you can't believe it until you start job hunting. You need two incomes *and* a pension!"
  H.N., Cape Coral

"The bugs! Pest control is not a luxury item. You have to spray every month or your house will fall down!"
  T.T., Miami

"I have never seen such big bugs in my life. And the termites can really do damage. You've got to get a pest control service."
  R.S., Gainesville

"We never thought we'd love it as much as we do. Our lives are so full and we've made some wonderful friends."
  H.A., Gainesville

"We see an awful lot of young people struggling to make a living here. Sometimes it seems you can't win for trying. Even good jobs don't pay very well, and owning a business guarantees nothing. Especially retail."
  M.Z., Ft. Lauderdale

"Everyone is so nice here. One person is nicer than the next. I hate to say it, but coming from New York, it kind of takes you by surprise."
  R.P., Plantation

"People seem to be very trusting here. Neighbors, the merchants. I thought for sure that no one would take my New York check when we first moved down, but nobody said boo."
  D.W., Delray Beach

"It's the south. You forget that. And it's a slower pace than you're used to. The way people drive can drive you nuts at first, but then you start to drive like everyone else and when you see a crazy driver doing 50 in a 30 mile zone, you know they just got here."
  B.B., Zephyrhills

"We've had to learn how to 'gear down'. The people at the supermarket are so nice and courteous. They take your bags to the car and everything, but by the time they finish, I could have been home and unpacked already. You don't want to seem ungrateful, but it's hard to be patient at first."

B.H., Gainesville

"Try not to drive behind an older man wearing a cap. And if he's smoking a cigar and wearing a cap, pull over. You're not going anywhere for a while."

H.H., Sarasota

"If you think they're old in Sarasota, you should see their parents in St. Pete."

H.H., Sarasota

"I wish I had more time to rest and relax. We've got so much going on, so many friends, we never seem to stop. I haven't read a book since I've been down here."

Everyone

Destination Florida...
The Guide to a Successful Relocation